The Great Entertainer Cookbook

The Great Entertainer Cookbook

Buffalo Bill Historical Center

ROBERTS RINEHART

Published by Roberts Rinehart Publishers
A Member of the Rowman & Littlefield Publishing Group
4720 Boston Way
Lanham, Maryland 20706

Distributed by National Book Network

British Library Cataloguing in Publication Information Available

Library of Congress Control Number: 2002109417
ISBN: 1-57098-408-5 (cl.: alk. paper)

Printed in the United States of America.

♾™ The paper used in this publication meets the minimum requirements of
American National Standard for Information Sciences—Permanence of
Paper for Printed Library Materials, ANSI/NISO Z39.48-1992.
Manufactured in the United States of America.

Contents

Trustees

Foreword

Originally founded as the Buffalo Bill Museum in 1927, this institution has served two generations of American and international guests in celebrating the history and art of the West. From its inception, the museum, known since 1958 as the Buffalo Bill Historical Center, has enjoyed vast popular appeal. A large and diversified audience has journeyed to Cody over the years to enjoy its collections. Those who took the time to step through the Historical Center's doors came away both better informed and pleasantly entertained.

In the same fashion that Buffalo Bill was much more than a great entertainer—he was a son of the West, an adventurer, an American hero in his own right, a visionary conservationist as well as a showman—the Historical Center was mandated to do more than simply entertain its vast public. Our role as an educational institution has expanded each year. Our responsibility in preserving and caring for the objects entrusted to us has long been a primary goal for the trustees and staff alike. And yet, without the spirit of entertainment—without imbuing our audience with a bit of drama—our task as educators and as preservers would be relatively mundane and uninviting.

The Buffalo Bill Historical Center, utilizing the rich resources of its collections and the diversity of the human element within the western experience, offers this testament to the culinary arts. It has provided an opportunity to expand our role as entertainers—and yours.

Peter H. Hassrick
Director
Buffalo Bill Historical Center

Acknowledgments

This cookbook is the culmination of a two-year project undertaken by the Historical Center's volunteers with love and dedication. My thanks to all who shared their ideas and recipes and gave unselfishly of their time, and my thanks also to those who gave continued encouragement and support—the Historical Center's staff, downtown businesses, and, of course, our families.

More than 1,200 recipes were submitted from throughout the country and abroad. All the recipes were tested at least twice and chosen for your pleasure. We hope that you will enjoy the wide range of selections from campfire simplicity to party elegance.

Robin M. Weiss

Chairman:	Robin Weiss
Vice Chairman:	Margot Belden Todd
Recipe Captions:	Marty Coe
	Frances Clymer
	Robert Deery
	Jane Dominick
	Barb Egan
	Nancy Fees
	Jim Herman
	Jan Hermann
	Mary McMillan
	Dee Oudin
	Shauna Poulsen
	K. T. Roes
	Pamela Stockton
	Liz Swanson
	Ann Way
	Robin Weiss
Editors:	K. T. Roes
	Dee Oudin
	Buzzy Hassrick
	Nancy Fees
	Margaret Martin

Special thanks to Shoshone Office Supply and the 150 testers.

For the third printing, Margot Belden Todd revised the index of the cookbook.

Buffalo Bill Historical Center

The Historical Center comprises four museums:

The Buffalo Bill Museum contains a vast collection of Cody memorabilia. William F. Cody, the best known American of his day, is depicted in his many roles—scout, hunter, soldier, entertainer, statesman, businessman, and, most important, portrayer of our Western heritage.

The Whitney Gallery of Western Art displays paintings and sculptures spanning the years 1830 to the present and depicting the reality, myth, and beauty of the West. Included are major artists of the Westward movement, many of whose works are represented in this cookbook.

The Plains Indian Museum preserves the Native American culture with extensive displays of Indian materials that reflect the artistic expression of the first Americans. The tribes represented include the Sioux, Cheyenne, Shoshone, Crow, Arapaho, and Blackfeet.

The Cody Firearms Museum houses the unique collection of Oliver F. Winchester, begun in 1860. The collection of more than five thousand projectile arms includes arms made by Winchester Repeating Arms Company and other major American and international manufacturers.

Hors d'Oeuvre

Avocado Crab Dip

1 large avocado, peeled and
  chopped
1 Tablespoon lemon juice
1 Tablespoon grated onion
2 teaspoons Worcestershire
  sauce
8 ounces cream cheese,
  softened
1/4 cup sour cream
1/4 teaspoon salt
2 (6-ounce) cans crab meat,
  drained

Blend together avocado, juice, onion and Worcestershire until smooth. Add cheese, sour cream and salt. Blend until smooth. Fold in crab and serve with taco chips.

Serves 12–16
Easy

Mrs. Will H. Hayes, Jr.
CRAWFORDSVILLE, INDIANA

Creamed Crab or Salmon

8 ounces cream cheese,
  softened
1 Tablespoon milk
2 teaspoons finely chopped
  onion
1/2 teaspoon prepared
  horseradish
1/4 teaspoon salt
  Dash pepper
1 (6-ounce) can crab or
  salmon
1/2 cup sliced almonds

"This is a specialty of the Seattle area."

Soften cheese in milk. Mix all ingredients but almonds and spoon into greased shallow baking dish. Cover with almonds. Bake at 350 degrees about 15 minutes. Serve hot with crackers. May be made ahead of time and heated when needed.

Serves 4–8
Easy
May do ahead

Ruth Carpenter
TETON VILLAGE, WYOMING

Spinach Dip

1 (10-ounce) package frozen
  chopped spinach
1 (1 5/8-ounce) package
  Knorr Swiss vegetable
  soup mix
1 cup sour cream
1 cup mayonnaise
1 Tablespoon lemon juice

Thaw spinach and squeeze out moisture. Put all ingredients in food processor and mix 6–8 seconds. Store in container in refrigerator for at least 24 hours. Serve with crudites, crackers or corn chips.

Yields 2 3/4 cups
Easy
Must do ahead

Leona Jensen
JACKSON, WYOMING

1

Cheese Fondue

"Festive for a cold winter's night."

1 clove garlic, halved
2 cups dry white wine
1/2 pound Gruyere cheese,
    shredded
1/2 pound Swiss cheese,
    thinly sliced
1/4 cup kirsch or dry sherry
1 teaspoon cornstarch
1/4 teaspoon grated nutmeg
    Dash pepper
    French bread, cut in
    1/2-inch cubes

Rub the inside of a heavy saucepan with the cut surface of garlic. Pour wine into pan and warm until bubbles rise and cover the surface. Stir constantly. Add handfuls of combined cheeses, stirring, and add more when melted. Do not boil. Stir kirsch into cornstarch until well mixed. After all cheese is blended and mixture is bubbling, add nutmeg while stirring. Add pepper and kirsch mixture. Transfer to a fondue pot on table and serve with bread. If it becomes too thick, add a little warm wine.

Serves 4–6

Danielle H. Reel
WILSON, WYOMING

Crudites with Special Sauce

CRUDITES:

4 carrots
1 bunch fresh broccoli
1 pint cherry tomatoes

Peel, slice and chill carrots. Break off flowerets of broccoli and blanch in 3 quarts boiling salted water 3 minutes. Plunge into ice water immediately. Wash cherry tomatoes, leaving stems. Drain and chill.

SAUCE:

3/4 teaspoon hot mustard
1–2 teaspoons lemon juice
1 teaspoon Worcestershire
    sauce
1/3 cup chili sauce
1 cup mayonnaise
3–4 drops Tabasco

For sauce, soften mustard in lemon juice. Add remaining ingredients. Refrigerate, covered, up to 10 days. To serve, place sauce in dish and arrange vegetables around it.

Serves 10–12
Easy
Must do ahead

Mrs. C.V. Whitney
SARATOGA SPRINGS, NEW YORK

Baba Ghannouj

"Wonderful served with pita bread and slices of onion."

2 large eggplants
1/2 cup tahini
3/4 cup lemon juice
2 cloves garlic, pressed
2 teaspoons salt
Olive oil
Parsley

Cut stems from eggplant and broil until skin is black and cracks open. Scoop out pulp and place in food processor. Add tahini, lemon juice, garlic and salt and blend. Arrange on serving dish. Top with a drizzle of olive oil and garnish with parsley.

Serves 10–12

Jane Dominick
CODY, WYOMING

Pate

"Also a pleasing spread on green apple slices."

1 pound chicken livers
3 Tablespoons butter
2 Tablespoons chopped
  green onions, chives or
  onion flakes
3 ounces cream cheese
4 Tablespoons margarine or
  butter, softened
4 Tablespoons brandy
4 Tablespoons bourbon
1/4 teaspoon salt
  Dash garlic salt
1/4 teaspoon freshly ground
  pepper
  Dash nutmeg
1–2 Tablespoons chopped
  parsley
  Chopped hard-boiled egg
  Paprika
  Minced parsley

Wash and dry chicken livers. Saute in butter with onions until cooked, about 5 minutes. Put into blender with next 9 ingredients. Mix until very smooth, then pour into a mold coated with non-stick spray or mayonnaise. Chill overnight. To serve, unmold and sprinkle with eggs, paprika and parsley.

Serves 12
Easy
Must do ahead

Marlene Farrell
DENVER, COLORADO

Pate Russe

1/4 cup oil
   1 pound calves' liver,
      trimmed and diced in
      1/2-inch cubes
   10 Tablespoons unsalted
      butter
   1 carrot, peeled and
      chopped
   1 cup chopped onion
   1/2 cup finely chopped
      parsley
1 1/2 teaspoons salt
   1/8 teaspoon black pepper
   1/8 teaspoon nutmeg

Heat oil in heavy skillet over high heat. Fry liver, stirring constantly until golden brown. Scrape liver into a mixing bowl. Melt 2 Tablespoons butter in same skillet and cook carrot and onions over medium heat until vegetables are soft but not brown. Add to liver and stir in parsley. Put entire mixture through finest blade of meat grinder. Beat in seasonings and then 8 Tablespoons softened butter, 1 Tablespoon at a time. Spoon into bowl and smooth top. Cover with plastic wrap and refrigerate a day before serving.

Serves 12
Easy
Must do ahead

Mrs. Henry H. Uihlein
MILWAUKEE, WISCONSIN

Mushroom Caviar

1 onion, chopped
2 Tablespoons butter
4 ounces fresh
   mushrooms, finely
   chopped
2 Tablespoons lemon juice
1 teaspoon Worcestershire
   sauce
   Salt and pepper, to taste
2/3–1 Tablespoon mayonnaise

Saute onions in butter until golden. Add mushrooms to onions and saute 5 minutes. Add lemon juice, Worcestershire, salt and pepper. Remove from heat. Cool and adjust seasoning. Add only enough mayonnaise to bind mixture. Pack in a jar or small bowl and refrigerate overnight. Unmold on serving platter and serve with small toast rounds.

Serves 6–8
Easy
Must do ahead

Mrs. C.V. Whitney
SARATOGA SPRINGS, NEW YORK

Crab Spread

1 small package
  unflavored gelatin
1 Tablespoon water
1 can cream of mushroom
  soup
8 ounces cream cheese
6–12 ounces crab meat
1 cup mayonnaise
1 cup chopped celery
1 cup chopped green onions
  Juice of 1/2 lemon

Dissolve gelatin in water and combine with soup and cheese. Heat the mixture 7–10 minutes, or until well blended, and let cool. Mix together the remaining ingredients and add to cooled mixture. Place in a crab or fish mold and refrigerate overnight. Serve with crackers.

Yields 6 cups
Easy   *"Diggie" Nelson*
Must do ahead   WHITTIER, CALIFORNIA

Smoked Salmon Ball

1 pound canned salmon,
  drained
8 ounces cream cheese,
  softened
1 Tablespoon lemon juice
2 teaspoons grated onion
1 teaspoon prepared
  horseradish
1/4 teaspoon salt, optional
1/4 teaspoon liquid smoke,
  optional
1/2 cup chopped pecans
3 Tablespoons chopped
  parsley

Flake salmon, removing skin and large bones. Mix well with remaining ingredients except pecans and parsley. Chill several hours. Shape salmon mixture into a ball and roll in pecans and parsley. Chill briefly. Serve with crackers.

Serves 10–12
Easy   *Norma Owsley*
Must do ahead   DUNCAN, OKLAHOMA

Smoked Fish Spread

1/2 pound smoked fish,
  broken in pieces
1 cup heavy cream
  Juice of 1/2 lemon
  Few drops Worcestershire
  sauce

In a blender or food processor, blend all ingredients a few seconds. Chill several hours or overnight. Serve with crackers.

Serves 6
Easy   *Carolyn Depue*
Must do ahead   WICKENBURG, ARIZONA

Christmas Balls

"Flavor improves with age."

2 (3-ounce) wedges
Roquefort or bleu
cheese
2 (5-ounce) jars
processed Cheddar
cheese spread
12 ounces cream cheese
2 Tablespoons minced
onion
1 teaspoon
Worcestershire sauce
1/2 cup snipped parsley
1 cup ground pecans

The day before serving, let cheeses soften at room temperature. Combine cheeses, onions and Worcestershire. Blend well. Stir in half the parsley and half the pecans. Shape into 1-inch balls. Place in a bowl lined with waxed paper. Roll in remaining parsley and pecans. Refrigerate until ready to serve.

Serves 20
Easy
Must do ahead

Lauretta Maxinne Hyatt
HYATTVILLE, WYOMING

Shrimp Cheese Balls

"A quick tasty appetizer. Always gets praise."

6 ounces cream cheese
1 1/2 teaspoons prepared
mustard
1 teaspoon grated onion
1 teaspoon lemon juice
Dash cayenne
Dash salt
1 (4-ounce) can shrimp,
drained and chopped
1/2–3/4 cup ground almonds

Combine first 6 ingredients and blend well. Add shrimp to cheese mixture and chill. Form into bite-sized balls. Roll in almonds. Keep chilled until ready to serve.

Serves 10–12
Easy
Must do ahead

Darlene McCarty
CODY, WYOMING

Brandied Cheese and Apple Slices

6 ounces cream cheese
1 (4-ounce) package bleu cheese
2 Tablespoons brandy
1/2 cup ground pecans
2 Tablespoons minced onions
3 red Delicious apples
2 Tablespoons lemon juice

Beat cheeses and brandy together until smooth. Add pecans and onions. Cover and refrigerate a few hours. Halve, pare and slice apples. Toss with lemon juice. Cheese may be formed into a ball or served in a crock. Surround with apple slices and crackers.

Serves 12
Easy
Must do ahead

Carolyn Depue
WICKENBURG, ARIZONA

Cheese Its

"Serve hot with drinks or any time."

1 (5-ounce) jar Old English cheese
1/4 cup butter
1/2 cup flour, white or whole wheat
1/4 teaspoon salt

Cream cheese and butter. Mix with flour and salt. Make roll 1-1/2 inches in diameter and slice 1/8-inch thick to make small circles. Place on ungreased baking sheet and bake at 450 degrees 10–15 minutes.

Serves 8–10

Ursula L. Kepler
CODY, WYOMING

Baked Rye Cheese Appetizers

12 ounces sharp Cheddar cheese, grated
1/2 cup finely chopped green onions
1/2 cup finely chopped ripe olives
1/2 cup mayonnaise
1 loaf party rye

Mix first 4 ingredients. Let stand 1 hour. Spread on sliced party rye. Freeze on baking sheet until needed. Bake at 375 degrees 8–10 minutes until cheese bubbles.

Serves 20
Easy
Must do ahead

Carolyn Depue
WICKENBURG, ARIZONA

Toasted Cheese Tidbits

"A versatile snack or appetizer to have on hand in the freezer."

1 large loaf Pepperidge
  Farm bread
4 jars Old English cheese
1 pound margarine,
  softened
1 teaspoon Tabasco
1 teaspoon onion powder
1 1/2 teaspoons dill weed
1 teaspoon Beau Monde
  seasoning

Remove crust from bread, Mix other ingredients together. Stack 3 pieces of bread. Ice between layers and outside, like a cake. Do not ice the bottom. Freeze on a baking sheet, uncovered. When sandwiches are very cold, cut each one in half lengthwise and twice across. Transfer to a plastic bag and freeze. Immediately before serving, bake on greased baking sheet at 350 degrees 20 minutes. Serve warm.

Serves 12
Easy
Must be frozen

Missy Hoster
Jackson, Mississippi

Super Crispy Crackers

"Delicious just for nibbling."

1 green box plain Bremner
  Wafers
1/2 cup butter, melted
  Salt
  Water

Arrange crackers, just touching each other, in a large, flat baking pan with 1-inch high edges. For a whole package of Bremner Wafers, use 2 large pans and 1 small one. Gently pour cold water over crackers until they are barely covered. Let them sit for half an hour or so, or until all the water is absorbed. Drizzle melted butter over crackers. Sprinkle lightly with salt. Bake at 350 degrees until golden brown and very crispy. It may be necessary to change pan positions in the oven to assure even browning. Bake about 1 hour. Serve hot or cold. If frozen, crisp in a moderate oven.

Serves 20
Easy
May be frozen

Margo Stratford
Cody, Wyoming

Sugared Nuts

"Good for bridge parties and buffets."

2 egg whites, stiffly
 beaten
1 cup sugar
1 (16-ounce) jar salted
 dry-roasted peanuts
6 Tablespoons margarine

Beat egg whites and slowly fold in sugar, beating after each addition. Add peanuts and stir well. Melt margarine in 9 × 13 × 2-inch pan. Add nut mixture. Bake at 300 degrees 45-60 minutes, stirring well every 10 minutes.

Serves 8   *Lois Miller*
Easy   CODY, WYOMING

Bacon-Wrapped Pineapple

1 (8-ounce, juice pack)
 can pineapple chunks
2 Tablespoons soy sauce
1/4 teaspoon ground ginger
 Dash garlic powder
6 strips bacon, cut in
 thirds

Marinate pineapple 1–2 hours in soy sauce, ginger, garlic powder and pineapple juice. Drain chunks from marinade and wrap bacon around pineapple chunks, securing with toothpicks. Bake at 300 degrees 10–15 minutes on top oven rack until bacon is slightly browned.

Serves 6–8
Easy   *Tina Wagner*
Must do ahead   CODY, WYOMING

Crab and Bacon Rolls

1 (6-ounce) package
 frozen crab
1–1 1/2 cups bread crumbs
1/4 cup freshly grated
 Parmesan cheese
1 egg, slightly beaten
1/4 cup tomato juice
1/3 cup finely chopped
 celery leaves
2 Tablespoons chopped
 parsley
1 Tablespoon chopped
 green onions
 Salt and pepper,
 to taste
12 strips bacon

Remove any shells from crab and flake. Put crab in bowl and add 1 cup bread crumbs. Add cheese, egg, juice, celery, parsley, onions, salt and pepper. Blend. Add more crumbs if necessary. Mixture should be moist but not soupy. Cut bacon in half. Place about 1 Tablespoon of crab on end of each bacon piece and roll up, fastening with toothpick. Arrange on rack in roasting pan and bake at 400 degrees 20 minutes until bacon is crisp.

Serves 6–10   *Robin Weiss*
                                           CODY, WYOMING

Escargots

1 can beef consomme
1 soup can white wine
1/2 bay leaf
1 clove garlic
1 can escargots
1/2 cup butter
1 clove garlic, minced
Pepper, to taste
2 Tablespoons parsley
Snail shells or
mushroom caps

In a saucepan, combine consomme, wine, bay leaf and garlic for a marinade and bring to a boil. Remove from heat and drop in snails. Marinate several hours. Melt butter and add garlic, pepper and parsley. Combine mixture with drained snails. Fill shells or mushroom caps and broil 5–10 minutes until bubbly.

Serves 4
Easy
Must do ahead

Mrs. John R. Woods
St. Louis, Missouri

Shrimp Toast

"Wonderful on their own or dipped into sweet and sour sauce."

1/2 pound fresh shrimp,
minced
5 water chestnuts, minced
1 teaspoon minced fresh
ginger
1 egg
1 1/2 teaspoons cornstarch
1 teaspoon sherry
1 loaf Pepperidge Farm
thin-sliced bread
Oil

Combine shrimp with chestnuts and ginger. Add egg, cornstarch, and sherry. Trim crusts off bread. Spread mixture firmly over bread and cut into three strips. Fry with shrimp side down in hot oil until crisp. Drain and serve.

Serves 6

Temptations
Cody, Wyoming

Artichoke Frittata

2 jars marinated artichoke
  hearts
1 small onion, chopped
1 clove garlic, minced
4 eggs
1/4 cup bread crumbs
1/4 teaspoon salt
1/8 teaspoon pepper
1/8 teaspoon oregano
2 cups shredded Monterey
  Jack cheese
2 Tablespoons minced
  parsley
  Small jar pimientos,
  optional

Drain marinade from only one jar of artichokes. Saute onion and garlic. In a bowl, beat eggs with a fork. Add bread crumbs and seasonings. Chop and stir in artichoke hearts and all other ingredients except pimientos. Turn into greased 9 × 9-inch pan. Bake at 325 degrees 30 minutes. Cool slightly. Decorate with pimientos cut in 1-inch pieces. Serve warm or slightly cooled.

Serves 8–10

Danielle H. Reel
WILSON, WYOMING

Artichoke Delight

1 (15-ounce) can
  artichokes (not
  marinated), rinsed,
  drained and chopped
1 cup mayonnaise
1 cup freshly grated
  Parmesan cheese
1 clove garlic, minced
1/2 teaspoon salt, optional
1 1/2 loaves party rye

Mix all ingredients except bread. Spread on rye slices and broil 3–5 minutes until bubbly and brown. Mixture may also be put into a 3-cup oven dish, baked at 375 degrees 15 minutes and served as a spread with rye bread.

Serves 10–20
Easy

Mrs. Henry Uihlein
MILWAUKEE, WISCONSIN

Spinach Squares

4 Tablespoons butter
3 eggs
1 cup flour
1 cup milk
1 teaspoon salt
1 teaspoon baking powder
1 pound mild Cheddar
 cheese, grated
2 packages frozen chopped
 spinach, thawed and
 drained
1 Tablespoon chopped
 onion

In a 350-degree oven, melt butter in a 9 × 13 × 2-inch baking dish. Remove from oven. Beat eggs in a large bowl. Mix in flour, milk, salt and baking powder. Add cheese, spinach and onion. Spoon into baking dish and bake 35 minutes. Remove from oven and let cool. Cut in bite-sized squares. If frozen, reheat at 325 degrees 12 minutes.

Serves 12
May be frozen

Helen M. Hobbs
ENGLEWOOD, FLORIDA

Stuffed Mushrooms

"Messy but delicious."

20 medium mushrooms
1 Tablespoon butter
1/4 pound ground pork
 sausage
4 ounces soft cream cheese
1/2 package Good Seasons
 Italian dressing mix or
 old-fashioned French
 dressing mix

Clean mushrooms and remove stems. Chop stems in small pieces and saute in butter. Saute sausage and drain well. Mix cream cheese and dressing mix, add sausage and stems. Stuff mushroom caps with mixture. Bake at 350 degrees 25–30 minutes.

Serves 6
Easy

Mrs. H. Earl Hoover, II
PASADENA, CALIFORNIA

Sausage Balls

1 1/2 cups hot sausage
1/2 cup prepared biscuit mix
1/2 cup grated cheese

Mix ingredients and form into small balls. Freeze on a baking sheet and store in an air-tight container. To serve, bake at 350 degrees 30 minutes. May be kept frozen for weeks.

Serves 10–12
Easy
May do ahead

Carolyn Depue
WICKENBURG ARIZONA

Hanky Panky Squares

1 pound sausage
1 pound ground lean beef
1 pound Velveeta jalapeño
  cheese, cubed
1 teaspoon garlic salt
1 teaspoon oregano
1 teaspoon Worcestershire
  sauce
1 loaf party rye
  Paprika
  Minced parsley

Brown meats, stirring until crumbly. Drain off fat. Stir cheese into meat, stirring and cooking over low heat until cheese melts. Add seasonings, mix well and remove from heat. Cut bread slices in squares and spread with meat and cheese mixture. Arrange on greased baking sheet and bake at 350 degrees 12–15 minutes. Sprinkle with paprika and parsley and serve. To make a batch in advance, freeze squares on baking sheet and then place in small, plastic bags for freezer storage.

Serves 20
Easy
May do ahead

Marlene Farrell
DENVER, COLORADO

Barbecued Chicken Wings

"Very economical and easily prepared in mass quantities."

5 pounds chicken wings
1 cup brown sugar
3/4 cup dry sherry
1/2 teaspoon dry mustard
1 cup soy sauce
2 cloves garlic, minced

Cut off tips of chicken wings and discard. Cut wings at the joint and place on baking sheet in a single layer. Bake at 350 degrees 30 minutes. Combine remaining ingredients in a saucepan and bring to a simmer. Pour over wings and continue baking 2 hours. Turn occasionally.

Serves 12
Easy
May be frozen

Nancy Shoop
CODY, WYOMING

Deviled Drumsticks

"A fun appetizer for an outdoor barbecue."

1/2 cup fine dry bread
    crumbs
  2 teaspoons onion powder
  2 teaspoons curry powder
3/4 teaspoon salt
1/2 teaspoon dry mustard
1/4 teaspoon garlic powder
1/4 teaspoon paprika
    Dash cayenne
    Milk
 16 chicken drumsticks

Mix together all ingredients except milk and chicken. Dip chicken in milk, then in crumb mixture. Place chicken, meaty side up, in greased, shallow baking pan. Bake at 375 degrees 1 hour or until done. Refrigerate until ready to eat.

Serves 3
Easy
May do ahead

Barbara Moran
ENGLEWOOD, NEW JERSEY

Buffalo Chicken Wings

  2 Tablespoons finely
    chopped onion
  1 small clove garlic,
    minced
1/4 cup minced fresh parsley
  1 cup mayonnaise
1/2 cup sour cream
1/4 cup finely crumbled bleu
    cheese
  1 Tablespoon lemon juice
  1 Tablespoon white wine
    vinegar
1/4 teaspoon salt
1/4 teaspoon black pepper
    Pinch cayenne
1/2 cup unsalted butter
1/4 cup Tabasco
4 1/2 pounds chicken wings
    About 1 1/2 quarts oil
    or lard
    Celery sticks

In a medium bowl, combine first 11 ingredients and whisk until blended. Cover and refrigerate until 30 minutes before serving. In a large skillet, melt butter over moderately low heat and add Tabasco. Mix well and set aside. Cut off tips of wings and discard, then cut wings into 2 pieces. In a deep fryer or a heavy, deep skillet, heat oil to 385 degrees. Fry wings in batches about 10 minutes, until brown and crisp. Drain on paper towels. Rewarm the Tabasco mixture in a large skillet. Add wings and toss to coat each piece thoroughly. Turn off heat, cover and let stand 5 minutes. Serve chicken with celery and chilled bleu-cheese mixture.

Serves 4–6
Must do ahead

Robin Weiss
CODY, WYOMING

Soups

Copenhagen Cucumber Soup

"A favorite summer refresher."

3 large cucumbers,
    peeled and thinly
    sliced
4 green onions,
    thinly sliced
4 Tablespoons butter
2 Tablespoons flour
4 1/2 cups chicken broth
1 cup milk
1/2 teaspoon salt, to
    taste
1/4 teaspoon white
    pepper, to taste
1 1/2–1 3/4 cups half and half
2 teaspoons bitters
Cayenne

Saute cucumbers and onions in 2 Tablespoons butter 10 minutes. In another pan, melt 2 Tablespoons butter and blend in flour. Heat broth and slowly stir into roux. Stir in milk, cooking over low heat 10 minutes, then add cucumber mixture and simmer gently 15 minutes. Season. Puree in blender, then strain and add cream and bitters. Chill overnight. Sprinkle with cayenne and serve.

Serves 6–10
Easy
Must do ahead

Margot Belden Todd
CODY, WYOMING

Curry Surprise Soup

8 ounces cream
    cheese, softened
1 teaspoon curry
    powder
2 cans consomme,
    at room
    temperature
Parsley

In blender, mix cheese, curry powder and half a can of consomme. Divide mixture evenly among 8 bouillon cups, cover and chill overnight. Next morning, carefully spoon the remaining consomme into the chilled cups, dividing evenly. Chill for an additional 6–8 hours. Serve with sprigs of parsley.

Serves 8
Easy
Must do ahead

Pat Ridgway
TUCSON, ARIZONA

Madrilene Bisque

"A delicious summer soup."

2 cans consomme
   madrilene
1 can tomato soup
1 soup can cream
   Salt and pepper, to taste
3 Tablespoons chopped
   chives

Mix soups and cream. Heat just through. Add seasonings and chives and chill. Stir twice during chilling period. Serve in individual cups, topping each serving with more chopped chives.

Serves 8
Easy
Must do ahead

Anne C. Tuckerman
BOSTON, MASSACHUSETTS

Old Drover's Lemon Soup

"With thanks to Charlie and Trav."

4 cups chicken stock
2 Tablespoons cornstarch
2 cups half and half
6 egg yolks, beaten
1 cup plus 2 Tablespoons
   lemon juice, to taste
   Dash cayenne

In a 3-quart saucepan, whisk stock and cornstarch, half at a time, until smooth. Whisk in cream until smooth. Place over low heat and stir constantly until thick, but do not boil. Gradually whisk a little of the hot mixture into the yolks, then blend yolks into soup. Cook a little longer until soup thickens, but do not boil. Add lemon juice and cayenne. Cool and refrigerate 8 hours. Serve garnished with lemon slices and parsley.

Serves 8–12
Must do ahead

Old Drover's Inn
DOVER PLAINS, NEW YORK

Cold Tomatoes Cobb

"Refreshing on a hot summer day."

5 Tablespoons mayonnaise
1 teaspoon minced parsley
1 teaspoon curry powder
6 large tomatoes, skinned
1 small white onion,
   peeled and grated
1 1/2 teaspoons salt
  1/4 teaspoon pepper

Mix first 3 ingredients for topping and refrigerate. Puree tomatoes and onion. Place in freezing tray of refrigerator until thoroughly chilled, but not frozen. Serve puree in bouillon, cups and garnish with 2 teaspoons of topping.

Serves 6
Easy
Must do ahead

Mrs. Chauncey Keep Hutchins
LAKE FOREST, ILLINOIS

Cold Tomato Soup

1 large can tomato puree
1 can consomme
3 cups half and half
1/2 teaspoon salt
1/4 teaspoon pepper
1 1/4 Tablespoons onion juice
1 1/2 Tablespoons sugar
1 teaspoon curry powder

Blend all ingredients and chill at least 3 hours. Serve in bouillon cups and garnish with chopped chives.

Serves 8
Easy
Must do ahead

Margo W. Stratford
CODY, WYOMING

14-Carrot Soup

3 Tablespoons butter
1 1/2 cups finely chopped onion
1 stalk celery, finely chopped
1 1/2 pounds carrots, peeled and cut in 1/4-inch rounds
2 medium potatoes, peeled and diced
1 teaspoon sugar
1 Tablespoon chopped fresh dill or 1 teaspoon dried
3 cups chicken broth
1 cup milk
1 cup heavy cream
Pinch cayenne
Salt and white pepper, to taste

Melt butter in 3-quart saucepan. Saute onion and celery until onion is translucent. Add carrots, potatoes, sugar, dill and broth. Cook, covered, on low heat 25 minutes. Cool slightly, then puree, a quarter at a time, in blender. If serving cold, cover and chill several hours and just before serving, add milk, cream and seasonings and garnish with parsley. For hot soup, return to saucepan and add milk, cream and seasonings but do not allow to boil. Garnish with chopped fresh parsley.

Serves 8
May do ahead

Mrs. W. Horace Schmidlapp
PALM BEACH, FLORIDA

Michel Mauphy's Cold Soup
with Avocados and Caviar

"Very elegant and superb in the summer."

4 or 5 very ripe avocados
  Juice of 1 lemon
3 cups chicken stock
2 cups heavy cream
1 shallot, finely chopped
  Salt and pepper, to taste
  Sour cream, optional
2–3 ounces golden caviar,
  optional

Puree avocados with juice. Combine chicken stock and cream in large saucepan and heat until just warm. Add avocado mixture, combining thoroughly. Add shallot and seasonings. Refrigerate. Serve with garnish of sour cream or caviar.

Serves 8–10
Easy
Must do ahead

Renate Szymanski
PASADENA, CALIFORNIA

Mulligatawny

3 large apples, quartered
2 small onions, quartered
3 cans consomme
1 1/2 cups cream
1 teaspoon curry powder
  Whipped cream
  Paprika

Cook apples and onions in consomme until apples are soft. Strain. Add cream and curry. Garnish with whipped cream and paprika. May be served hot or cold.

Serves 6–8
Easy
May do ahead

Mrs. W. Horace Schmidlapp
PALM BEACH, FLORIDA

Senegalese Soup

"A '21' Club favorite."

2 apples, peeled and
  chopped
2 stalks celery, chopped
2 onions, chopped
  Butter
1 Tablespoon curry
  powder
1–2 Tablespoons flour
8 cups cold chicken stock
2 cups half and half
  Salt, to taste
1/2 cup finely chopped
  cooked chicken

Brown apples, celery and onions in butter. Add curry powder and flour. Simmer 5 minutes. Add stock and cook 30 minutes. Strain and chill. When cold, add cream and seasoning. When ready to serve, sprinkle soup with chicken. May also be served hot.

Serves 8–10
Must do ahead

"21" Club
NEW YORK, NEW YORK

Sorrel Soup

"Denise Browne Hare brought this recipe from southern France to Deer Creek Ranch near Cody."

2 medium potatoes, boiled
6 cups chicken broth
1 Tablespoon butter
3 green onions, finely chopped
1 cup shredded sorrel
Juice of 1/2 lemon
Salt and pepper, to taste

Puree potatoes and broth in blender until smooth. In a saucepan, melt butter and cook green onions and sorrel until soft but not brown. Add puree, then juice and seasonings. Serve hot or cold. Sorrel may be cooked and frozen, like spinach, to have on hand for soup at any time of the year.

Serves 4–6
Easy

Anne Y. Model
CODY, WYOMING

Yogurt Soup

"This Armenian soup recipe was given to me by a friend. It's a distinctive taste blend of yogurt, mint and lemon."

3 ounces hulled whole wheat
6 cups chicken broth or water
1/2–1 teaspoon salt, to taste
1 medium onion, finely chopped
4 Tablespoons butter
1 Tablespoon dried mint leaves
1 cup plain yogurt
1 egg, beaten
2 Tablespoons lemon juice
Dash black pepper

Rinse wheat in cold water and add to broth or water in a saucepan. Bring to boil and reduce heat. Add salt. Cover and simmer about an hour and a half. Saute onion in butter in a skillet until golden brown. Remove skillet from heat, add mint and stir. When wheat is tender, add onion and mint. Beat yogurt until smooth, then thoroughly blend in egg. Gradually add a little of the hot liquid from the saucepan to the yogurt mixture, stirring to prevent curdling. After about 2 cups of liquid have been added, pour mixture back into saucepan and continue stirring. Remove from heat. Do not allow to boil. Add lemon juice and pepper. Some cooks prefer to add the mint on top of the soup after adding the yogurt. May be served hot or cold.

Serves 4–6
May do ahead

Jane Dominick
CODY, WYOMING

Borscht

"The longer it sits, the better it is."

4 slices bacon
1 pound ground beef
1 large onion, chopped
2 (16-ounce) cans sliced
    beets
1 (8-ounce) can sliced beets
2 (1-Pound, 12-ounce) cans
    tomatoes
1/4 cup sugar
1 Tablespoon lemon juice

Cook bacon, drain and crumble, reserving 2 Tablespoons fat. Brown beef and onions in fat. Cut beets in half and tomatoes in bite-sized pieces and add with their liquid. Add bacon. Bring to boil and simmer 2 hours, stirring in sugar and lemon juice after first hour. Chill and skim fat. Reheat and serve with dollops of sour cream.

Serves 8–10
Easy
Must do ahead

Buzzy Hassrick
CODY, WYOMING

Cream of Almond Soup

2 Tablespoons butter
2 Tablespoons flour
3 cups chicken broth
1 teaspoon salt
1/2 teaspoon sugar
1/4 teaspoon dry mustard
1/4 teaspoon paprika
2 pinches thyme
1 pinch powdered cloves
1/2 teaspoon ground mace
1 clove garlic, speared with
    a toothpick
2/3 cup finely ground
    blanched almonds
1 cup heavy cream
    Cayenne, to taste
1 teaspoon toasted slivered
    almonds

Melt butter, stir in flour until smooth and slowly stir in chicken broth, stirring well until smooth and heated. Stir in seasonings. Add the garlic and almonds. Just before serving, remove garlic and add cream and cayenne. Sprinkle almonds on each serving.

Serves 4–6

William E. Weiss
CODY, WYOMING

Cream of Broccoli Soup

1 cup chopped onion
1 Tablespoon butter
1 1/2 pounds broccoli or
2 packages frozen
4 cups chicken broth
2 medium potatoes,
  chunked
1/2 cup celery, chunked
1/2 teaspoon bouquet garni
Salt, to taste
1/2 teaspoon curry powder
3 Tablespoons sherry
2 cups half and half

In a saucepan, lightly saute onions in butter. Trim broccoli, peel stems and slice, reserving 1/2 cup tops, and add with broth, potatoes, celery, garni and salt to onions. Cook until vegetables are tender. Cool slightly and puree until smooth. Return mixture to pan and add reserved tops. Simmer until tender. Add curry and sherry with cream. Heat, but do not boil. Garnish with a dab of sour cream, minced parsley and shredded carrot. For variations, add 12 ounces thawed crab meat and omit curry powder after vegetables have been pureed or substitute cauliflower or Brussels sprouts for broccoli.

Serves 8

Marge Simonton
CODY, WYOMING

Cream of Mushroom Soup

"From the Woman's Athletic Club of Chicago."

8 ounces fresh mushrooms,
  finely chopped
10 Tablespoons butter
6 Tablespoons flour
1 cup milk
1 cup half and half
2 cups chicken stock
Salt and pepper, to taste
1 egg yolk, beaten with a
  little half and half

Saute mushrooms in 4 Tablespoons butter. In another saucepan, melt 6 Tablespoons butter and add flour. Remove from heat and make a roux. Add milk, cream and stock. Bring to a boil, stirring constantly, then simmer 5 minutes. Add mushrooms and seasonings. Remove from heat and add yolk, stirring constantly. Serve with dollops of whipped cream.

Serves 4–8
Easy

Diana M. Senior
CHICAGO, ILLINOIS

Moot House Soup

1 pound ground beef
1 cup chopped onions
1 cup diced celery
1 cup sliced carrots
1 cup pared, cubed
   potatoes
6 tomatoes or 1 large can
   whole tomatoes
4 cups water
2 teaspoons salt
1/4 teaspoon pepper
1 teaspoon bouquet sauce
1 bay leaf
1/8 teaspoon basil
1 cup cooked elbow
   macaroni, optional

Brown beef in a large skillet and drain thoroughly. Add vegetables, water and seasonings. Cover and simmer 30–40 minutes until vegetables are tender. Add macaroni just before serving. The soup may be simmered in a crock pot all day for better flavor, with macaroni added at serving time.

Serves 4–6
Easy

Chris Young
STEAMBOAT SPRINGS, COLORADO

Crab Meat Bisque

6 Tablespoons butter
4 Tablespoons finely
   chopped green pepper
4 Tablespoons finely
   chopped onion
1 green onion, chopped
1 1/2 cups sliced fresh
   mushrooms
2 Tablespoons chopped
   parsley
2 Tablespoons flour
1 cup milk
1 teaspoon salt
1/8 teaspoon white pepper
Dash Tabasco
1 1/2 cups half and half
1 1/2 cups cooked crab meat
3 Tablespoons dry sherry

In 4 Tablespoons butter, saute vegetables about 5 minutes until soft. In a separate saucepan, heat 2 Tablespoons butter, stir in flour and add milk. Cook and stir until thick and smooth. Stir in salt, pepper and Tabasco. Add sauteed vegetables and cream. Bring to boil while stirring, then reduce heat. Add crab meat and simmer, uncovered, for 5 minutes. Just before serving, stir in sherry. Cooked, deveined shrimp may be substituted for crab.

Serves 4

William E. Weiss
CODY, WYOMING

"Lunch Hour" by Charles M. Russell. *Courtesy of Buffalo Bill Historical Center, Cody, WY; Charles Ulrick and Josephine Bay Foundation Inc.; 65.50*

Crab Meat Chowder

"A little dill weed on top adds a special touch."

1 (10 3/4-ounce) can
   asparagus soup
1 (10 3/4-ounce) can
   mushroom soup
1 can crab meat or
   1 box frozen crab meat
1 1/2 cups milk
   1 cup half and half
   1/8 cup sherry

Combine all ingredients and simmer until hot.

Serves 4   *R.W. Stockton*
Easy   SHAWNEE MISSION, KANSAS

Mushroom and Onion Soup

4 Tablespoons butter
12 green onions, sliced
   paper thin
1 clove garlic, minced
3 Tablespoons flour
3 cups hot chicken broth
2 cups minced mushrooms
   Salt and white pepper,
   to taste
1 cup heavy cream
1 teaspoon minced parsley

Melt butter in a heavy saucepan, saute onions and garlic until soft. Stir in flour to make a smooth paste and gradually add hot broth, stirring over medium heat until mixture is thick and smooth. Rub through a fine sieve and return soup to saucepan. Add mushrooms and cook 5 minutes. Add seasonings. Stir in cream and parsley.

Serves 4–6   *William E. Weiss*
                            CODY, WYOMING

Mushroom Shrimp Bisque

"Rich in flavor but not in calories."

8 ounces mushrooms,
   sliced
1 cup diced onion
2 Tablespoons water
2 cups skim milk
2 chicken bouillon cubes
1 (7-ounce) package
   frozen, peeled, deveined
   shrimp
1/4 teaspoon marjoram
1/4 teaspoon mustard
   Dash white pepper

In a medium saucepan, cook mushrooms and onion with water until onion is transparent. Add milk and bring just to a boil. Add cubes, shrimp and seasonings. Cook, uncovered, only until shrimp turn pink. Serve hot.

Serves 4   *Yvonne Nielson*
Easy   CODY, WYOMING

Potato Soup

3 1/2 cups chopped onions
  2–3 carrots, chopped
    8 Tablespoons butter or
      rendered chicken fat
    8 cups chicken stock or
      bouillon
    3 cups diced potatoes
1/4 teaspoon basil, to taste
1/4 teaspoon thyme, to taste
1/4 teaspoon dried parsley,
      to taste
    Salt and pepper, to taste

Saute onions and carrots in butter in a large pot. Add stock and potatoes, simmering until potatoes are done. Puree, then add herbs and seasonings. Serve hot.

Serves 8–10   *Betsey Hassrick*
Easy   BOULDER, COLORADO

Portuguese Tomato Soup

"Given to me by the chef at Reed's Hotel on the island of Madeira."

2 medium onions, sliced
      paper thin
2 cloves garlic, mashed
2 Tablespoons olive oil
4 cups rich beef broth
1/4 teaspoon freshly ground
      pepper
1 Tablespoon sugar
4 fresh tomatoes, finely
      chopped
1 teaspoon salt
1/4 teaspoon oregano
1/2 teaspoon marjoram
1 Tablespoon minced
      parsley
4 poached eggs
    Paprika

Saute onions and garlic in olive oil until tender. Add all other ingredients except eggs and paprika and simmer 20–25 minutes. Just before serving, poach eggs. Top each serving with a poached egg and sprinkle with paprika.

Serves 4   *Margot Belden Todd*
Easy   CODY, WYOMING

Savory Steak Soup

"A meal in itself when served with crisp tossed salad, crusty French bread and dessert of fresh fruit and sharp cheese."

2–3 Tablespoons butter or
   margarine
3 cloves garlic, minced
2 pounds chopped or
   coarsely ground round
   steak
1 cup butter or margarine
1 cup flour
2 cups water
2 large carrots, diced
1 large onion, coarsely
   chopped
2 stalks celery, diced
1 (20-ounce) package frozen
   mixed vegetables
2 (16-ounce) cans whole
   tomatoes with liquid,
   chopped
4 Tablespoons granulated
   beef soup base
1/2 teaspoon allspice
2 teaspoons thyme
2 teaspoons basil
1/2 teaspoon coarsely ground
   pepper
   Salt, to taste, optional

In a heavy skillet, melt 2–3 Tablespoons butter. Add garlic and saute 15–20 seconds. Add meat and brown. Drain and set aside. In a large soup pot, melt butter. Add flour and make a roux. Gradually stir in water until smooth and bubbly. Add meat and remaining ingredients, except salt, and stir well. Simmer, stirring occasionally, about 1 1/2 hours or until vegetables are tender but still crisp. Adjust seasoning. Soup should be thick. If too thin, add more roux. If too thick, add water. Note: ask butcher for "chili grind," a very coarse grind that will keep its body after simmering. Regular hamburger is acceptable but loses its texture.

Serves 12

Dick Ludewig
DENVER, COLORADO

California Cabbage Soup

8 slices bacon
1 cup diced onions
1/2 cup flour
8 cups beef or chicken stock
1/2 cup tomato puree
   Salt and pepper, to taste
1 (2-pound) cabbage,
   shredded
2 cups diced potatoes

Fry bacon crisp. Saute onions in drippings until transparent. Add flour, stirring well, and cook 5 minutes. Add broth and cook over low heat, stirring constantly. Add puree and seasonings. Simmer 30 minutes. Add cabbage and potatoes. Simmer about 45 minutes until tender. Crumble bacon and sprinkle over top of each serving.

Serves 8

Pat Trewasser
TURTLE CREEK, PENNSYLVANIA

Trout Chowder

"A summer tradition in northern Michigan."

5 or 6 trout, at least 10 inches
    long
1 pound salt pork, cubed
1 medium onion, finely
    diced
1/2 cup minced green pepper
1/2 cup minced celery
1/2 cup minced carrots
1 cup peeled, cubed raw
    potatoes
2 Tablespoons butter
2 cups drained whole
    tomatoes
Salt and pepper, to taste
2 large potatoes, cooked
    and mashed or riced
Tomato juice, optional

Gently poach trout 10–15 minutes until tender. Cool slightly, skin and fillet. Fry salt pork until crisp. Remove from pan with slotted spoon and set aside. Reserve 1/2–1/3 cup fat, add minced vegetables and cook slowly 10–15 minutes until carrots are nearly done. Add raw potatoes and butter and cook gently until tender. Add tomatoes and seasonings. Simmer about 5 minutes, then add cooked potatoes. Thin with a little tomato juice if necessary. Bring to a boil and add trout. To serve, sprinkle with reserved salt pork.

Serves 4–6
Time-consuming

William E. Weiss
CODY, WYOMING

Zucchini Soup

1 onion, chopped
1/4 cup butter
3 cups chicken stock
A few celery leaves
1 sprig parsley
Dash thyme
6 medium zucchini,
    sliced crosswise
1 1/2 cups half and half
1/3–1 cup dry white wine,
    to taste
Salt and pepper, to taste

Saute onions in butter. Add stock, celery leaves, parsley, thyme and zucchini. Simmer until zucchini is soft. Puree in blender. Add cream, wine and seasonings and serve. The pureed ingredients can be frozen or refrigerated a day before using. If so, heat puree and add last 3 ingredients before serving.

Serves 6
Easy
May do ahead

Harriet G. McGee
CODY, WYOMING

Bread and Breakfast

Dill Bread

"For dill fans."

2 envelopes dry yeast
1 cup warm water
4 Tablespoons sugar
2 cups creamed cottage
  cheese
2 Tablespoons butter,
  softened
2 eggs, slightly beaten
4 Tablespoons chopped
  onion or 2 Tablespoons
  dried flakes
4 Tablespoons dill seed
3 Tablespoons fresh or dried
  dill
2 teaspoons salt
1/2 teaspoon baking soda
5 cups unbleached flour

In a small bowl, dissolve yeast in warm water with 1 Tablespoon sugar. Set aside 5 minutes until bubbly. Heat cottage cheese in saucepan to lukewarm, then put in large bowl. Add remaining ingredients but flour to yeast mixture. Mix well. Add flour to make a stiff dough. Let rise in bowl until doubled. Stir down and turn into greased loaf pans or round souffle dishes. Allow to rise another 40–50 minutes. Bake at 350 degrees about 50 minutes. Delicious with stews and egg dishes.

Yields 2–3 loaves

Anne Y. Model
Cody, Wyoming

Bitter End Bread

"This bread is a favorite with all our guests at The Bitter End Yacht Club, a sailing resort in the British Virgin Islands."

1 Tablespoon yeast
1/4 cup warm water
1 (14 1/2-ounce) can
  evaporated milk
1/2 cup butter
1/2 cup sugar
5–6 cups flour
1/4 teaspoon salt
1 teaspoon vanilla

Soften yeast in water. Heat milk and add butter and sugar until dissolved. Set aside to cool. Add yeast and fold in flour and salt, a little at a time. Add vanilla while blending. Knead about 20 minutes. Place in a bowl, cover and let rise about 30 minutes. On a floured surface, knead again 2–3 minutes and let rise until doubled. Form into loaves and place in greased loaf pans. Let rise about 20 minutes and bake at 350 degrees 30 minutes.

Yields 2 loaves
Easy

Don and Janis Neal
St. Johns, British Virgin Islands

Pepper Bread

1 envelope active dry yeast
1/4 cup warm water
1/2 cup butter or margarine
1 cup milk
1/4 cup plus 2 Tablespoons sugar
1/2 teaspoon salt
1 Tablespoon coarsely ground pepper
1 teaspoon nutmeg
1 egg, slightly beaten
About 4 1/2 cups flour
1 Tablespoon butter, softened
1/2 cup sliced almonds

In a large bowl, dissolve yeast in water and let stand 5 minutes. Combine 1/2 cup butter, milk, sugar and salt in 1-quart saucepan and heat to 110 degrees. (Butter need not melt completely.) Add to yeast with pepper, nutmeg, egg and 2 cups flour. Mix until well blended, then stir in 2 more cups flour until incorporated. Scrape dough onto board coated with remaining 1/2 cup flour and knead about 15 minutes until smooth and elastic. Gradually knead in more flour, as needed to prevent sticking. Place dough in greased bowl, turning to grease top. Cover with plastic and let rise in a warm place about 1 1/2 hours until doubled. Smear 1 Tablespoon butter over bottom and sides of a 5–6 quart, straight-sided Dutch oven and press almonds onto buttered surface. Punch down dough, knead briefly on lightly floured board, shape into smooth ball and place in Dutch oven. Cover with plastic and let rise again about 1 hour until doubled. Bake, uncovered, at 325 degrees about 1 1/4 hours until bread sounds hollow when tapped. Cool in pan 10 minutes, then invert on a rack and cool completely. To serve, cut bread in quarters and thinly slice each quarter. Uncut bread may be wrapped and frozen up to a month. Allow frozen bread to thaw, wrapped, at room temperature 8 hours before serving.

Serves 12

Robin Weiss
CODY, WYOMING

Pepperoni Roll

1 envelope dry yeast
1/2 cup warm water
1 1/4 cups water
1/4 cup oil
1 Tablespoon sugar
1 teaspoon salt
About 5 cups flour
2 sticks pepperoni, chopped
1/2 cup chopped green pepper
1/4 cup chopped onion
8 ounces mozzarella cheese
Dashes oregano, garlic salt and parsley flakes

Dissolve yeast in warm water in large bowl. Add remaining water, oil, sugar and salt and mix well. Add enough flour to make a soft dough. Cover and let rise 15 minutes. Fry pepperoni a few minutes and drain. Mix pepper, onion and cheese with pepperoni. Divide dough in half and roll on floured surface. Sprinkle on spices and top with pepperoni mixture and, starting with long end, roll up like a nut roll. Bake at 425 degrees 15 minutes.

Yields 2 loaves

Dorothy Marchezak
EXPORT, PENNSYLVANIA

Shredded Wheat Bread

"Good texture and unusual flavor."

2 cups boiling water
2 large Shredded Wheat biscuits, crumbled
2/3 cup molasses
1 teaspoon salt
3 Tablespoons butter
1 envelope yeast
1/2 cup lukewarm water
5–6 cups flour

Pour boiling water over cereal. Add molasses, salt and butter. Let cool to lukewarm. Dissolve yeast in lukewarm water and blend thoroughly with cereal mixture. Add flour gradually until a firm dough forms. Turn onto lightly floured board. Cover and let rest 10 minutes, then knead until smooth. Place in greased bowl, turning to grease top. Cover and let rise in warm place about 1 hour until doubled. Punch down. Shape into 2 loaves. Place in greased 8 1/2 × 4 1/2 × 2 1/2-inch loaf pans. Cover and let rise about 50 minutes until doubled. Bake at 325 degrees 50 minutes until loaves sound hollow when tapped. Turn out onto wire rack.

Yields 2 loaves

Joanie Icenogle
CODY, WYOMING

Whole Wheat Bread Plus

"This recipe evolved over the years as I was trying to make bread that tasted good and was healthy and filling."

2 Tablespoons dry yeast
2 1/2 cups warm water
1/4–1/2 cup honey or molasses
    or a mixture
1 egg
1 cup yogurt
1/2 cup wheat germ
1/4 cup cracked soybeans,
    optional
1/4 cup cracked whole
    wheat, optional
1/4 cup cracked sunflower
    seeds, optional
1/4 cup cracked millet,
    optional
4–6 cups whole wheat
    flour
1/4 cup margarine, melted
2 teaspoons salt
1 cup rye flour, optional
2–3 cups unbleached
    white flour

Proof yeast in 1/2 cup warm water with 1 Tablespoon honey. Stir in egg, yogurt, wheat germ, optional grains cracked in blender, honey and remaining warm water. Stir in whole wheat flour, 1 cup at a time. Add margarine and salt. Add remaining wheat or rye flour until too stiff to stir. Turn out on floured surface and knead in white flour until no longer sticky. Continue kneading until smooth and elastic. Place in greased bowl covered with damp towel in warm, draft-free place and let rise about 1 hour until doubled. Punch down, divide in 3 pieces, shape into loaves and put into greased 9 1/4 × 5 1/4 × 2 3/4-inch pans to rise until nearly reach tops of pans. Put in unheated oven, bake at 400 degrees 15 minutes and then bake at 350 degrees for another 20 minutes. Turn out on wire racks.

Yields 3 large loaves

Jane Dominick
CODY, WYOMING

French Bread

"One of the easiest and most successful recipes I've tried."

2 envelopes dry yeast
2 3/4 cups warm water
7 cups unbleached
    white flour
4 1/2 teaspoons salt

Soften yeast in 1/4 cup warm water. Mix flour and salt. Add yeast and remaining water and mix well. Knead until smooth. Place in covered bowl and let rise until double. Punch down and let rise again. Place on floured board and shape. Cover with plastic wrap and let rise. Make diagonal slashes across tops of loaves. Bake at 400 degrees 25 minutes. For a crisp crust, spray with water several times during baking.

Yields 6 loaves

Douglas Clark Sunderland
CODY, WYOMING

Southern Spoon Bread

"Wonderful texture and taste."

4 cups milk
1 cup corn meal
2 Tablespoons butter
1/2 teaspoon salt
3 eggs, separated
1/2 teaspoon baking powder

Scald milk in double-boiler insert. Slowly sift in corn meal and cook 15 minutes. Add butter and salt and cook a little longer, stirring often. Beat egg whites with baking powder. Remove pan from heat and add beaten egg yolks. Fold in egg whites, pour into greased 1 1/2-quart dish and bake in slow oven an hour and 15 minutes. Serve at once with plenty of butter.

Serves 4–6
Easy

Mrs. Samuel C. Hyatt
HYATTVILLE, WYOMING

Heavenly Popovers

Butter
1 cup flour
1/4 teaspoon salt
2 cups milk
4 eggs, at room temperature

Using a cast-iron popover pan or ovenproof glass custard cups, put a scant 1/4 teaspoon of butter in each cup and heat until sizzling. Prepare pan on top of stove or in an auxiliary oven. Put flour and salt in bowl and slowly add 1 cup milk, stirring in with a whisk or fork. Batter will be lumpy. Stir in eggs, 1 at a time. Add the second cup of milk. Fill sizzling hot cups 3/4 full, put into cold oven and heat to 300 degrees. Bake 15 minutes. During the next 15 minutes, increase heat gradually to 425 degrees and bake 10–15 minutes more (45 minutes total cooking time).

Serves 6
Easy

Margot Belden Todd
CODY, WYOMING

No-Fail Popovers

1 cup milk, at room
   temperature
1 cup flour
2 eggs, at room temperature
Pinch salt

Combine all ingredients and mix lightly with a fork. Batter should be lumpy. Pour batter into 4 or 5 well-buttered, ovenproof glass cups, filling 3/4 full. Place on rack in cold oven and heat to 450 degrees. Bake 20 minutes, reduce heat to 375 and bake another 20–25 minutes. Do not open oven during baking.

Serves 4
Easy

Thomas D. McCall
SAN FRANCISCO, CALIFORNIA

Pretzels

"These are fun!"

1 envelope yeast
1 1/2 cups warm water
1 teaspoon salt
1 Tablespoon sugar
4 cups flour
2 large eggs, beaten
Coarse salt

Dissolve yeast in water. Combine with salt and sugar. Blend in flour. Shape into pretzels. Place on baking sheet, brush with egg, sprinkle with coarse salt and bake at 425 degrees 15 minutes. Serve hot with spicy mustard.

Serves 4
Easy

Ally Tilden
CODY, WYOMING

Baking Powder Biscuits

"This old-fashioned recipe was passed down from my grandmother, Laura Ritts."

2 cups flour
4 teaspoons baking
    powder
1/2 teaspoon cream of tartar
1/2 teaspoon salt
2 Tablespoons sugar,
    to taste
1/2 cup shortening
1 egg
2/3 cup milk

Gently work together the first 6 ingredients. Stir in egg and milk only until moistened. Turn dough onto lightly floured board and, quickly and lightly, knead briefly. Dough should be soft and tender, but not sticky. Pat to 3/4-inch thickness and cut into biscuits. Bake at 450 degrees 12–15 minutes.

Yields 15
Easy

Deanna Matteson
CODY, WYOMING

Bran Muffins

1 cup brown sugar
1/2 cup oil
1 egg
1 teaspoon vanilla
Dash salt
1 cup All Bran
1 1/2 teaspoons baking
    powder
1 cup flour
1 teaspoon soda
1 cup milk
3/4 cup raisins

Mix all ingredients together well, put in tins for large muffins and bake at 450 degrees 15 minutes.

Serves 12
Easy

Angie Lalonde
WINNIPEG, CANADA

Sour Cream Muffins

2 cups cake flour, sifted
3 teaspoons baking
   powder
1 1/2 Tablespoons sugar
3/4 teaspoon salt
1 teaspoon soda
1 large egg, beaten
1 1/4 cups heavy cream
   soured with
   1 Tablespoon lemon
   juice

Sift together dry ingredients. Combine egg and sour cream and mix in quickly. Batter will be lumpy. Fill greased muffin tins about half full. Bake at 425 degrees 15–20 minutes.

Serves 8–12   *Margot Belden Todd*
Easy   CODY, WYOMING

English Muffins

1 envelope yeast
1/4 cup warm water
1/2 cup milk
4 teaspoons sugar
1 1/4 teaspoons salt
1 cup water
3 Tablespoons butter,
   melted and cooled
1 egg, slightly beaten
3 1/2–4 cups flour
   Melted butler
   Cornmeal

Dissolve yeast in warm water and set aside. Scald milk. Add sugar and salt to milk and stir until sugar is dissolved. Add water and butter and mix well. Add egg, then add to dissolved yeast with 1 cup flour, stirring well to mix. Work in remaining flour, as needed, until dough is smooth and elastic. Put in lightly greased bowl, brush top of dough with melted butter, cover and let rise in a warm place about 1 1/2 hours until doubled. Punch down well and turn onto a board lightly sprinkled with cornmeal. Roll dough 1/4-inch thick, cut with 3-inch round cutter and put on baking sheet that has been greased lightly and sprinkled with cornmeal. Sprinkle cornmeal on muffins. Cover and let rise 45 minutes until doubled. Heat ungreased griddle or cast-iron skillet to medium hot. Cook muffins 7–8 minutes per side until golden.

Yields 24   *Pamela Stockton*
                                         CODY, WYOMING

Refrigerator Muffins

"Great for expected—or unexpected—houseguests."

2 cups oatmeal
2 cups Shredded Wheat
2 cups All Bran
1 cup boiling water
1 cup oil
1 pound brown sugar
4 cups buttermilk
4 or 5 eggs, beaten
5 cups flour
5 teaspoons soda
1 scant Tablespoon salt

Combine cereals in large bowl and pour in boiling water. Add oil, brown sugar and buttermilk. Add eggs. Sift flour, soda and salt and mix into batter. Fill greased muffin tins half full and bake at 400 degrees 20–25 minutes. Batter can be kept in refrigerator, covered, for several weeks.

Serves 12
Easy
May do ahead

Ann Simpson
MCLEAN, VIRGINIA

Angus Loaf

"Slices of this fruit loaf are traditionally served in the Scottish County of Angus at tea time, liberally spread with butter."

1 pound mixed dried fruit
1 teaspoon cinnamon
1/2 teaspoon nutmeg
1/2 teaspoon ginger
1/2 teaspoon cloves
1/2 teaspoon allspice
8 ounces soft brown sugar
1 1/2 cups cold tea
1 egg, beaten
1 pound self-rising flour

Put fruit, spices and sugar in mixing bowl, add tea and let stand overnight. Add egg and flour and mix well. Put mixture into greased tins or 8 × 4 1/2 × 2 1/2-inch pans. Bake at 300 degrees 30 minutes, then at 250 degrees 1 1/2 hours longer.

Yields 2 loaves
Easy
Must do ahead

Mrs. R. Steuart-Fothringham
MURTHLY CASTLE, SCOTLAND

Brown Bread

"Good as a sweet breakfast bread or a snack with cream cheese."

1 1/2 cups boiling water
   8 ounces raisins or dates
     or mixture of both
   2 Tablespoons vegetable
     shortening
   1 cup sugar
2 1/2 cups flour
   1 teaspoon salt
   2 teaspoons baking soda
  1/2 cup chopped nuts
   1 egg, beaten

Pour water over fruit, add shortening and let stand 30 minutes. Combine sugar, flour, salt and baking soda. Add nuts. Add to fruit with egg. Fill 4 well-greased, 8-ounce coffee cans half full and bake at 300 degrees 20–30 minutes or longer if baked in larger cans.

Yields 4 loaves

Al Smith
CODY, WYOMING

Pumpkin Bread

"Rich and moist."

  2 cups sugar
1 1/2 cups oil
  4 eggs
  3 teaspoons cinnamon
  3 cups flour
  1 teaspoon soda
  1 teaspoon salt
  2 cups cooked or canned
    pumpkin
  1 cup walnuts, chopped

Stir together sugar, oil and eggs. Add cinnamon, flour, soda and salt. Add pumpkin and nuts. Pour into 2 greased, floured loaf pans and bake at 350 degrees 1 hour.

Yields 2 loaves
Easy

Sandy Montgomery
CODY, WYOMING

Zucchini Bread

4 extra-large eggs
2 cups sugar
1 cup oil
3 1/2 cups flour
1 1/4 teaspoons baking soda
1/2 teaspoon baking powder
1 1/2 teaspoons salt
1 teaspoon allspice
1/2 teaspoon freshly ground
    nutmeg
4 cups grated zucchini
1 cup broken walnuts
1 cup dark raisins
1 teaspoon vanilla

Whisk eggs and sugar in large bowl until lemon colored. Mix in oil. Sift dry ingredients and blend a little into egg mixture. Add 2 cups zucchini and then remaining dry ingredients. Mix in remaining zucchini. Add walnuts, raisins and vanilla. Bake in 2 greased, floured loaf pans at 350 degrees 55–60 minutes.

Yields 2 loaves
Easy
May be frozen

Sylvia Wasmuth
Cody, Wyoming

Applesauce Raisin Bread

"A sweet bread, ideal for teas or mid-day snacks."

1 egg, slightly beaten
1 cup applesauce,
    preferably homemade
1/4 cup butter or margarine,
    melted
1/2 cup sugar
1/4 cup firmly packed
    brown sugar
2 cups flour
2 teaspoons baking powder
3/4 teaspoon salt
1/2 teaspoon baking soda
1/2 teaspoon cinnamon
1 teaspoon nutmeg
1/2 teaspoon ginger
1/2 cup raisins
    Pecans or walnuts,
    optional

In a bowl, combine egg, applesauce, butter and sugars. Blend well. Stir in flour, baking powder, salt, soda and spices and stir until smooth. Stir in raisins and nuts. Bake in well-greased loaf pan at 350 degrees about 1 hour. Cool before removing from pan.

Yields 1 loaf
Easy
May be frozen

Anne Hassrick-Morales
South Lake Tahoe, California

Pear Bran Bread

3 fresh Bartlett pears,
  cored, peeled and
  chopped or 6 canned
  pear halves, drained
2 eggs, beaten
1 cup Bran Buds
1 1/2 cups flour
1/2 cup sugar
  1 teaspoon baking powder
1/2 teaspoon salt
1/2 teaspoon soda
1/4 cup oil
3/4 cup pecans, chopped

Combine pears, eggs and Bran Buds and let stand. Combine dry ingredients. Add oil and pear mixture, mixing only until flour is moistened. Stir in pecans. Bake in greased 8 × 4-inch loaf pan on lower oven rack at 350 degrees about 1 hour until tester comes out clean.

Yields 1 loaf   *Mrs. C.V. Whitney*
Easy   SARATOGA SPRINGS, NEW YORK

Susan's Sour Cream Coffee Cake

1 cup butter, softened
2 cups sugar
2 eggs
1 cup sour cream
1/2 teaspoon vanilla
2 cups flour
1 teaspoon baking powder
1/4 teaspoon salt
4 teaspoons sugar
1 cup chopped walnuts or
  pecans
1 teaspoon cinnamon

Cream butter and sugar, beating until fluffy. Add eggs, 1 at a time, beating thoroughly after each addition. Fold in cream and vanilla, then flour sifted with baking powder and salt. Combine remaining sugar with nuts and cinnamon. Place 1/3 batter in well-greased, floured bundt or 9-inch tube pan. Sprinkle with 3/4 of nut mixture. Spoon in remaining batter. Sprinkle remaining nut mixture on top and bake at 350 degrees 1 hour. Cool on rack.

Serves 10   *Celeste B. Shepard*
Easy   CODY, WYOMING

Coffee Cake

1 cup brown sugar
1 cup chopped nuts
1 Tablespoon cinnamon
1 (3-ounce) package
  butterscotch pudding
  mix
1 cup water
3/4 cup oil
1 teaspoon vanilla
4 eggs, slightly beaten
2 cups flour
1 teaspoon salt
2 teaspoons baking
  powder
1 cup sugar
1 (3-ounce) package instant
  vanilla pudding mix

Mix together brown sugar, nuts and cinnamon. Set aside. Mix together butterscotch pudding, water, oil, vanilla and eggs. Mix together remaining ingredients, combine with butterscotch mixture and beat 2 minutes. Butter 9 × 13-inch baking pan and pour in half the batter. Spread half the nut mixture evenly over batter. Cover with remaining batter and top with remaining nut mixture. Bake at 350 degrees about 45 minutes until springy to touch.

Serves 10–12

Vera Osborne
CODY, WYOMING

Coffee Crumb Cake

1 1/2 cups sifted flour
1 cup sugar
1/2 cup butter, softened
1/2 cup sour milk or milk
  soured with 1 teaspoon
  vinegar
1 Tablespoon molasses
1/4 teaspoon cloves
1/2 teaspoon cinnamon
1 egg
1 teaspoon vanilla
1/2 teaspoon baking soda
  dissolved in small
  amount of water

Mix flour and sugar. Cut in butter until crumbly and set aside 1/2 cup for topping. Combine remaining ingredients with flour mixture. Pour batter into greased 9-inch cake pan and sprinkle with topping. Bake at 375 degrees 30 minutes.

Serves 8–10
Easy

Susan Blaisdell Coe
RED BANK, NEW JERSEY

Danish Puff

"Just right with morning coffee."

3 cups flour
1 cup margarine or butter
2 Tablespoons water
1 cup water
1 teaspoon almond extract
3 eggs

In a bowl, cut butter into 1 cup flour. Sprinkle with 2 Tablespoons water and mix with a fork. Shape into a ball and divide in half. Pat dough with hands into 2 long 12 × 3-inch strips. Place strips 3 inches apart on an ungreased baking sheet. Mix remaining butter and water in a medium saucepan and bring to a rolling boil. Add almond flavoring and remove from heat. Stir in flour all at once. Beat until smooth and thick. Add eggs, one at a time, beating until smooth. Spread evenly over each piece of pastry. Bake at 350 degrees about 60 minutes, until topping is crisp and browned. Frost with confectioners' sugar icing and sprinkle with toasted slivered almonds.

Makes 2 puffs

Mary Jo Barr
LOVELAND, COLORADO

Sourdough Pancake Tea Cakes

1 cup sourdough starter
2 cups water
2 cups flour
3 Tablespoons sugar
2 eggs, slightly beaten
1 teaspoon salt
3 Tablespoons sugar
1 1/2 teaspoons baking soda
   dissolved in small
   amount of warm water
4 Tablespoons melted
   shortening
   Butter
   Sugar

The night before serving, combine first 3 ingredients and 1 1/2 Tablespoons sugar in large bowl. Let stand overnight in a warm place. The next day, remove 1 cup of mixture and return it to refrigerator. To remainder, add eggs, salt and remaining sugar. Fold in completely, but do not beat. Mix in baking soda and stir in shortening. Bake cakes, 8–10 inches in diameter, on 350-degree griddle. Butter each cake and sprinkle with sugar. Make a stack about 8 cakes high. Using a bread knife, cut stack into 6 or 8 pie-shaped wedges. Serve one wedge per person. Vary some stacks by spreading jelly, jam or maple-sugar butter between layers. Any remaining portions may be heated in microwave for a few seconds.

Serves 6–8
Easy
Must do ahead

Richard S. Dumbrill
NEWCASTLE, WYOMING

Pancakes

"Light and thin like Swedish pancakes."

1/2 cup oat flour
1 egg
1/2 cup whole wheat flour
1 cup buttermilk
1/2 teaspoon soda
1 teaspoon vanilla
1/2 cup chopped nut meats,
   optional
1/2 cup blueberries, optional
1 1/2 cup strawberries,
   optional

Prepare oat flour by grinding rolled oats in a blender. Beat egg and add other ingredients. Blend well. Cook on hot griddle and serve immediately with syrup, strawberries, jam, jelly or eggs.

Serves 2–4
Easy

Waneta Judy
CODY, WYOMING

Whey Pancakes

"While making cottage cheese one morning, I wondered if the whey could also be used in a tasty fashion. Here is the result."

2 cups flour
1 teaspoon salt
1 1/2 teaspoons soda
2 eggs
1/4 cup butter, softened
2 cups whey

Combine dry ingredients. Sift and set aside. Beat eggs, butter and whey together and add to dry mixture. Stir just to moisten dry ingredients. Batter will be thick and lumpy. Bake on a hot griddle until golden.

Serves 5–6
Easy

Salli Allen
CODY, WYOMING

Rice Waffles

"Unusual and delicious for breakfast."

1 cup flour
2 teaspoons baking powder
2 Tablespoons sugar
3/4 teaspoon salt
1 cup milk
2 eggs, separated
2 Tablespoons melted
   butter
1 cup cooked rice
Honey and maple syrup

Combine dry ingredients. Add milk, beaten yolks, butter and rice. Carefully fold in stiffly beaten egg whites. Bake until brown in hot waffle iron. Make a mixture of half honey and half maple syrup, heat and serve with waffles.

Serves 4
Easy

Mrs. Donald Young
SCOTTSBLUFF, NEBRASKA

Very Crispy Waffles

1 cup sifted flour
1 Tablespoon sugar
1/2 teaspoon salt
1 cup top milk or mixture
  of milk and cream
2 eggs, separated
3 Tablespoons butter,
  melted
1 1/2 teaspoons baking
  powder

Resift flour with sugar and salt. Slowly stir in milk, keeping batter very smooth. Beat egg yolks slightly and add to batter. Add butter, beating well. Let batter stand 10 minutes, then stir in baking powder until blended. Beat egg whites until stiff and fold into batter. Bake in very hot waffle iron and serve immediately.

Serves 4–6
Easy

Margot Belden Todd
CODY, WYOMING

Cinnamon Twists

TWISTS:

1 cup sour cream
3 Tablespoons sugar
1 teaspoon soda
1 teaspoon salt
1 envelope dry yeast
1/4 cup warm water
1 egg
2 Tablespoons shortening,
  softened
3 cups sifted flour
2 Tablespoons butter,
  softened
1/3 cup brown sugar
1 teaspoon cinnamon

FROSTING:

1 cup confectioners' sugar
1–2 Tablespoons milk
1/2 teaspoon vanilla

"Perfect with a cup of coffee."

Heat sour cream to lukewarm in large saucepan. Remove from heat and stir in sugar, soda and salt. Stir in yeast dissolved in warm water. Add egg, shortening and flour. Mix well. Turn onto floured board and fold over several times. Roll into 24 × 6-inch oblong. Spread with butter. Sprinkle half with mixture of brown sugar and cinnamon. Fold over other half. Cut into 24 strips, 1-inch long. Hold strip at both ends and twist. Place on greased baking sheet, 2 inches apart. Bake at 375 degrees 12–15 minutes. Partially cool, mix frosting ingredients and ice.

Yields 24

Mary Jo Barr
LOVELAND, COLORADO

Lucile's French Toast

"The combination of brandy and cinnamon produces a unique flavor."

Butter
2 eggs
1/2 cup milk
1 Tablespoon brandy or
sherry, to taste
2 Tablespoons sugar
1/8 teaspoon salt
1/2 teaspoon cinnamon or
nutmeg, optional
Sliced bread

Heat a frying pan to 360 degrees and grease generously with butter. Mix remaining ingredients in blender. Dip slices of bread into mixture, thoroughly saturating each. Slowly brown bread in butter, 3–4 minutes per side. Serve toast hot and sprinkled with confectioners' sugar or with syrup, honey or jelly.

Serves 2–4
Easy

Mrs. Lucile S. Barnes
JACKSON, WYOMING

Dutch Baby

"Great for a Sunday brunch."

6 large eggs
1 cup flour
1/2 teaspoon salt
1 cup milk
2 Tablespoons butter, melted
2 Tablespoons solid
vegetable shortening

Make batter a day before or at least 1 hour before baking. Blend all but shortening about 30 seconds until smooth. Scrape sides and blend again. (Batter can stand, covered, 4 hours at room temperature or may be chilled overnight.) In a 450-degree oven, heat two 9-inch metal pie pans or iron skillets, each greased with 1 Tablespoon shortening. Heat in oven 5 minutes. Remove and fill with batter. Bake 20 minutes. Reduce heat to 350 degrees and bake 5–10 minutes longer until fluffy and brown. Serve with fruit sauces or honey.

Serves 6–8
Easy
Must do ahead

Barbara Schmidlapp
NEW YORK, NEW YORK

Eggs Vichy

4 Tablespoons butter
2 Tablespoons flour
1 cup chicken stock
5 Tablespoons Gruyere or
  Swiss cheese, melted
1/2 cup cold chicken, cut in
  strips
1/2 cup sliced button
  mushrooms
2 teaspoons minced
  pimiento
2 teaspoons paprika
1 teaspoon Worcestershire
  sauce
1 teaspoon celery salt
2 pinches cayenne
6 eggs

In a saucepan, heat butter, blend in flour and slowly add stock. Stir in 4 Tablespoons cheese and, when melted, add next 7 ingredients. Cook 5 minutes. Pour some sauce in bottoms of individual dishes, put 1 egg in each, cover with remaining sauce, sprinkle with remaining cheese and bake at 350 degrees 10 minutes until set and brown.

Serves 6

William E. Weiss
CODY, WYOMING

Breakfast Casserole

"Mexican food lovers will enjoy the addition of diced green chiles and salsa."

12 slices extra-thin white
  bread
  Butter
1 pound bulk sausage
8 ounces grated sharp
  Cheddar or Swiss cheese
4 eggs
3 cups milk

Trim crusts from bread and lightly butter 1 side of each slice. Saute sausage until lightly browned. Place 6 slices, buttered-side-up, in greased 9 × 13-inch pan. Spread half the sausage and grated cheese over bread. Place remaining slices on top and spread with remaining sausage and cheese. Slightly beat eggs and milk. Pour over bread until milk comes to the top. Refrigerate, uncovered, overnight. Bake at 350 degrees 1 hour.

Serves 6
Easy
Must do ahead

Diana Seabeck
LARAMIE, WYOMING

Wiley's Asparagus Dish

6 Tablespoons butter or
  margarine
3/4 cup flour
  1 teaspoon dry mustard
1/2 teaspoon salt
3 1/2 cups milk
  4 eggs, separated
  1 pound fresh asparagus
    (or 1 package frozen
    asparagus or 2 cans
    green asparagus)
  1 cup shredded Swiss or
    Gruyere cheese

Line bottom of greased 10 × 15-inch pan with foil, then grease and flour foil. In a saucepan, melt butter and stir in flour, mustard and salt. Gradually stir in 3 cups milk. Cook 5–10 minutes until thick, stirring constantly. Remove from heat and set aside 1 cup of white sauce. Beat egg yolks and gradually beat in all but reserved sauce. Beat whites until stiff but moist and fold into yolk mixture. Pour into pan and bake at 325 degrees 40 minutes. Cook asparagus until tender, drain and keep warm. In a saucepan, combine reserved sauce, remaining milk and cheese. Stir until cheese melts. When souffle is done, invert onto a towel. Spoon half of cheese sauce across width of souffle. Top with an arrangement of asparagus spears. Roll up. Serve seam-side-down and pass remaining cheese sauce separately.

Serves 6–8   *Nancy Fees*
Time-consuming   CODY, WYOMING

Hashed Brown Omelet

4 slices bacon
2 cups finely shredded
  potatoes or 1 package
  hashed brown potatoes,
  cooked
1/2 cup chopped onion
1/4 cup chopped green pepper
  4 eggs
1/4 cup milk
1/2 teaspoon salt
  Dash pepper
  1 cup shredded sharp
    American cheese

In a 10 or 12-inch skillet, cook bacon until crisp. Remove bacon and crumble, leaving 2 Tablespoons drippings in pan. Mix potatoes, onions and green pepper. Pat into skillet. Cook over low heat until underside is crisp and brown. Blend eggs, milk, salt and pepper. Pour over potatoes. Top with cheese and bacon, cover and cook over low heat. When eggs are done, loosen with spatula and fold in half.

Serves 4   *Four Bear Ranch*
                                      CODY, WYOMING

Turkish "Breakfast"

3 slices bacon, cut in small
    pieces
1 small onion, finely diced
1 cup plain yogurt
3 eggs, beaten
1/2 cup grated Monterey Jack
    cheese
1/2 cup milk
1/2 teaspoon salt
2 Tablespoons minced
    parsley, optional
12 phyllo sheets

Over medium-low heat, fry bacon and onions until bacon is almost crispy. Drain off half the grease. Mix together yogurt, eggs, cheese, milk and salt. Mix with bacon, onions and bacon grease from pan. Add parsley. Layer 3 or 4 phyllo sheets, separated, in bottom of buttered baking dish and spread each layer with some filling. Repeat layers of phyllo and filling. Pour any unused liquid over top layer of phyllo. Press top of last layer with broad spatula until liquid flows over the phyllo. Bake at 350 degrees 40 minutes until almost set. Cool slightly before cutting in squares. Serve hot or cold.

Serves 6–8

Sharon McNicol
CODY, WYOMING

Cream Cheese and Bacon Pie

"Good for breakfast, lunch or picnics."

1 (9-inch) unbaked pie crust
4 slices bacon, cut in
    1/4-inch strips
1 egg
3 egg yolks
8 ounces cream cheese,
    softened
1/2 cup plus 2 Tablespoons
    heavy cream
    Celery salt, to taste
    Pepper, to taste
10 cherry tomatoes, halved
6 slices bacon
    Parsley

Line flan or pie pan with crust. Fry bacon pieces, drain and sprinkle on bottom of crust. Beat egg, yolks and cream cheese until smooth. Add cream gradually, then salt and pepper. Pour into crust. Arrange tomatoes in a circle along outer edge of crust. Bake at 400 degrees 20 minutes, then at 350 degrees another 10 minutes. Fry 6 slices of bacon and roll into curls. Garnish pie with bacon rolls and parsley.

Serves 6
Easy

Nancy Fees
CODY, WYOMING

Chicken Livers Supreme

"May change the minds of even inveterate liver haters."

12 slices bacon
1 medium onion, thinly
  sliced
1 medium green pepper,
  sliced
1/3 cup sliced green olives
1/3 cup sliced black olives
2–3 Tablespoons sherry
1 pound chicken livers
3 Tablespoons butter
  English muffins, toasted
  and buttered

Fry bacon until crisp. Remove from pan, crumble and place in bowl. Saute onions and peppers in bacon fat and add to bacon with olives and sherry. In a separate pan, saute chicken livers in butter and add bacon mixture. Ladle over English muffins for brunch or serve as an appetizer.

Serves 6–8
Easy

Helen L. Cashman
MINNEAPOLIS, MINNESOTA

Chipped Beef with Sour Cream

"An old favorite with a new twist."

3 (4-ounce) packages
  chipped beef, cut up
2 Tablespoons butter
4 cups sour cream
8 ounces cream cheese
2 packages frozen artichoke
  hearts
1/2 cup dry white wine
2 Tablespoons Parmesan
  cheese
  Paprika

Saute beef in butter. Add sour cream and cream cheese. In a separate saucepan, cook artichoke hearts until just tender and add with wine. Combine in casserole, top with Parmesan and paprika and bake at 350 degrees 20 minutes.

Serves 8
Easy

Mrs. H. Lansing Vail, Jr.
SHAKER HEIGHTS, OHIO

Imperial Tenderloin

1 (4–6 pound) beef
    tenderloin
1/4 cup melted butter
1 clove garlic
1 Tablespoon Worcestershire
    sauce
4 ounces bleu cheese
1/2 cup butter

Trim surface fat from tenderloin and brush with melted butter. Roast on a rack at 450 degrees 45–60 minutes or until meat thermometer registers 140 degrees. In Worcestershire, mash garlic and add bleu cheese and butter. Remove meat from oven and spread garlic mixture over top. Serve immediately. Note: half the mixture is sufficient for the average loin.

Serves 8–10
Easy

Mrs. Clifford Hansen
JACKSON, WYOMING

Chateaubriand Valentine

"Most elegant of steaks."

1/2 cup butter, softened
1 medium clove garlic,
    minced
4 Tablespoons sliced green
    onions, white sections
1/2 teaspoon dry mustard
1/2 teaspoon fines herbes or
    Italian herbs
    Salt and pepper, to taste
1 medium Chateaubriand

Cream butter and add remaining ingredients, except meat, mixing well. Place Chateaubriand in preheated broiler approximately 4 inches from heat source. Brush often with sauce as meat cooks. Total cooking time for medium is about 35 minutes. Serve on preheated platter and carve in diagonal slices, 1/4-inch thick.

Serves 4–5
Easy

Maxinne Hyatt
HYATTVILLE, WYOMING

Individual Beef Wellington

"Make both the mushroom and the pate varieties, to please everyone."

1 Tablespoon oil
4 fillets mignons, about 1-inch thick
Salt and pepper, to taste

MUSHROOM FILLING:

4 ounces fresh mushrooms, minced
2 Tablespoons onion, minced
2 Tablespoons butter
1 Tablespoon sherry
2 packages frozen patty shells, thawed
1 small can pate
1 egg
1 Tablespoon milk

Oil a skillet and sear fillets on high heat 1 minute on each side. Season and set aside. In the same skillet, saute mushrooms and onions in butter 2 minutes, then add sherry and stir. Set aside. On a board, roll thin 4 patty shells, one large enough to wrap around individual fillets. Spread 2 Tablespoons of mushroom mixture or pate on each shell and top with a fillet. Wrap shell around the fillet and place, seam-side-down, on greased cookie sheet. Brush shells with mixture of egg beaten with milk. Roll out another shell and cut out decorative shapes. Decorate each wrapped fillet and brush again with egg mixture. Bake at 375 degrees 20 minutes. Pastry will be golden brown, and meat will be medium rare.

Serves 4

Liz Swanson
CODY, WYOMING

Foolproof Rib Roast

"This easy, never-fail method allows the hostess to spend an afternoon away from home and still serve an elegant dinner, even to guests who are hours late."

1 rib roast, any size, at room temperature
Salt and pepper, to taste
Garlic, optional

Rub roast with seasonings. Place in open roasting pan, rib-side-down. Roast at 375 degrees 1 hour. Turn off oven and keep door closed until ready to continue cooking, taking care that door is not opened. Between 30–40 minutes before dinner, turn on oven again to 375 degrees. Potatoes may be added at this point. Regardless of the size of the roast, it will be well browned outside and rare inside. For more well-done meat or at high altitude, add more time in the final reheating.

Easy
Must do ahead

Mrs. Josephine S. Montgomery
HILLSBORO, VIRGINIA

Steak and Bacon Tournedos

1 1/2 pounds flank steak
   Instant, unseasoned
   meat tenderizer
8 ounces bacon
1/4–1 teaspoon garlic salt
1/2 teaspoon ground pepper
1–2 Tablespoons parsley

Pound steak to 1/2-inch thick. Use tenderizer according to directions. Cook bacon, not too crisp. Sprinkle steak with garlic salt and pepper. Score meat diagonally in both directions, in a crosshatched pattern. Place bacon strips lengthwise on steak and sprinkle with parsley. Roll up and skewer with toothpicks at 1-inch intervals. Cut into 1-inch slices and grill.

Serves 4
Easy

Adelaide D. Valentine
DENVER, COLORADO

Marinated Flank Steak

1 1/2 pounds flank steak
1/2 cup ketchup
3/8 cup red wine vinegar
1/2 cup dry red wine
1 Tablespoon
   Worcestershire sauce
2 Tablespoons finely
   chopped onion
1 clove garlic, chopped
1 Tablespoon prepared
   mustard
1/2 teaspoon salt
2 Tablespoons oil

Put steak in flat glass pan. Combine marinade ingredients and pour over steak. Marinate in refrigerator overnight or all day. Cook on grill about 3 inches above heat, 3 minutes on each side for rare and 4–5 minutes for medium. To serve, slice diagonally in thin strips.

Serves 4
Easy
Must do ahead

Ann Scarlett Daley
DENVER, COLORADO

Flank Steak Teriyaki

2 pounds flank steak
3/4 cup oil
1/4 cup soy sauce
3 Tablespoons honey
2 Tablespoons vinegar
1 1/2 teaspoons ginger
1 clove garlic, pressed

Slash steaks diagonally, in one direction, about 3/4-inch apart. Mix remaining ingredients and place in shallow pan with steak. Marinate 6–8 hours, turning frequently. Broil steak 3 inches from heat. Allow 3–4 minutes on each side for rare, 5–6 minutes for medium. To serve, cut steaks in narrow strips at right angles to diagonal slashes.

Serves 4
Easy
Must do ahead

Nan Thorne Fogle
BOULDER, COLORADO

Rolled and Stuffed Flank Steak

"Tasty and inexpensive."

2 pounds flank steak
1/2–1 teaspoon salt
1/4 teaspoon pepper
4 ounces sausage or
    bacon, diced
2 medium onions, finely
    chopped
2 cups soft bread crumbs
    Milk
1/2 cup water, stock or
    tomato juice

Score steak and pat dry. Sprinkle with salt and pepper. Prepare stuffing by sauteing sausage or bacon and onions until onions are browned. Pour off fat. Add bread crumbs and enough milk to moisten. Spread thin layer of stuffing on steak. Roll tightly and fasten with skewers or tie with string. Brown meat. Place on rack in roasting pan. Add water, stock or juice. Cover and bake at 300 degrees for 2 hours. A roasting bag may also be used.

Serves 4–6
Easy

Nita Winterink
CHARLES CITY, IOWA

Baked Corned Beef

"Very tender with a fine flavor."

3 to 4-pound corned beef
    brisket
1/2 teaspoon rosemary
1 teaspoon pickling spice
1 bay leaf, crumbled
    A few peppercorns
4 orange slices
4 onion slices
1 carrot, cut in strips
1/2 green pepper, cut in
    strips
2 stalks celery
2 cloves garlic
1 teaspoon instant beef
    broth crystals dissolved
    in 1/2 cup water

Put brisket in a heavy pot and cover with cold water. Cook 2 minutes at a rolling boil. Remove from water and place on a large piece of double-heavy aluminum foil, large enough to wrap the meat and make a tight seal. Spread all the other ingredients evenly over meat, adding broth last. Seal the foil package carefully and tightly. Bake at 300 degrees 4–5 hours or until quite tender. Check after 4 hours. Serve with traditional vegetables: boiled potatoes, onions, carrots, cabbage and creamed horseradish sauce.

Serves 8
Easy

Ralph Anthony
MEETEETSE, WYOMING

"21" Burgers

"An after-theater favorite."

2 pounds lean ground sirloin
1/4 teaspoon nutmeg
    Dash Worcestershire sauce
    Salt and freshly ground
    pepper, to taste
1/4 cup bread crumbs
1/4 cup finely chopped cooked
    celery
    Oil

In a mixing bowl, combine all the ingredients by hand, using rapid motions, without overworking mixture. Shape into round patties, about 8–10 ounces each. Heat a little oil in a skillet with a metal handle. When the pan is very hot, brown the patties quickly on both sides. Bake, in the skillet, at 350 degrees until done as desired, about 5 minutes for rare. Serve with "21" Sauce.

Serves 3–4
Easy

"21" Club
NEW YORK, NEW YORK

Hamburger Sharon

HAMBURGERS:

5 slices Pepperidge Farm
    white bread
3 Tablespoons
    Worcestershire sauce
1 pound lean ground beef
    Salt and pepper, to taste
    Butter

SAUCE SHARON:

Hollandaise sauce
Tarragon vinegar
2 Tablespoons minced fresh
    tarragon or 1 teaspoon
    dried, crushed
1 Tablespoon parsley,
    chopped
1 large tomato, finely
    chopped

Break 1 slice bread into fine pieces and soak in Worcestershire. Squeeze out and discard sauce. Add soaked bread to beef, then add salt and pepper. Gently shape into 4 patties. Cut 4 rounds of bread and saute in butter. Broil hamburgers about 10 minutes and place on bread rounds.

For Sauce Sharon, prepare Hollandaise sauce, substituting tarragon vinegar for lemon juice. Add tarragon and parsley. Top hamburgers with sauce and tomatoes.

Note: this may easily be expanded to serve more. The dish is good for luncheons served with a mixed green salad.

Serves 4

Mrs. Byron Ramsing
CODY, WYOMING

"Beer-y" Beef

5 pounds stewing beef, cut
  in 1 1/2-inch cubes or
  5 pounds meat from boned
  beef shortribs, cubed
  Flour seasoned with salt
  and pepper
1/4 cup olive oil
1/4 cup butter
  8 medium onions, sliced
  2 cloves garlic, sliced
  3 Tablespoons flour
  4 cups dark beer
1/4 cup brandy Bouquet garni
  of 1 garlic clove, 4 pieces
  celery, 5 sprigs parsley and
  2 bay leaves
1/2 teaspoon thyme
  2 teaspoons Worcestershire
  sauce
  Salt and pepper to taste
  1 cup parsley, chopped

Dredge beef in flour. Heat half the oil in 5–6 quart ovenproof casserole or Dutch oven. Brown meat, a small portion at a time, over medium heat. Add remaining oil as needed. When all meat is browned, return reserved meat to casserole. In large, heavy skillet, melt butter over low heat. Saute onions and garlic until golden and add to meat. Add 3 Tablespoons flour to skillet in which onions were cooked, stirring over medium heat to make light-brown roux. Add more butter if necessary, making sure butter and flour are present in equal proportions. Cook roux about 5 minutes or until light brown. Remove from heat. Slowly add beer and brandy, stirring constantly, and return to heat until slightly thickened. Add sauce to meat. Tie bouquet garni ingredients in cheesecloth and place in casserole. Stir in thyme and Worcestershire. Cover and bake at 350 degrees 2–2 1/2 hours or until meat is tender. Remove bouquet garni. Adjust seasoning. Garnish with parsley. Serve with buttered, parsley noodles.

Serves 8–10   *Dick Ludewig*
May be frozen   CODY, WYOMING

Sergeant Major's Stew

"This stew helps keep the A-Team in shape."

2 pounds stew meat, cut in
  1-inch cubes
1 cup flour seasoned with
  salt and pepper
2 Tablespoons oil
3 (14 1/2-ounce) cans whole
  tomatoes
3 medium onions, cut in
  eighths
2 packages brown gravy mix
2 cups water
2 cups sliced mushrooms

Roll meat in seasoned flour and fry in oil, searing outside only, in a very hot skillet. Place remaining ingredients into a 3 or 4 quart pot and add meat and drippings. Stir vigorously with spoon so tomatoes are cut into thirds. Adjust seasoning. Cover and simmer until onions have a slight crunch left, about 2 hours. If crock pot is used, cook on low 12 hours. Stir occasionally. Serve with hot biscuits.

Serves 4   *George Peppard*
Easy   BEVERLY HILLS, CALIFORNIA

Marshal Dillon's Stew

2 pounds beef chuck, cut
   in 1 1/2-inch cubes
2 Tablespoons fat
4 cups boiling water
1 teaspoon Worcestershire
   sauce
1 clove garlic
1 medium onion, sliced
1–2 bay leaves
1 Tablespoon salt
1 teaspoon sugar
1/2 teaspoon pepper
1/2 teaspoon paprika
   Dash allspice or cloves
6 medium carrots
1 pound (or 18) small
   white onions
   Cubed potatoes, optional

Thoroughly brown meat on all sides in hot fat, turning often. Add water, Worcestershire, garlic, sliced onions, bay leaf and seasonings. Cover and simmer 2 hours, stirring occasionally to prevent sticking. Remove bay leaf and garlic. Add carrots, whole or, if they are large, quartered or halved. Add onions and potatoes. Cover and simmer 30 minutes more or until vegetables are done. Remove meat and vegetables and thicken gravy if desired.

Serves 6–8

James Arness
LOS ANGELES, CALIFORNIA

Cock and Bull Stew

1 large onion, chopped
   Oil
1 pound beef chuck, cubed
2 1/2 cups water
4 Tablespoons A-1 sauce
2 chicken bouillon cubes
2 beef bouillon cubes
1 teaspoon salt
1/2 teaspoon pepper
1 teaspoon sugar
1 (2 1/2 to 3-pound) frying
   chicken, cut in serving
   pieces
3 medium potatoes, cubed
3 large carrots, chunked
1 (16-ounce) can stewed
   tomatoes

Saute onions in oil until clear and set aside. Brown the meat in oil. Pour off extra fat and return onions to pan with the meat. Add the water, A-1, bouillon cubes, salt, pepper and sugar. Simmer 1 hour, then add chicken and cook 1–2 hours more. Approximately 45 minutes before serving, skim off excess fat, then add potatoes, carrots and tomatoes. Thicken broth, if desired, before serving.

Serves 4–6

Sallie Chase
CODY, WYOMING

Mediterranean Stew

2 pounds chuck steak, cut
  in 1 1/2-inch cubes
1 pound sweet Italian
  sausage
1 1/2 cups dry red wine
2 cups water
1 (6-ounce) can tomato
  paste
2 teaspoons salt
3/4 teaspoon pepper
2 teaspoons paprika
1 small jar pimiento
3 medium onions,
  coarsely chopped
1 sweet red or green
  pepper, coarsely chopped
1/4 cup chopped fresh
  parsley
1–2 (1-pound) cans garbanzo
  beans, drained
1 teaspoon grated lemon
  rind
1 head cabbage, cut in
  wedges

In large skillet, saute beef and sausage until brown. Drain meats and slice sausage and transfer to Dutch oven. Add wine, water, tomato paste, salt, pepper and paprika. Bring to boil, cover and simmer 1 1/2–2 hours or until meat is tender. Add remaining ingredients except cabbage. Cover and cook about 20 minutes. Refrigerate overnight to develop flavors. Skim off fat and bring stew to a boil. Add cabbage and cook until tender but still crisp, about 20 minutes. Serve cabbage in separate bowls.

Serves 6–8
Must do ahead

Paddy Chase
CODY, WYOMING

Beef Stroganoff

"This recipe comes from Heinzey Ost, maitre d'hotel at The Red Onion in Aspen, Colorado."

1 1/2 pounds fillet of beef, cut
  in 1 × 1/2-inch cubes
1 pound fettucine noodles
8 Tablespoons butter
1 small onion, grated
4 Tablespoons cognac
8 ounces mushrooms,
  sliced
  Salt and pepper, to taste
1/4 cup dry white wine
1 cup sour cream

Pound the beef thin. Cook noodles until tender. Drain and toss with 5 Tablespoons butter, setting aside in warm place. In a 12-inch frying pan, melt 1 Tablespoon butter. Add onions and saute 1 minute. Add beef and continue to saute 2 minutes. Add cognac and simmer 1 minute. Remove from pan and reserve. Melt remaining butter in the same pan and add mushrooms. Saute until tender. Return meat mixture to pan with salt and pepper. Add wine and simmer briefly. Add sour cream and heat just through, but do not allow mixture to boil. Serve over noodles.

Serves 4–6

Steven Lopata
CLAYTON, MISSOURI

"Building the Fire" by Alfred Jacob Miller. *Courtesy of Buffalo Bill Historical Center, Cody, WY; Gift of the Coe Foundation; 30.64*

Tomato Beef Stroganoff

"An easy party dish."

2 Bermuda onions, finely
   chopped
1/4 cup butter
  2 pounds beef tenderloin,
   cut in thin strips
  1 pound mushrooms,
   sliced
   1 (6-ounce) can tomato
   paste
  1 can tomato soup
1/2 cup dry red wine
  1 teaspoon Tabasco
  1 teaspoon salt
  2 Tablespoons chopped
   parsley
1/4 teaspoon oregano
  1 cup sour cream
   Wild rice

Saute onions in butter. Add meat and brown well. Add remaining ingredients, gradually stirring in sour cream last. Mix well and simmer until tender, about 2 hours. Serve with wild rice. May be made ahead and reheated.

Serves 6
May do ahead

Leann Wassam
SAN PEDRO, CALIFORNIA

Veal Saint Anne

2 1/2 pounds veal, very thinly
   sliced
  4 Tablespoons butter
  4 Tablespoons flour
1 1/2 cups heavy cream
1 1/2 cups consomme
1/2 cup sherry
1/2 teaspoon salt
1/4 teaspoon freshly ground
   pepper

Put veal between 2 sheets of heavy waxed paper and pound it paper-thin with a wooden mallet or the flat side of a cleaver. Melt butter in a heavy skillet and lightly brown both sides of the veal over medium heat, about 2 minutes to a side (overcooking toughens veal). As veal pieces are browned, remove and arrange them in a shallow glass baking dish. When all pieces are browned, add flour to the pan juices, blending well and cooking over low heat until the roux is a golden brown. Stir in the cream until smooth, then add the consomme. Cook only until smooth and well heated, not boiling. Stir in sherry and take from heat. Sprinkle veal with salt and pepper, then pour sauce over all. If doing ahead, cover with foil, cool and refrigerate until an hour before cooking time. Bake at 250–300 degrees 45–60 minutes. Serve with curly noodles.

Serves 6
Easy
May do ahead

Anne C. Tuckerman
BOSTON, MASSACHUSETTS

Veal with Strawberries

"A wonderful spring dish."

4 Tablespoons butter
4 slices veal, pounded
    thin
    Salt and pepper, to taste
1/4 cup sliced almonds
1/2 cup Amaretto
1/4 cup heavy cream
4 sliced strawberries

Melt butter and saute veal until browned. Add seasonings. Remove veal and place on warm platter. In remaining butter, saute almonds. Add Amaretto and flame. Allow liquid to simmer until reduced by half. Add cream. Return veal to pan and garnish with strawberries.

Serves 4

Temptations
CODY, WYOMING

Veal Crepes

2 pounds veal, cubed
1 large onion, chopped
1 can tomatoes
    Garlic salt and pepper,
    to taste
3/4 pound fresh
    mushrooms, sliced
1 green pepper, chopped
    Butter
2 cups sour cream
8 crepes

Brown veal with onion, then add tomatoes and seasonings. Cover and simmer 1 1/2 hours. Saute mushrooms and green pepper in butter, then mix in half the sour cream. Put veal mixture in crepes, cover with remaining sour cream and bake at 300 degrees 20 minutes.

Serves 4–6

William E. Weiss
CODY, WYOMING

Lazy Lamb Shanks

1 package Lipton onion
    soup mix
1/2 cup bourbon
3/4 cup strong coffee
4 or 5 lamb shanks

Mix soup mix, bourbon and coffee and let stand 30 minutes. Arrange shanks in shallow baking dish and pour mixture over them. Cover with foil and bake at 350 degrees 2 1/2 hours, turning occasionally. Uncover and baste during the last half hour of cooking.

Serves 4–5
Easy

Margaret O'B. Smith
SOMERS, NEW YORK

Barbecued Butterflied Lamb

1 (14-ounce) bottle ketchup
1/4 cup mint sauce
1 teaspoon dry mustard
2 Tablespoons brown sugar
4 whole cloves
Juice of 1 lemon
1 leg of lamb, butterflied

Mix all ingredients but lamb and cook until simmering for marinade. Cool overnight. Marinate lamb 24 hours. Grill 15–20 minutes on each side.

Serves 6–8
Easy
Must do ahead

Mrs. Richard N. Young
BERWYN, PENNSYLVANIA

Grilled Butterfly Lamb

1 leg of lamb, butterflied
1/2 cup olive oil
2 Tablespoons lime juice
1 teaspoon cracked pepper
1 teaspoon salt
1 clove garlic, crushed
1/2 cup prepared mint sauce
1/2 cup Escoffier Sauce
    Diable

Marinate meat in a deep serving pan with the next 5 ingredients for at least 2 hours. Broil over charcoal or on a preheated, stove-top broiler about 15–20 minutes on each side, depending on thickness of meat. Combine sauces and serve with meat. The meat differs in thickness, so everyone's taste can be served, from quite rare to well done. Thin slices arranged with garnishes on a platter are attractive.

Serves 6–8
Easy
Must do ahead

Mrs. William G. Cluett
PALM BEACH, FLORIDA

Lamb Curry

"Adapted from a recipe discovered in Turkey."

2 pounds cubed lamb
1 cup water
1/2 cup ketchup
1 medium orange, thinly
  sliced
1 teaspoon minced orange
  rind
1 clove garlic, minced
1 medium onion, sliced
1/2 teaspoon salt
1 cup raisins
2 apples, diced
1/2 teaspoon powdered
  ginger
1 Tablespoon curry powder

Combine all ingredients in a stew pan or large frying pan with tight cover. Simmer 3–4 hours, stirring occasionally. Serve over brown rice with traditional curry condiment dishes: chutney, pickles, shrimp, crumbled bacon, chopped green onions, peanuts, cashews, coconut, chopped hard-boiled eggs, chopped tomatoes, raisins or pineapple chunks. Serve condiments in small dishes beside rice and curry.

Serves 6
Easy

Anita Iceman
DUBOIS, WYOMING

Barbecued Spareribs

3 pounds lean meaty
  spareribs
1 1/2 cups water
1/2 teaspoon salt
1/4 cup margarine
2 Tablespoons finely
  chopped onion
2 Tablespoons prepared
  mustard
1 Tablespoon
  Worcestershire sauce
1/2 cup ketchup
1 Tablespoon vinegar
1 teaspoon sugar
Dash garlic powder,
  optional

Place first 3 ingredients in large kettle and simmer 1 1/2 to 2 hours. Remove ribs from kettle and place in large baking dish. Melt margarine in small saucepan and saute onions until light golden brown. Add remaining ingredients, heat and stir until all is blended. Spread sauce over ribs and bake at 350 degrees 30 minutes or until lightly browned.

Serves 4–6
Easy

Mrs. Felix Bedlan
FAIRBURY, NEBRASKA

Sherry Roast Pork

5 pounds loin of pork
1/2 cup cooking sherry
1/2 cup firmly packed brown
  sugar
1 Tablespoon grated orange
  rind
1/3 cup orange juice
1 teaspoon prepared
  horseradish
1 teaspoon prepared
  mustard

Ask the butcher to saw away part of the bone, which makes roast easier to carve. Place pork, with ribs down, in a shallow roasting pan. In a saucepan, combine other ingredients and bring to a boil. Pour sauce over pork and roast at 325 degrees 35 minutes per pound or about 3 hours for a 5-pound loin, basting often during the first two hours. The pork will have a slightly charred appearance. If desired, roast pork an hour before adding sauce to prevent darkening.

Serves 8–10

Mrs. Florence Dais
CODY, WYOMING

Sweet and Sour Pork

2 pounds boneless pork loin,
  cut in 1/2-inch cubes
1/4 cup soy sauce
  Cornstarch
2 eggs, beaten
  Flour
  Oil
1 large onion, cut in eighths
1 large green pepper, cut in
  1-inch squares
1 cup pineapple chunks,
  drained, juice reserved
2 small tomatoes, cut in
  thin wedges
2/3 cup pineapple juice
1/4 cup wine vinegar
2 Tablespoons oil
3 Tablespoons brown sugar
1 Tablespoon soy sauce
1/2 teaspoon pepper
1 teaspoon cornstarch
2 teaspoons water

Toss pork cubes with soy sauce. Roll in cornstarch, then in eggs, and then in flour. Fry in hot oil until golden brown. Drain on paper towels and keep warm in 350-degree oven. Heat 1 Tablespoon oil in wok or skillet over high heat. Add onion and stir-fry 2 minutes. Add green pepper and stir-fry an additional 2 minutes. Add pineapple and tomatoes and stir-fry 1 minute. Make sauce by combining pineapple juice, vinegar, oil, brown sugar, soy sauce and pepper in saucepan. Bring to boil and add cornstarch which has been mixed with water. Stir until clear and slightly thickened. Return pork to wok, add sauce and stir until thoroughly heated. Serve with hot steamed rice.

Serves 6

Elizabeth C. Heins
FORT COLLINS, COLORADO

Quick Pork Chow Mein, Hunan Style

1 teaspoon salt
1 can chicken broth
2 Tablespoons dry white
  wine
1 Tablespoon sesame oil
2 Tablespoons cornstarch
  Dash pepper
1/4 cup vegetable oil
1 cup thinly sliced pork or
  meat of 3 or 4 center-cut
  pork chops
3 stalks celery, cut
  diagonally
1 medium onion, thinly
  sliced
1 package frozen pea pods
1 can chow mein
  vegetables, drained
1 can sliced mushrooms
1 can sliced water chestnuts
  Sesame oil
1 can dry chow mein
  noodles

Combine first 6 ingredients for sauce, mix thoroughly and set aside. Heat wok or frying pan over high heat and add vegetable oil. Add pork and stir until meat lightens in color. Add celery, onions and pea pods and stir until coated, 1–2 minutes. Add remaining vegetables and heat through. Add sauce and continue stirring until sauce thickens. Sprinkle sesame oil onto vegetables. Serve over dry noodles, accompanied by steamed rice.

Serves 4   *Peg Frisby*
Easy   CODY, WYOMING

Oriental Barbecue

10 ounces plum jam
1/3 cup dark corn syrup
1/3 cup soy sauce
1/4 cup chopped green onion
 2 cloves garlic, minced
 2 teaspoons powdered
   ginger
 2 pounds country-style
   spareribs

Heat all ingredients except ribs in a 13 × 9 × 2-inch baking pan on stove until jam is melted. Trim excess fat from ribs, place in pan and coat heavily with jam mixture. Bake at 350 degrees 1 hour, basting and turning ribs every 15 minutes.

Serves 4   *Gwen T. Coe*
Easy   CODY, WYOMING

Sausage and Rice Royal

2 packages chicken noodle
   soup mix
4 cups water
1 pound ground sausage
1 large onion, chopped
1 green pepper, chopped
1 bunch celery, chopped
1 cup rice
1 package slivered almonds

Bring soup and water to boil and boil 4 minutes. Set soup aside. Saute sausage until light brown and add vegetables and rice. Coat vegetables and rice in drippings, stir in almonds, mix in soup, then pour into casserole. Bake, covered, at 350 degrees 1 hour and uncover for last 5 minutes.

Serves 6–8
Easy
May be frozen

Peg Shreve
CODY, WYOMING

Sausage-Vegetable Pie

1 (10-ounce) package frozen
   chopped broccoli
1 (13 3/4-ounce) package
   refrigerated roll dough
8 ounces Italian bulk
   sausage
8 ounces ground beef
1/4 cup chopped green onions
1 egg, beaten
1/2 teaspoon salt
1/4 teaspoon pepper
1/4 teaspoon basil
3/4 cup soft bread crumbs
2 cups grated cheese (use a
   mixture of 2 or 3 cheeses
   such as Swiss, Cheddar,
   Fontina, Tilsit or
   Monterey Jack)
1 cup ricotta
1/4 teaspoon nutmeg
2 cups thinly sliced carrots,
   cooked until just tender

Cook and drain broccoli. Prepare roll mix through first rising. Meanwhile, cook meats and onions in heavy skillet 10–15 minutes and drain. Reserving 1 Tablespoon of egg in a cup, combine remaining egg with salt, pepper, basil, crumbs and meat mixture. Roll out three fourths of the risen dough and line a spring form pan. Spread the meat mixture evenly on bottom of pan. Combine broccoli, cheeses and nutmeg, spoon over meat mixture, then top with carrots. Roll out remaining dough to cover top of pie. Brush top with reserved egg and cut several slits in top of dough. Bake at 350 degrees 50 minutes, covering top with foil after 30 minutes. Cool 10 minutes before cutting into serving wedges.

Serves 10–12

Carolyn Waller
CODY, WYOMING

Ham Loaf

2 pounds ground ham
1 pound ground pork
1 1/2 cups bread crumbs
1 egg, slightly beaten
1 cup milk
1 cup brown sugar
1 teaspoon dry mustard
1/4 cup water
1/2 cup cider vinegar

SAUCE, OPTIONAL:

1 cup heavy cream,
  whipped
1 small bottle horseradish,
  drained
Salt and pepper, to taste

Combine the first 5 ingredients for loaf and place in large, oiled pan, approximately 9 5/8 × 5 1/2 × 2 3/4-inches. Bake at 375 degrees 15 minutes. Combine last 4 ingredients for basting sauce. Before basting, drain off grease. Bake 45 minutes longer. Serve with horseradish sauce. If prepared loaf has been frozen, allow to thaw completely before baking.

Serves 6–8
Easy   *Adelaide M. Donnan*
May be frozen   WILSON, WYOMING

Ham and Broccoli Royale

1 cup rice
2 packages frozen broccoli
  spears
6 Tablespoons butter
2 cups fresh bread
  crumbs, about 4 slices
2 large onions, chopped
3 Tablespoons flour
1 teaspoon salt
1/4 teaspoon pepper
3 cups milk
1 1/2 pounds cooked ham,
  cubed, about 4 cups
8 ounces sliced American
  cheese

Cook rice and put into greased 13 × 9 × 2-inch baking dish. Cook broccoli and drain well. Place in a layer over rice. Melt 2 Tablespoons of the butter and drizzle over bread crumbs. Set aside. Cook onions in remaining butter until soft. Add flour, salt and pepper and cook until bubbly. Stir in milk. Cook and stir until thick and boil 1 minute. Stir in ham and heat until bubbly. Pour sauce over all layers in dish. Place cheese slices over the sauce and crumbs over all. Cover and chill. Bake at 350 degrees 45 minutes.

Serves 8   *Yvonne Nielson*
Must do ahead   CODY, WYOMING

Horn Headresses, ca. 1860, Northern Plains. *Courtesy of Buffalo Bill Historical Center, Cody, WY; Catherine Bradford McClellan Collection, Gift of the Coe Foundation; NA.203.18*

Baked Ham

"From The Palace Hotel in San Francisco."

1 (9–10 pound) ham, with
  bone
Cloves
Bourbon
Butter
English marmalade
1/8 cup dry mustard
1 cup currant jelly
1/2 cup vinegar
1/4 cup sugar

Score ham, stud with cloves and bake at 450 degrees, about 30 minutes or until fat opens. Pour a mixture of 2 parts bourbon, 1 part butter and 1 part marmalade over ham. Continue baking at 325–350 degrees until done. Serve with a sauce made of mustard mixed with some of the liquid and added to the last 3 ingredients.

Serves 10–12
Easy

John Sinai
SAN FRANCISCO, CALIFORNIA

Spanish Sandwiches

1 small can green olives,
  chopped
1 small can pimientos,
  chopped
1 (4-ounce) can chopped
  green chiles
1 small can tomato sauce
1 (6–8 ounce) package sliced
  ham, chopped
8 ounces Cheddar cheese,
  grated
  Salt and pepper, to taste
12 French rolls

Mix all ingredients except rolls. Refrigerate overnight. Cut off top thirds of rolls and hollow them out. Fill rolls with cheese mixture and replace tops. Wrap in waxed paper and bake at 250 degrees 1 hour.

Serves 8–12
Easy
Must do ahead

Pamela Stockton
CODY, WYOMING

Sauce for Baked Ham

1/2 cup butter, melted
1 Tablespoon flour
1/4 cup orange juice
1/3 cup brown sugar
2 Tablespoons sugar
1/4 teaspoon cinnamon
1/4 teaspoon nutmeg
1/8 teaspoon cloves
1/2 cup apple jelly

Blend all ingredients and bring to a boil, stirring constantly. Serve hot with baked ham.

Easy

Nancy L. Allen
WHEATLAND, WYOMING

Rose Hill's Steak Butter

1 cup butter, slightly
  softened
4 dashes Worcestershire
  sauce
4 dashes Maggi's
3 dashes salt
3 dashes pepper
2 dashes soy sauce
1 Tablespoon parsley
1 Tablespoon A-1 sauce

Combine all ingredients and mash thoroughly. Form into a large ball or small balls for individual servings. Store tightly wrapped or in airtight container in refrigerator or freezer. Serve with hot meats like steak, elk or venison.

Yields 1 cup
Easy
May be frozen

Mrs. John R. Woods
ST. LOUIS, MISSOURI

Cal's Macho Mustard

"Keeps for weeks in the refrigerator."

2 (4-ounce) cans Colman's
  dry mustard
6 eggs
1 pound brown sugar
2 cups wine vinegar
  Juice of 1 lemon

Mix thoroughly in blender. Put in top of double boiler over simmering water. Beat with wire whisk until thick.

Yields 1 quart
Easy

Calvert Moore
SAN FRANCISCO, CALIFORNIA

Fluffy Mustard Sauce

"Wonderful and light!"

2 egg yolks, beaten
1 Tablespoon sugar
3 Tablespoons prepared
  mustard
2 Tablespoons vinegar
1 Tablespoon water
1/2 teaspoon salt
1 Tablespoon butter
1 Tablespoon prepared
  horseradish
1/2 cup heavy cream, whipped

Mix first 6 ingredients well and cook about 5 minutes in double boiler over hot, not boiling, water, stirring constantly until mixture thickens. Remove from heat and blend in butter and horseradish. Cool thoroughly. Fold in whipped cream and store in refrigerator. To serve with warm meat, remove from refrigerator 30 minutes before serving.

Yields 1 1/3 cups
May do ahead

Anita Iceman
DUBOIS, WYOMING

Mustard Mold

"Especially good with ham, hot or cold."

1 envelope unflavored
  gelatin
4 teaspoons dry mustard
1/2 teaspoon salt
4 eggs, beaten
1/4 cup white vinegar
1 (7-ounce) bottle lemon-
  lime carbonated beverage
  or tonic
2 cups sour cream

Combine gelatin, mustard and salt and stir into eggs. Stir in vinegar and carbonated beverage. Cook in heavy saucepan or double boiler over very low heat until mixture is thickened, stirring constantly. Gently stir in sour cream. Pour into a lightly oiled 1 quart mold and chill until firm.

Serves 10
Easy
Must do ahead

Katie Downes
ENGLEWOOD, NEW JERSEY

Dennis Day Marinade

"This superior marinade for any meat came from Dennis Day's barbecue book published many years ago."

2 cloves garlic, crushed
1/2 cup soy sauce
1/4 cup brown sugar
2 Tablespoons olive oil
1/2 teaspoon cracked pepper
2 small pieces ginger root,
  grated

Mix all ingredients thoroughly. Use to marinate about 3 pounds of meat or to brush on barbecued hamburgers or chicken.

Yields 3/4 cup
Easy

Margaret S. Coe
CODY, WYOMING

Linda's Barbecue Sauce

1/2 cup white vinegar
1 cup water
4 Tablespoons sugar
2 Tablespoons mustard
1 teaspoon pepper
1/2 teaspoon red pepper
2 slices lemon
2 slices onion
1/2 cup butter
1/2 cup ketchup
4 Tablespoons
  Worcestershire sauce
2 teaspoons liquid smoke

Combine first 8 ingredients and simmer 20 minutes. Remove from heat, add remaining ingredients and blend well. Remove lemon and onion slices. Serve warm.

Yields 2 cups
Easy

Mrs. Lewis S. Robinson, III
WEST YELLOWSTONE, MONTANA

Hot Apple Chutney

12 apples, peeled and cored
2 large green peppers,
  finely chopped
2 large onions, finely
  chopped
3 ounces green chiles,
  stemmed, seeded and
  chopped
3 cloves garlic, minced
1/2 cup fresh ginger, finely
  grated
2 teaspoons salt
1/2 teaspoon cayenne
3 1/2 cups brown sugar
2 1/2 cups cider vinegar
1 1/2 cups raisins

Place all ingredients in a large kettle. Cook uncovered over low heat 3 hours, stirring often. Keep refrigerated. For milder version use fewer chiles and less ginger.

Yields 8 cups

Susan Blaisdell Coe
RED BANK, NEW JERSEY

Chicken Chasseur

1/4 cup flour
  1 teaspoon salt
1/4 teaspoon oregano
1/8 teaspoon pepper
  4 chicken breasts or equal
    amount of cubed chicken
  4 Tablespoons butter
2/3 cup dry white wine
  1 Tablespoon lemon juice
1/2 cup chopped onion
  1 cup sliced fresh
    mushrooms
  2 medium tomatoes, peeled
    and diced
  1 teaspoon sugar
1/4 cup water

Blend first 4 ingredients. Set aside 1 Tablespoon flour mixture and coat chicken with remainder. Brown chicken in 3 Tablespoons butter. Combine wine and juice and pour over chicken. Add onion. Bring to a boil, reduce heat, cover and cook over low heat 45 minutes or bake at 350 degrees 45 minutes. Set aside chicken and keep warm. In a separate pan, cook mushrooms in remaining butter and drain. Add tomatoes, sugar, and wine mixture from pan and simmer 5 minutes. Blend reserved flour with water, add to sauce and simmer until thickened. Pour over chicken and serve immediately with wild, brown or white rice.

Serves 4

Ally Tilden
CODY, WYOMING

Chicken Imperial

6 boneless chicken breasts,
  halved
1 cup sherry
1 cup bread crumbs
1 teaspoon salt
1/4 teaspoon pepper
  1 cup grated Parmesan
    cheese
  2 Tablespoons minced
    parsley
  1 clove garlic, crushed
  1 cup chopped almonds
3/4 cup melted butter

"Makes a nice dinner party dish."

Marinate chicken in sherry 2–3 hours. Combine remaining ingredients except butter. Dip chicken in butter, roll in crumb mixture and arrange in 13 × 9-inch pan. Sprinkle with remaining crumb mixture. Bake at 350 degrees 1 hour.

Serves 6
Easy
Must do ahead

Anita Renee DiGiorgio
ELLICOTT CITY, MARYLAND

Chicken Dijon

"Tomato adds a touch of color."

6–8 boneless chicken
   breasts, skinned
3 Tablespoons margarine
3 Tablespoons flour
1 cup chicken broth
1/2 cup half and half
2 Tablespoons Dijon
   mustard
Fresh tomato wedges,
   optional
Fresh parsley, optional

In a large skillet, cook chicken in margarine over medium heat about 20 minutes until tender and lightly browned. Set chicken aside. Stir flour into skillet drippings and add chicken broth and cream. Cook and stir until thick and bubbly and stir in mustard. Return chicken to pan. If serving immediately, heat about 10 minutes and garnish with tomatoes and parsley. Dish may be prepared ahead and reheated, covered, about 15 minutes.

Serves 4
Easy
May do ahead

Ruth Carpenter
TETON VILLAGE, WYOMING

Herbed Chicken Breasts

4 large boneless chicken
   breasts, halved and
   skinned
1 teaspoon rosemary
1 teaspoon thyme
1 teaspoon marjoram
1 teaspoon Accent
2 teaspoons salt
3/4 cup butter
3/4 cup butter
3 Tablespoons lemon juice
1 1/2 cups sherry
4 cups cooked wild rice

Rub breasts with mixture of herbs and salt. Melt first 3/4 cup butter in heavy pan or skillet and cook breasts slowly, 30–35 minutes or until tender. Turn often and watch carefully. When done, remove breasts to a warm serving dish. Melt the second 3/4 cup butter and add the lemon juice and sherry, stirring and simmering for 5 minutes. Return breasts to pan and keep warm (no more cooking). Serve breasts on wild rice, spooning sauce over them.

Serves 6
Easy

Lazy L&B Ranch
DUBOIS, WYOMING

Breast of Chicken Gismonde

4 chicken breasts,
  skinned and boned,
  if desired
  Salt
2 or 3 eggs
1 Tablespoon olive oil
1/3 cup finely grated bread
1/3 cup grated Parmesan
  cheese
  Flour
9 Tablespoons butter or
  margarine
8 ounces sliced
  mushrooms
3 cups cooked spinach

Sprinkle chicken with salt. Beat eggs and oil together. Combine bread and cheese. Dip chicken in flour, then in egg mixture and finally in bread mixture. Brown in 6 Tablespoons butter about 45 minutes or until chicken is cooked, turning once. Saute mushrooms in 3 Tablespoons butter. Arrange chicken on hot spinach and top with mushrooms.

Serves 4

William E. Weiss
CODY, WYOMING

Chicken and Almond Delight

4 boneless chicken breasts
1 teaspoon salt
1/4 teaspoon pepper
4 Tablespoons flour
1 egg, slightly beaten
1 cup finely chopped
  almonds
2 Tablespoons vegetable
  shortening
1/4 cup butter
2 Tablespoons flour
1/2 teaspoon salt
2 Tablespoons sherry
1 cup half and half

Season chicken with salt and pepper and dust lightly with flour. Dip chicken in egg, then roll in almonds. Heat shortening with half the butter in skillet and brown chicken on both sides. Place chicken in a foil-lined baking pan. Pour 2 Tablespoons drippings over chicken. Fold edges of foil together over chicken and bake at 350 degrees 1 hour. Melt remaining butter with remaining drippings. Stir in flour and salt and blend. Add sherry and cream and cook, stirring constantly, until thick. Saute remaining almonds in butter until golden brown. Serve chicken topped with gravy and almonds.

Serves 6–8
May be frozen
May do ahead

Mrs. Phillip V. Carroll
CHARLES CITY, IOWA

Chicken Breasts with Artichokes

3 boneless chicken
breasts, halved and
skinned
Salt, pepper and
paprika, to taste
1/2 cup butter or margarine
1 (15-ounce) can
artichoke hearts,
drained and halved
1/2–1 pound fresh
mushrooms, halved
3 Tablespoons flour
1/2 cup dry white wine
1 1/2 cups canned chicken
broth

Dust chicken with salt, pepper and paprika. In skillet, saute chicken quickly in butter until brown, then place in casserole. Scatter artichoke hearts over chicken. In same skillet, saute mushrooms slightly and add to casserole. Sprinkle flour gently into remaining butter in skillet, mixing slowly while adding wine and broth. Simmer 5 minutes until thickened slightly. Pour sauce over chicken. Cover and bake at 375 degrees about 40 minutes. Serve over rice or egg noodles.

Serves 4–6
Easy

Paddy Chase
CODY, WYOMING

Chicken Breasts with Seafood Sauce

"An elegant party dish."

1/2 cup butter
4 boneless chicken
breasts halved and
skinned
2 Tablespoons sherry
1 pound mushrooms,
sliced
2 Tablespoons flour
1 1/2 cups chicken stock
1 bay leaf
1 Tablespoon tomato
paste
2 Tablespoons chopped
chives
Salt and pepper, to taste
2 or 3 medium lobster tails
or 4–5 king crab legs,
cooked and cut in
bite-sized pieces
3 ripe tomatoes,
quartered

Heat butter in large skillet until foamy. Add chicken and cook until golden brown. Sprinkle with sherry and remove to shallow baking dish. Cover with foil and bake at 300 degrees 25–30 minutes. To the skillet, add mushrooms and more butter, if needed, and saute until tender. Remove mushrooms. Add flour and chicken stock and simmer until thickened. Season with bay leaf, tomato paste, chives, salt and pepper. Add lobster, tomatoes and reserved mushrooms. Heat thoroughly. Arrange chicken in chafing dish, pour sauce over and serve. If desired, sauce may be prepared in advance, but lobster and vegetables not added until just before serving.

Serves 6–8

Liz Swanson
CODY, WYOMING

Stuffed Chicken Breasts

1 medium onion, finely
  chopped
6 green onions, minced
2 Tablespoons butter
1 large can artichoke hearts,
  chopped
1 large can pitted black
  olives, chopped
1/2 cup slivered almonds
1 Tablespoon tarragon
  Salt and pepper, to taste
4 boneless chicken breasts

Brown onions in butter. Add remaining ingredients except chicken and mix well. Loosen skin of chicken and place stuffing between skin and meat. Chill. When breasts are cold, cut in half lengthwise. Bake at 350 degrees 45 minutes. Serve hot or cold with hollandaise sauce.

Serves 8
Must do ahead

Robin Weiss
CODY, WYOMING

Italian Chicken

6–8 chicken breasts, halved
  and skinned
5–6 large carrots, scraped and
  chunked
4–5 medium potatoes,
  unpeeled, cut in 1-inch
  cubes
  Salt and pepper, to taste
1 (16-ounce) bottle zesty
  Italian dressing
1 cup broccoli flowerets
1 cup cauliflower flowerets
1 medium green pepper,
  thinly sliced
1 cup sliced fresh
  mushrooms
1 cup sliced zucchini,
  optional

Arrange chicken, meat-side-down, in a well-buttered casserole dish. Cover with carrots, then potatoes. Sprinkle with salt and pepper. Pour dressing over all, cover with foil and bake at 375 degrees 30–40 minutes. Remove from oven, turn chicken and add broccoli and cauliflower. Cover again and bake 30–45 minutes more, adding green pepper, mushrooms and zucchini during the final 10 minutes.

Serves 6–8
Easy

Gloria Cottle
CODY, WYOMING

Greek Chicken with Zucchini

1 Tablespoon margarine
1 (3-pound) chicken, cut up
1 clove garlic, crushed
1/4 cup chicken broth
2 medium zucchini, cut in
    1/4-inch slices
1/4 teaspoon salt
1/8 teaspoon pepper

SAUCE:

2 egg yolks
2 teaspoons cornstarch
1/8 teaspoon salt
    Dash red pepper
3/4 cup chicken broth
2 Tablespoons lemon juice

In a Dutch oven, melt margarine over low heat. Add chicken, a few pieces at a time, and brown slowly on all sides. Pour off fat. Add garlic and chicken broth, cover tightly and simmer 10 minutes. Add zucchini, salt and pepper. Cover and simmer about 15 minutes until chicken is fork tender.

For sauce, combine yolks, cornstarch, salt and pepper in saucepan and stir until smooth. Add chicken broth and cook over medium heat, stirring constantly until mixture just starts to boil. Remove from heat and stir in lemon juice. Do not reheat. Transfer chicken and zucchini to serving platter and spoon on sauce.

Serves 4
Easy

Lois Miller
CODY, WYOMING

Chicken with Orange Glaze

"Also wonderful with duck."

2 chickens, cut up
    Salt and pepper, to taste
3/4 cup frozen orange juice
    concentrate
3 Tablespoons butter
1/2 teaspoon ginger
1/4 cup white wine or sherry
2 teaspoons cornstarch

Sprinkle chicken with salt and pepper and place pieces, skin-side-up, in shallow baking dish. Bake at 350 degrees 30 minutes. In saucepan, combine 1/2 cup concentrate, butter and ginger, heat and spoon over chicken. Bake 30 minutes longer, basting occasionally. Remove from oven, add remaining concentrate, wine and cornstarch to pan drippings and simmer a few minutes. Serve sauce separately.

Serves 6–8

Joan S. Richardson
LAKE FOREST, ILLINOIS

Chicken in Wine with Lemon Sauce

1 1/2 pounds white chicken
    meat, sliced
1/2 cup flour
  6 Tablespoons unsalted
    butter
    Salt, to taste
1/2 cup dry white wine
    Juice of 1/2 lemon
1–2 Tablespoons sugar
    Parsley sprigs

Pound chicken slices to make them uniform and tender. Press pieces in flour and pat them gently to work in as much as possible. Melt butter in large frying pan over medium heat and add chicken. Turn and salt. When meat is done, pour in wine and heat to bubbling. Add lemon juice and stir. Add sugar to taste. If a tangier sauce is desired, add more lemon and sugar and cook a little longer. Arrange chicken with sauce and parsley on a serving platter.

Serves 4–5
Easy

Millie Jones
CODY, WYOMING

Chicken Divan

"A dish with dash."

2 (10 3/4-ounce) cans
    condensed cream of
    chicken soup
1 cup sour cream
1 cup mayonnaise
1 cup shredded sharp
    Cheddar cheese
1 Tablespoon lemon juice
1 teaspoon curry powder,
    to taste
    Salt and pepper, to taste
2 (10-ounce) packages
    frozen broccoli, cooked
    and drained
    Grated Parmesan cheese
    Meat from 3 cooked
    chicken breasts
    Butter
    Paprika

Mix first 7 ingredients. Arrange broccoli in bottom of greased, shallow 3-quart casserole. Sprinkle with Parmesan. Spread meat over broccoli and sprinkle with Parmesan. Pour sauce over all. Dot with butter and sprinkle with Parmesan and paprika. Bake at 350 degrees 30–40 minutes or until bubbly and thoroughly heated.

Serves 6–8
Easy

Elizabeth C. Heins
FORT COLLINS, COLORADO

Chicken Curry Madras

"Spicy dishes make a person feel cool in a steamy climate."

1 thin slice ginger root
2 cloves garlic
2 (1–1 1/2 pound) chickens, cut up
1 teaspoon turmeric
1 teaspoon crushed red pepper
1 1/2 teaspoons salt
2 cups cottage cheese
6 whole cloves
4 whole cardamom seeds
4 (2–3 inch) cinnamon sticks
2 Tablespoons oil
8 green chiles
1 large white onion, coarsely chopped
15 green onions, coarsely chopped
1 Tablespoon poppy seeds
4 teaspoons coriander
2 cups coconut milk or substitute (see procedure)
10 cashew nuts
Shredded coconut
Raisins

Grind ginger and garlic and mix with chicken. Add turmeric, red pepper and salt. Cover with cottage cheese and allow to marinate 30–60 minutes. Fry cloves, cardamom and cinnamon in oil in a heavy iron skillet over low heat. After 5 minutes, discard whole spices and add green chiles and onions and fry until onions are golden. Add chicken mixture and simmer, stirring occasionally. Grind poppy seed and coriander into a soft paste and blend with coconut milk. When chicken is tender, slowly add poppy seed mixture. Simmer until liquid thickens to gravy. Add cashews and mix well. Garnish with coconut and raisins. Serve over rice and with side dishes of coconut, ground peanuts, currants, chutney, and other traditional curry condiments.

For coconut milk substitute, place 1 cup fresh or dry shredded coconut into 3 cups boiling water. Puree in blender or processor 1 minute, then squeeze out all liquid using either a food mill or doubled cheesecloth. Pulp can be frozen and used later for other recipes. Makes 2 1/2 cups. Substitute may be prepared ahead.

Serves 4
Time-consuming
Must do ahead

Steven Lopata
CLAYTON, MISSOURI

Chicken Curry

"A super recipe for parties, as it may easily be doubled."

1 Tablespoon garlic powder
2 medium onions, chopped
1 cup tomato puree or
   2 tomatoes, peeled and
   chopped
1 large can apple pie
   filling
1/2 cup butter, melted
1 Tablespoon flour
2 Tablespoons curry
   powder
1 Tablespoon sugar
1/4 teaspoon dry mustard
   Pinch ground ginger
2 cups chicken broth
   Juice and rind of 1 lime
1 cup raisins
2 1/2 cups cubed chicken
1/2 cup cream
2 Tablespoons chopped
   chutney

Saute first 4 ingredients in butter. Add remaining ingredients and simmer 30 minutes. Reduce heat and cook 15 minutes more. Serve with hot rice.

Serves 8–12

Katrina Demme
CODY, WYOMING

Sweet and Sour Chicken

"Finger lickin' good."

2 chickens, cut up
1 (16-ounce) can jellied
   cranberry sauce
1 (8-ounce) bottle
   Catalina salad dressing
1 package dry onion soup
   mix

Place chicken in baking dish in single layer. Mix remaining ingredients well and pour over chicken. Bake at 350 degrees 1 1/2 hours.

Serves 6–8
Easy

Rawan Guest Ranch
JELM, WYOMING

Chinese Chicken Almond

2 cups finely sliced
uncooked breast of
chicken
1/4 cup peanut oil
3 (5-ounce) cans diced
bamboo shoots, drained
2 cups diced celery
1 cup diced romaine
2 (5-ounce) cans water
chestnuts, drained and
sliced
1/2 cup blanched almonds
2 Tablespoons soy sauce
3 cups chicken broth
1/4 cup cornstarch
1/2 cup cold water
Salt

Over high heat, quickly fry chicken in oil in large, heavy skillet or wok, taking care not to overcook. Stir frequently. Add next 7 ingredients. Mix thoroughly. Cover and steam 5 minutes. Blend cornstarch and cold water. Add to chicken mixture and cook, stirring constantly, until thick. Adjust seasoning. Garnish with extra almonds. Serve immediately with rice or Chinese fried rice.

Serves 8

Peg Garlow
CODY, WYOMING

Aunt Donna's Sesame Chicken

"A great prepare-ahead dish."

3–4 pounds chicken breasts,
skinned and boned
1/4 cup sesame seeds
3 Tablespoons oil
1/4 cup soy sauce
2 Tablespoons brown sugar
1 1/2 teaspoons minced fresh
ginger or 3/4 teaspoon
ground
1/4 teaspoon pepper
1 clove garlic, minced
4 green onions, thinly
sliced

Tenderize breasts, if desired, by pounding them between pieces of waxed paper. Cut meat in 1-inch chunks and set aside. Combine sesame seeds and oil in heavy skillet and cook over medium heat about 2 minutes or until seeds turn golden. Cool. Stir in remaining ingredients, reserving half the onions. Mix in the chicken, cover and refrigerate 1–4 hours. Arrange chicken mixture in a single layer in a baking pan and broil 10 minutes, 6 inches from heat. Turn mixture and broil 5 minutes longer. Serve on a bed of hot rice and garnish with reserved onions.

Serves 4–5
Easy
Must do ahead

Jonathan Thorne
VALLEY RANCH, WYOMING

Hawaiian Island Chicken

15 boneless chicken
breasts, skinned
1 bottle chutney,
chopped
1/2 cup dark rum
2 cups bread crumbs
Butter or margarine
Chicken broth

Pound breasts and spread with chutney. Roll and skewer. Roll in rum and bread crumbs and brown in butter or margarine. Put in flat casserole. Partially cover chicken with rum and broth. Cover with foil and bake at 375 degrees 30 minutes. Add more rum during the final 10 minutes.

Serves 15
Easy

Helen M. Hobbs
STONINGTON, CONNECTICUT

Chicken with Snow Peas and Peanuts, Szechuan Style

1 Tablespoon peanut oil
1 slice fresh ginger root,
minced
1 clove garlic, finely
chopped
2 green onions, chopped
1 tiny dried hot chile
pepper, minced
2 boneless chicken
breasts, skinned and
cut in bite-sized pieces
1/2 cup unsalted peanuts
or cashews
8 to 10 large fresh
mushrooms, sliced
8 ounces fresh snow
peas or broccoli
1 cup chicken stock
2 Tablespoons soy sauce
2 Tablespoons sake or
sherry
1 Tablespoon cornstarch
3 Tablespoons cold
water

Heat oil in wok or large skillet. Add next 4 ingredients and cook over high heat 1–2 minutes. Add chicken and saute 2–5 minutes, only until cooked through. Add nuts, mushrooms and snow peas and continue cooking another 3–4 minutes, stirring constantly. Combine stock, soy sauce and sake in a small bowl and add to the chicken mixture. Heat through. Combine cornstarch and water and add to the wok. Stir until mixture thickens. Serve over or with Chinese-style rice. Serves 4 when served as a main dish or 8 as part of a Chinese dinner.

Serves 4–8

Shirley Wilkerson
CODY, WYOMING

"21" Chicken Hash

BECHAMEL SAUCE:

2 cups milk
2 Tablespoons butter
2 Tablespoons flour
1/4 teaspoon white pepper
Salt, to taste
Dash Tabasco
Dash Worcestershire
sauce

HASH:

1 cup bechamel sauce
1/2 cup half and half
1/4 cup sherry
2 cups cooked diced
white chicken meat
2 egg yolks

For sauce, scald milk. Melt butter in a heavy-bottomed saucepan with a metal handle. Add flour, stirring with whisk for a couple of minutes. Gradually stir in milk and continue to whisk until thick. Season with remaining ingredients and place the saucepan, covered, in a preheated 300-degree oven. Bake 1 1/2 hours and strain the sauce, which should be very thick and fluffy. Adjust seasoning. Yields 1 1/2 cups.

For hash, combine bechamel and cream in a saucepan, whipping with whisk until fluffy. Add sherry and mix well. Stir in chicken and cook over low heat until mixture is hot. Adjust seasoning. Stir in yolks, blending well with a spoon. Serve hot over toast, waffle, baked potato shell or wild rice or incorporate into an omelet or crepe.

Serves 4–6   *"21" Club*
Must do ahead   NEW YORK, NEW YORK

Baked Chicken Salad

2–2 1/2 cups cooked chicken
breast, chunked
2 cups diced celery
1 cup cream of chicken
soup
1 cup mayonnaise
1 can water chestnuts,
drained and diced
1 teaspoon lemon juice
1 heaping Tablespoon
grated onion
Salt and pepper,
to taste
Mushrooms, slivered
almonds, and
pimientos, optional
1/2 cup grated cheese
1/2 cup canned French-
fried onions

Combine all ingredients but cheese and onions in casserole. Top with cheese, then onions. Bake at 350 degrees 30–40 minutes.

Serves 6–8   *Mrs. John R. Woods*
Easy   ST. LOUIS, MISSOURI

"Outlet at Lake Tahoe" by Albert Bierstadt. *Courtesy of Buffalo Bill Historical Center, Cody, WY; Gift of Mr. and Mrs. Richard J. Cashman; 18.80*

Mock Chicken Souffle

"Good for brunch or summer luncheon."

2 cups cooked, cubed,
  well-seasoned chicken
1 cup chopped celery
2/3 cup chopped onion
1/2 cup chopped green pepper
1/4 cup chopped pimiento,
  drained
1/2 cup mayonnaise
4 eggs, beaten
3 cups milk
1 teaspoon salt
1/2 teaspoon thyme
1/2 teaspoon marjoram
  Pinch curry powder
4 slices white bread, cubed,
  crusts removed
6 slices white bread, whole,
  crusts removed
1 can cream of mushroom
  soup
1/2 cup grated sharp Cheddar
  cheese

Combine first 12 ingredients and mix slightly. Place cubed bread in bottom of greased 9 × 12-inch baking dish. Pour chicken mixture over bread, cover and refrigerate overnight. About 1 hour before serving, remove the casserole from the refrigerator and adjust seasoning. Bake at 375 degrees 15 minutes. Remove from oven and arrange bread slices on top. Spread soup over bread and sprinkle with cheese. Reduce oven to 350 degrees and bake 45–60 minutes until puffed and golden.

Serves 6–8
Time consuming
Must do ahead

Gina Guy
PORTLAND, OREGON

Special Chicken Sandwiches

REMOULADE SAUCE:

1 cup mayonnaise
1/4 cup milk
2 1/2 Tablespoons chopped
   dill pickle
1 Tablespoon capers
1 1/2 teaspoons Dijon
   mustard
1/2 teaspoon anchovy paste
1/2 teaspoon chopped parsley
1/2 teaspoon tarragon
1/2 teaspoon basil

SANDWICHES:

4 large slices dark rye
   bread
4 slices Swiss cheese
1 cup shredded lettuce
4 large slices cold cooked
   chicken or turkey breast
8 slices bacon, crisply
   cooked
2 hard-boiled eggs, finely
   chopped
1/4 cup sliced green olives

Make remoulade sauce by mixing all ingredients well. Chill. Dividing ingredients in 4 equal parts, assemble sandwiches by layering in the following order: cheese, lettuce, remoulade sauce, chicken, a smaller quantity of sauce, bacon, egg and olive. Garnish each plate with tomato quarters.

Serves 4   *Carolyn Depue*
Must do ahead   WICKENBURG, ARIZONA

Cornish Hens Stuffed with Grapes

"Elegant, but quick, easy and inexpensive."

6 Cornish game hens
  Salt and pepper, to taste
  Seedless grapes
4 Tablespoons parsley flakes
2 Tablespoons tarragon
1/2 cup butter, melted

Wash and dry hens. Rub with salt and pepper. Stuff with grapes until full. Place in shallow roasting pan. Grind parsley and tarragon with mortar and pestle until fine and add to melted butter. Roast at 350 degrees 1 hour, basting with butter mixture every 15 minutes until done.

Serves 6
Easy

Mrs. C. H. Kibbee
SHERIDAN, WYOMING

Long Island Duck Montmorency

1 (5-pound) Long Island
  duckling
  Salt
2/3 cup each diced onions,
  carrots, and celery
4 bay leaves
1–2 Tablespoons flour
1/2 cup Madeira
2 cups brown sauce

MONTMORENCY SAUCE:

1/2 cup currant jelly
1/2 cup sugar
1/2 cup red wine vinegar
  Cornstarch, optional
1 dozen pitted black cherries
1/2 cup port

Clean, wash and truss duckling. Sprinkle salt in bottom of roasting pan to keep duckling from sticking. Roast at 400 degrees 1 1/2 hours. Remove excess fat as it accumulates. During the last 15 minutes of roasting, place vegetables and bay leaves around duckling. Remove duckling to serving platter and keep warm. Pour excess fat from pan and place pan over medium heat. Remove bay leaves and sprinkle flour over vegetables, stirring to absorb remaining fat. Stir in Madeira and brown sauce. Simmergently 10–15 minutes. Strain, discard vegetables and keep sauce warm.

For Montmorency sauce, combine jelly, sugar and vinegar in a saucepan. Cook over medium heat, stirring constantly until mixture is reduced to the consistency of caramel. Add to the strained sauce mixture and simmer 30 minutes. If sauce becomes too thin, thicken with a little cornstarch. Strain into a gravy boat. Heat cherries in port and add to sauce.

Serves 4
Time-consuming

"21" Club
NEW YORK, NEW YORK

Turkey Pancakes

1 cup flour
2 teaspoons baking powder
1/4 teaspoon nutmeg
   Dash pepper
1/2 teaspoon salt
1 cup thin turkey or chicken
   gravy
1/8 teaspoon thyme
2 cups finely chopped turkey
3 Tablespoons melted butter
1 small onion, grated

Sift together first 5 ingredients. Stir in remaining ingredients. Cook on a greased, 350-degree griddle.

Serves 4–6   *William E. Weiss*
Easy   Cody, Wyoming

Garlic Sauce

1 medium potato, boiled
   and peeled
2 cloves garlic, pressed
1 cup olive oil
2 Tablespoons wine vinegar
   Salt and pepper, to taste

"This sauce is traditionally served in Lebanon with grilled chicken."

Mash potato and combine with remaining ingredients.

Yields 1 1/2 cups   *Robin Weiss*
          Cody, Wyoming

Fish

Crab Meat au Gratin

1 Tablespoon butter
2 Tablespoons flour
1 (10 1/2-ounce) can
  cream of mushroom
  soup
3/4 cup water
1 1/2 cups soft bread
  crumbs
18 ounces crab meat
  Dash pepper
7–8 ounces grated sharp
  Cheddar cheese

Melt butter and mix with flour. Add soup and water, stirring until smooth and thick. Add remaining ingredients. Bake at 350 degrees 45–60 minutes, until bubbly.

Serves 6 *Ally Tilden*
Easy CODY, WYOMING

Crab Meat Newburg

2 1/2 cups crab meat
4 Tablespoons cooking
  sherry
2 teaspoons lemon juice
2 Tablespoons butter
1/4 teaspoon paprika
  Dash nutmeg
  Dash cayenne
1 cup cream or
  evaporated milk
2 egg yolks, slightly
  beaten
1/4–1/2 teaspoon salt

Flake crab and combine with sherry and lemon juice. Let stand in refrigerator 30 minutes. Melt butter and add crab, paprika, nutmeg and cayenne. Stir lightly. Cover and cook over low heat 8 minutes. Heat cream very slightly and pour over yolks. Add gradually to crab mixture and continue to cook about 5 minutes longer, stirring until thickened. Do not boil. Add salt. Serve on toast points or patty shells. Newburg may also be prepared with shrimp.

Serves 4–6 *Peg Garlow*
Must do ahead CODY, WYOMING

Crab Burgers

1 cup flaked crab meat
1/4 cup diced celery
2 Tablespoons chopped
  onion
1/2 cup shredded
  Cheddar cheese
1/3 cup mayonnaise
4 hamburger buns,
  buttered

Combine ingredients and spread on buttered buns. Broil until hot, bubbly and brown. "Burgers" may be prepared ahead of serving time.

Serves 4
Easy *Mrs. Kelly Howie*
May do ahead BIG HORN, WYOMING

Hot Crab Meat and Avocado Salad

"Crab salad with a flair."

8 ounces crab meat
1/3 cup chopped celery
3 hard-boiled eggs,
  chopped
2 Tablespoons chopped
  pimiento
1 Tablespoon chopped
  onion
1/2 teaspoon salt
1/2 cup Thousand Island
  dressing
3 large avocados
  Lemon juice
3 Tablespoons bread
  crumbs
1 Tablespoon melted
  butter
2 Tablespoons slivered
  almonds

Mix first 7 ingredients. Cut unpeeled avocados in half, brush with lemon juice and fill with crab mixture. Toss crumbs in butter and spoon over crab mixture. Place in a baking dish and bake at 400 degrees 5 minutes. Sprinkle with almonds and bake 5 more minutes.

Serves 6–8
Easy

Mary McMillan
CODY, WYOMING

Old-fashioned Scalloped Oysters

"Good accompaniment to a traditional Thanksgiving or Christmas turkey dinner."

2/3 cup soft bread crumbs
1 cup fine cracker crumbs
1/2 cup butter, melted
1 1/2 pints fresh oysters
3/4 teaspoon salt
  Freshly ground black
  pepper, to taste
2 Tablespoons chopped
  parsley, optional
1/2 teaspoon Worcestershire
  sauce
3 Tablespoons milk or
  cream

Mix bread and cracker crumbs with butter and place half the crumb mixture on bottom of a greased 1-quart casserole. Add half the oysters, cutting up if large. Reserve the liquor, and sprinkle with half the salt, pepper and parsley. Add remaining oysters and sprinkle with remaining salt, pepper and parsley. Mix 1/3 cup oyster liquor with Worcestershire sauce and milk and pour over oysters. Top with remaining crumb mixture. Bake, uncovered, at 350 degrees about 45 minutes until puffy and brown.

Serves 4
Easy

Jane Dominick
CODY, WYOMING

Don's Oregon Bar-B-Q Salmon

"Outstanding!"

1 (10-pound) Chinook or
   silver salmon
1 cup butter
1 medium jar honey
3–6 fresh lemons, sliced
8–12 ounces bacon
   Honey
   Lemon butter

Clean fish and stuff with butter, honey and lemon slices. Place bacon on a piece of foil and lay the fish on top. Wrap loosely with an additional piece of foil, to prevent disasters, and cook on a gas or charcoal grill 45 minutes to 1 1/2 hours, depending on the size of the fish. Turn after 30 minutes and baste with additional honey and lemon butter.

Serves 8–10
Easy

Donald Bosley
PORTLAND, OREGON

French Embassy Scallops

1 pound scallops
3 Tablespoons butter
   Salt and pepper
1/4 cup chopped green onions
2 Tablespoons chopped
   parsley
6 large fresh mushrooms,
   sliced
1 can Cheddar cheese soup
1/3 cup sherry or brandy
1/2 cup slivered toasted
   almonds

Rinse scallops and pat dry with paper towel. Saute in a skillet in 1 1/2 Tablespoons butter, stirring, 5 minutes or until golden and tender. Season lightly. Remove to heated casserole and keep warm. In the skillet, saute and stir the remaining butter, onions, parsley and mushrooms 2–3 minutes. Combine soup and sherry and blend into mixture. Pour over scallops and bake at 350 degrees 30 minutes. Garnish with almonds and serve immediately with rice.

Serves 4
Easy

Marilyn Montville
CODY, WYOMING

Scampi au Champagne

"Fresh chervil makes all the difference."

2 Tablespoons butter
16 large shrimp, peeled and deveined
2 Tablespoons finely chopped green onions
1 1/2 cups dry champagne
3/4 cup heavy cream, not whipping cream
1/2 teaspoon salt
Freshly ground pepper
Fresh chervil sprigs or parsley

Heat butter in large, heavy skillet over high heat until sizzling. Add shrimp and onion and saute until shrimp turn pink, 2–3 minutes. Add champagne and heat to boiling. With skillet on heat, remove shrimp with slotted spoon to ovenproof plate and keep warm in oven set at lowest setting. Boil champagne, uncovered, 6–7 minutes until reduced by two thirds. Add cream and boil, uncovered, until liquid is reduced by one third, about 5 minutes. Remove from heat and add salt and pepper to taste. Arrange shrimp on warmed platter and pour sauce over. Serve immediately as a main course or an appetizer. Garnish with chervil.

Serves 4

Ralph Stewart
BILLINGS, MONTANA

Hot Shrimp Salad

1 1/2 cups croutons
Butter
1 (4 1/2-ounce) can shrimp
1 (4 1/2-ounce) can crab meat
1 1/2 cups finely chopped celery
1 small onion, finely chopped
1 large green pepper, finely chopped
1 teaspoon Worcestershire sauce
1 cup mayonnaise
Dash salt
Freshly ground pepper

Brown croutons in butter and combine with remaining ingredients. Pour into a well-buttered 6 × 10-inch or 8 × 8-inch casserole. Bake at 350 degrees 30 minutes. Serve on lettuce leaves with hot rolls.

Serves 6–8
Easy

Gloria Cottle
CODY, WYOMING

Louisiana Shrimp

"An informal dish with zip!"

3/4 cup butter
1 bay leaf
1/4 cup fresh lemon juice
1 teaspoon garlic powder
1 teaspoon cayenne
1 1/2 teaspoons lemon pepper
1/2 cup water
1 pound raw shrimp

Place all ingredients but shrimp in a pot and heat until butter melts. Place shrimp in one layer in an ovenproof, shallow glass dish. Pour butter mixture over shrimp and bake at 350 degrees 40 minutes. Serve at table from the glass dish directly from the oven with plenty of French bread for dunking in the butter sauce.

Serves 4
Easy

Mrs. Paul Koeppe
FORT WORTH, TEXAS

Shrimp Capri

"Make it as spicy as you wish."

1–2 teaspoons crushed red
 pepper flakes
3 cloves garlic, peeled
1/3 cup olive oil
1 pound large shrimp,
 shelled and deveined
1 Tablespoon capers,
 rinsed and drained
12 black pined olives,
 halved
12 cherry tomatoes, halved
1/2 cup dry white wine
1 Tablespoon fresh lemon
 juice
1 Tablespoon chopped
 fresh parsley
1/2 teaspoon salt
 Several dashes freshly
 ground black pepper
3 Tablespoons unsalted
 butter

Saute pepper flakes and garlic in the oil in a large skillet, then discard. Saute shrimp in the hot oil 1 minute. Add capers, olives and tomatoes and cook only until tomatoes are soft but still hold their shape. Add wine, lemon juice, parsley, salt and pepper. Boil 1 minute. Stir in butter, a Tablespoon at a time, until well blended. Serve immediately.

Serves 4

Tami McGinty
FORT LAUDERDALE, FLORIDA

Shrimp Creole

"Preparing a doubled or tripled recipe means leftovers that are particularly good the next day when spices have mingled."

1 onion, finely chopped
2 cloves garlic, finely
  chopped
1/4 cup chopped green
  pepper
3 Tablespoons bacon
  grease
1 large can stewed
  tomatoes
1 teaspoon chili powder
1 teaspoon sugar
1 teaspoon salt
1/4 teaspoon pepper
1 bay leaf
3/4–1 pound cleaned shrimp

Brown onion, garlic and green pepper in bacon grease. Add tomatoes and spices and simmer 50 minutes. During the last 15 minutes, add shrimp. Serve over rice.

Serves 4   *Sheila Peterson*
Easy   CODY, WYOMING

Shrimp Curry

"This is HOT!"

2 1/4 cups hot water
  3 cans shredded coconut
1 1/2 cups margarine
  3 garlic cloves
1 1/2 cups flour
1 1/2 teaspoons cayenne
  5 Tablespoons curry
    powder
1 1/2 Tablespoons ginger
1 1/2 Tablespoons saffron
1 1/2 Tablespoons sugar
  6–9 teaspoons salt
  3/4 cup lemon juice
  5 pounds shrimp, cleaned

Soak water and coconut. Squeeze and strain. Melt margarine, add garlic, stir in half the flour and add the coconut water, spices and lemon juice. Boil 30 minutes, stirring frequently. Add shrimp and boil until shrimp are done, about 5 minutes. Add remaining flour if needed to thicken.

Serves 12   *Mrs. Atlee W. Davis*
                                BARTOW, FLORIDA

Shrimp Gumbo

1/2 cup chopped onion
5 Tablespoons butter
3 Tablespoons flour
4 1/2 cups chicken broth or
    bouillon
1 (16-ounce) can tomatoes
1 teaspoon salt
2 teaspoons minced parsley
1/4 teaspoon thyme
1 clove garlic, minced
2 bay leaves
2 cups cooked okra
1 teaspoon gumbo file
1 1/2 pounds shrimp, shelled
1 (6-ounce) package frozen
    crab meat, thawed

Saute onions in 2 Tablespoons butter 5 minutes. Add remaining butter and melt. Blend in flour. Add broth, stirring until smooth. Add tomatoes, salt, parsley, thyme, garlic and bay leaves. Simmer, covered, 1 hour. Add okra, gumbo file, shrimp and crab meat. Simmer 10 minutes. Remove bay leaves and serve over hot rice.

Serves 5–6

William E. Weiss
CODY, WYOMING

Can-opener Gumbo

1 can condensed pepper
    pot soup
1 can condensed chicken
    gumbo soup
1 1/2 soup cans water
1 small can white flaked
    crab meat
1 small can tiny shrimp
1/4 teaspoon onion salt

"A working spouse's delight for a simple supper or a great dude ranch lunch."

Combine all ingredients in a saucepan, cover and simmer 10 minutes.

Serves 4
Easy

Mrs. Atlee W. Davis
BARTOW, FLORIDA

Seafood Strudel

"Worth the time and effort."

2 Tablespoons butter
2 Tablespoons flour
Salt
1/2 teaspoon Dijon mustard
Ground red pepper
3/4 cup milk, at room
   temperature
2 Tablespoons heavy cream
1 cup bread crumbs
1/4 cup grated Parmesan
   cheese
1/4 teaspoon dry mustard
8 ounces phyllo sheets
3/4 cup butter, melted
1 pound crab, shrimp,
   lobster, halibut or scallops,
   cooked and chunked
1/2 cup grated Swiss cheese
2 hard-boiled eggs, chopped
3/4 cup sour cream
1/4 cup chopped parsley
1/4 cup diced green onions
2 Tablespoons chopped
   green olives
1 clove garlic, minced
2 Tablespoons parsley,
   chopped
2 Tablespoons grated
   Parmesan cheese

For sauce, melt butter, add flour and heat until bubbling. Remove from heat, stir in salt, mustard and red pepper, then add milk and cook, stirring, over medium heat until thick. Add cream, take from heat and chill 2 hours. Combine crumbs, Parmesan and dry mustard. Place phyllo sheet on waxed paper, brush with some melted butter and sprinkle with some of the crumb mixture. Continue with 12 layers. Arrange cooked seafood lengthwise in rows on the lower third of the top phyllo sheet. Sprinkle with Swiss cheese, then continue with rows of chopped egg, sour cream, parsley, green onions, olives, garlic and chilled sauce. Make a packet by first folding in the short outside edges, next folding in the long edge of the lower third (near the filling). Using the waxed paper, roll lengthwise, as tightly and carefully as possible. Place the roll, seam-side down, on a buttered baking sheet and brush with melted butter. Bake at 375 degrees 12 minutes. Remove from oven, brush with more butter, cut into 8 slices and gently push together again. Brush top of roll with remaining melted butter and parsley. Top with Parmesan. Return to oven and bake 35–40 minutes longer, basting 3 times with butter. Remove from oven, cool 10 minutes and serve.

Serves 6–8
Time-consuming
Must do ahead

Temptations
Cody, Wyoming

Scandia Seafood Souffle

SOUFFLE:

> 1 pound halibut, turbot or
>   pike
> 2 cups half and half
> 4 slices soft bread, cubed
> 2 Tablespoons butter
> 1 teaspoon salt
> 1/4 teaspoon celery salt
> 1/4 teaspoon dill weed
> 4 eggs, separated

SAUCE:

> 4 Tablespoons butter
> 4 Tablespoons flour
> 1/4 teaspoon salt
>   Dash white pepper
> 1 3/4 cups half and half,
>   warmed
> 1 cup crab, shrimp or
>   lobster
> 1/4 cup dry white wine

Put fish through food grinder. If using pike, be sure all bones are removed. Scald cream, add bread, butter and seasonings and mix well. Add slightly beaten egg yolks and fish and heat thoroughly, stirring constantly. Fold in stiffly beaten egg whites. Pour into a buttered, 3-quart casserole, set in pan of hot water and bake at 350 degrees 1 hour.

For sauce, melt butter over low heat, stir in flour and seasonings and stir to a smooth paste. Add half and half and cook over low heat until thickened. Add seafood and wine. Adjust seasoning. Cook until well heated but not boiling. Serve in sauce dish with hot souffle.

Serves 6

Margot Belden Todd
CODY, WYOMING

All-Star Casserole

CASSEROLE:

> 2 cups cooked wild rice
> 1 cup cooked white rice
> 1 1/2 cups crab meat, flaked
> 1 1/2 cups chopped celery
> 1 large green pepper,
>   chopped
> 1 medium onion, chopped
> 1 (4-ounce) jar pimiento,
>   chopped
> 4 (10 1/2-ounce) cans
>   mushroom soup
> 1 1/2 cups cooked shrimp,
>   broken

SAUCE:

> 1 pound fresh mushrooms,
>   sliced
>   Butter

Combine first 7 ingredients. Add 1 1/2 cans mushroom soup and 1/2 cup shrimp. Place mixture in baking dish and bake at 350 degrees 1 1/2 hours or until brown and crusty on top. (If using glass baking dish, bake at 325 degrees.)

For sauce, brown mushrooms in butter. Add remaining soup and remaining shrimp and heat through. Serve with casserole.

Serves 8–10
Easy

Carolyn Karsten
WAPITI, WYOMING

Cantonese Seafood Noodles

2 Tablespoons peanut oil
1 teaspoon sesame oil
1/4 teaspoon salt
1/4 teaspoon pepper
3 packages ramen noodles
7 Tablespoons peanut oil
5 Tablespoons soy sauce
5 Tablespoons sake
2 cups chicken broth
10 Tablespoons oyster sauce
1 teaspoon sugar
1/2 teaspoon pepper
3 teaspoons minced ginger
  root
3 teaspoons minced garlic
4 green onions, chopped
2 cups shrimp or scallops
1/2 cup julienne-cut celery
1 bunch broccoli
10 mushrooms, regular or
  Chinese
2 Tablespoons cornstarch
6 Tablespoons water
1 teaspoon sesame oil

Combine first 4 ingredients in a small dish and set aside. Boil noodles 1 minute, drain and toss with the oil and seasoning mixture. Heat 3 Tablespoons peanut oil in large skillet. Add noodles in a solid mass and cook about 5 minutes. Invert onto a plate, add another Tablespoon oil and cook on other side until golden brown. Remove to plate. Combine soy sauce, sake, broth, oyster sauce, sugar and pepper in large pan and keep warm. Heat 3 Tablespoons peanut oil in wok. Stir-fry ginger, garlic and onions 1 minute. Add shrimp and stir-fry another 1–2 minutes (raw baby scallops may take a bit longer). Add celery and broccoli and cook 3–4 minutes. Add mushrooms and cook 1 minute more. Pour all into large pan containing broth mixture and simmer. Add a combination of cornstarch and water and stir until thickened. Stir in sesame oil and pour entire mixture over noodles. Serve immediately.

Serves 6–8
Time-consuming

Shirley Wilkerson
CODY, WYOMING

Salmon Stuffed Trout

"Best when prepared with native brook trout."

4 small to average trout
Salt and pepper
1 (7-ounce) can salmon,
 drained, with skin
 and bones removed
2 Tablespoons chopped
 chives
2 Tablespoons chopped
 parsley
2 Tablespoons lemon
 juice
4 slices wheat bread,
 crumbled
1 egg
1/2–3/4 cup dry white wine
1/8 teaspoon thyme
1 (11-ounce) package
 pie crust mix
 Rind of 1 lemon,
 grated
2 Tablespoons chopped
 dill, or to taste
1 egg, well beaten

Sprinkle trout with salt and pepper. Mix salmon, chives, parsley, lemon juice, bread crumbs, and egg. Stuff body cavities of trout with mixture. Lay trout in shallow pan and add equal amounts of wine and water to cover trout halfway. Sprinkle thyme into liquid. Cover and bake at 350 degrees 20 minutes. Cool and drain. Remove trout carefully and strip off skin. Remove backbones by loosening them at tail and carefully extracting them. Combine pie crust mix with lemon rind and dill and prepare according to package directions. Cut dough into 4 sections on floured surface and roll into flat pieces large enough to cover each trout completely. Wrap each trout in pie crust and place, seam-side-down, on greased cookie sheet. To decorate with fish scales, first brush with beaten egg, then mark scales on the pie crust with the tip of a spoon or a melon scoop. Bake at 375 degrees 25–30 minutes.

Serves 4
Time-consuming

Laurie J. Rufe
CODY, WYOMING

Spinach Sauce

8 ounces fresh spinach
1/2 cup watercress leaves
1 Tablespoon chopped
green onions
1 Tablespoon chopped
garlic
3 leaves fresh basil
1 1/2 teaspoons nutmeg
Salt and pepper, to taste
1 cup melted butter
1/2 cup Pernod

Wash spinach and cook 3 minutes in the water that clings to the leaves. Drain and put into food processor or blender with watercress, green onions, garlic and seasonings. Blend until pureed. Transfer puree to a bowl and gradually beat in butter and Pernod. Serve with hot fish or meats.

Yields 2–3 cups
Easy

William E. Weiss
CODY, WYOMING

Cucumber Dill Sauce

"A great sauce for any cold fish mold."

1 large cucumber, peeled
and grated
1 cup mayonnaise
1/4 cup heavy or sour cream
1/2 teaspoon salt or more, to
taste
1/4 teaspoon white pepper
1 1/4 teaspoons dill
Dash cayenne
1/2 teaspoon Dijon mustard
1 Tablespoon lemon juice
1 Tablespoon minced
onion or chives
1 Tablespoon minced
parsley

Set grated cucumber aside 30 minutes, then press out most of the juice. Mix remaining ingredients together, combine with cucumber, mix well and chill overnight.

Serves 8
Easy
Must do ahead

Margot Belden Todd
CODY, WYOMING

"Sacagawea" by Harry Andrew Jackson. *Courtesy of Buffalo Bill Historical Center, Cody, WY; Gift of Mr. and Mrs. Richard J. Cashman; 5.80*

Vegetables

Asparagus Casserole

4 Tablespoons butter
4 Tablespoons flour
2 (15-ounce) cans green
　asparagus, drained and
　juice reserved
1 cup plus 4 Tablespoons
　grated American cheese
6 to 8 hard-boiled eggs, sliced
　Pepper, optional
1 Tablespoon finely
　chopped pimiento,
　optional

Melt butter in saucepan, add flour and then asparagus juice. Boil until thick. Add 1 cup cheese and stir until melted. In a buttered casserole, alternate asparagus, eggs and cheese sauce, sprinkling eggs with pepper or pimiento. Top with remaining cheese and bake at 350 degrees 20–30 minutes. Casserole may be made ahead and reheated before serving.

Serves 6–8
Easy *Lucille Clarke Dumbrill*
May do ahead NEWCASTLE, WYOMING

Broccoli with Caper Vinaigrette

2 pounds broccoli
　Juice of 1/2 lemon
　Pinch dry mustard
　Salt and pepper, to taste
2-inch squeeze of anchovy
　paste or 4 mashed
　fillets
1 shallot, peeled and
　minced
1 Tablespoon capers,
　minced
4 Tablespoons olive oil
　Dash Tabasco

Cut stems and flowers of broccoli in bite-sized pieces. Steam stalks 5 minutes. Add flowers and steam 5 minutes. Refresh with cold water. Combine other ingredients for sauce and serve immediately over broccoli.

Serves 4 *Douglas Clark Sunderland*
Easy CODY, WYOMING

Cabbage Casserole

4 cups shredded cabbage
1/2 cup margarine, melted
1 1/2 cups crushed corn
   flakes
1/2 cup mayonnaise
1 cup milk
1 can cream of celery
   soup
1 cup grated sharp
   Cheddar cheese
1 cup crushed corn
   flakes

Soak cabbage in cold water 30 minutes and drain. Combine margarine and corn flakes, mix and place in bottom of casserole dish. Cover with cabbage. Mix mayonnaise, milk and soup and pour over all. Spread with cheese and top with corn flakes. Bake at 325 degrees 35 minutes.

Serves 6–8
Easy

Mrs. Mary S. Banks
MARIETTA, GEORGIA

Cody Carrots

2 1/2–3 pounds carrots, cut in
   strips
1 1/2 cups chicken broth
1 teaspoon minced onion
2 Tablespoons butter
1–2 Tablespoons
   horseradish
1/2 cup mayonnaise
1 cup crushed saltine
   crackers
3 Tablespoons butter
Pepper
Parsley

Steam carrots in broth until barely tender. Remove carrots and transfer to 9 × 13-inch baking dish. To broth, add onions, butter, horseradish and mayonnaise. Blend with whisk until smooth and pour over carrots. Sprinkle crackers over carrots, dot with butter and sprinkle with pepper and parsley. Bake at 350 degrees 20 minutes.

Serves 6–8
May do ahead

Karla Carr
CODY, WYOMING

Carrot Casserole

4 cups sliced carrots
1 medium onion,
   chopped
4 Tablespoons butter
1 can celery soup
1/2 teaspoons salt
   Dash pepper
1/2 cup grated cheese
1/2 cup seasoned croutons
1/3 cup butter, melted

Cook carrots until done, but still firm, and drain. Saute onions in butter. Stir in soup, spices, cheese and carrots. Place in casserole dish. Toss croutons in melted butter, sprinkle on top and bake at 350 degrees 35 minutes.

Serves 8
May do ahead

Lois N. Goppert
CODY, WYOMING

Carrot Quiche

"A great dish for vegetarians."

PASTRY:

2 1/4 cups flour
  1/2 teaspoon salt
  3/4 cup butter, softened
    1 egg
      About 1/4 cup sour
      cream

FILLING:

1 1/2 pounds carrots, peeled
    and grated
  6 Tablespoons butter,
    melted
  2 teaspoons sugar
  5 eggs
1 1/2 cups half and half
    1 teaspoon salt
  1/4 teaspoon mace
      Chopped parsley

Sift together flour and salt. Add butter, egg and 2 Tablespoons sour cream. Knead gently in bowl until mixture forms soft ball, adding a little more sour cream if necessary. Wrap in foil or waxed paper and chill before rolling out.

Blanch carrots in boiling water 2 minutes and drain well. Roll out pastry and line two 9-inch pie pans or one 12-inch pan. Prick with fork. Cover inside of shell with foil and weight with uncooked rice or beans. Bake at 425 degrees 12–15 minutes. Remove rice and foil and bake a little longer until center is firm. Toss carrots in butter and sugar and arrange in pie shell. Slightly beat eggs and cream. Add salt and mace and pour over carrots. Sprinkle with parsley. Bake at 375 degrees 20–25 minutes for 2 quiches or 35–40 minutes for a large one.

Serves 8   *Yvonne Nielson*
Must do ahead   CODY, WYOMING

Chestnut Puree

1 1/2 pounds chestnuts,
      shelled and peeled
  3 stalks celery
  1 teaspoon salt
  2 cups water
  1 cup milk or chicken
    broth
  1/2 teaspoon sugar
      Salt and pepper, to taste
1–2 Tablespoons butter
      About 1/4 cup half and
      half

Simmer chestnuts with celery, salt, water and milk in a covered saucepan 30 minutes or until chestnuts are very soft and tender. Drain chestnuts, reserving 1/4 cup cooking liquid, and puree together in a food processor. Whisk in seasonings and butter, adding enough cream to make a light, fluffy mixture. Serve with any poultry or game birds.

Serves 4   *William E. Weiss*
                                                        CODY, WYOMING

Fresh Corn Pudding Souffle

12 ears sweet, young and
   tender corn
2 eggs, separated
2 teaspoons sugar
1/2 teaspoon salt
1/4 teaspoon pepper
1 Tablespoon melted butter
1/4 cup half and half
2 teaspoons sherry

Scrape corn from ears and combine with egg yolks, sugar, seasonings, butter and cream. Beat egg whites until stiff and fold into corn mixture with sherry. Pour into buttered, 2-quart casserole, place in a pan of hot water and bake at 350 degrees 30 minutes until top is a delicate brown and slightly firm to touch.

Serves 4–6

Margot Belden Todd
CODY, WYOMING

Grilled Corn

"Wonderful and easy to prepare for a large cookout."

1/2 cup unsalted butter,
   melted
2 Tablespoons lemon juice
1/8 teaspoon cayenne
1/8 teaspoon chili powder
12 ears of corn, husked

Mix butter, lemon juice and spices in small bowl for basting mixture. Place corn on grill. Cook 10 minutes, or until golden, turning and basting often. Serve with extra butter, salt and pepper.

Serves 8
Easy

Mrs. R. W. Martin
BOZEMAN, MONTANA

Eggplant Souffle

1 medium eggplant, peeled
   and cubed
1 egg, well beaten
1/3 cup bread crumbs
1 medium onion, finely
   chopped
1/4 cup melted butter
Salt and pepper, to taste
Few drops Tabasco

Cook eggplant in salted water until tender and drain thoroughly. Mix together remaining ingredients and combine with eggplant. Put in buttered baking dish and bake at 350 degrees 45–60 minutes until lightly browned on top. May serve with broiled tomato halves.

Serves 4
Easy

John Sinai
SAN FRANCISCO, CALIFORNIA

Eggplant Italienne

2 eggs
1/4 cup milk
1 cup flour
1/4 teaspoon salt
2 medium eggplants,
 sliced 1/2-inch thick
4–6 Tablespoons oil
4 cups marinara sauce
2/3 cup water
2 Tablespoons ricotta
1 1/2 cups grated Romano or
 Parmesan cheese
12 ounces mozzarella
 cheese, sliced

Beat eggs and milk together. Mix flour and salt. Dip eggplant into egg, then into flour mixture. Saute in oil until golden brown and drain on paper towel. Thin sauce with water. Warm sauce and ladle a small quantity on the bottom of a 9 × 14-inch glass baking dish. Add a layer of half the eggplant and spread with ricotta cheese. Follow with half the remaining sauce and sprinkle generously with Romano. Make another layer of eggplant and cover with remaining sauce. Cover with foil and bake at 350 degrees about 30 minutes, until bubbly. Uncover and bake 30 minutes longer. Place mozzarella cheese on top and bake 10 minutes more until cheese melts.

Serves 8–10

Helen M. Hobbs
ENGLEWOOD, FLORIDA

Marvelous Mushrooms

"An excellent accompaniment to prime rib or any red meat."

1 pound fresh mushrooms
1/3 cup butter, softened
1 Tablespoon minced
 parsley
1 Tablespoon minced onion
1 Tablespoon Dijon
 mustard
1 teaspoon salt
Pinch cayenne
1 1/2 Tablespoons flour
Pinch nutmeg
1 cup heavy cream

Wipe mushrooms clean with damp paper towel and trim stem ends. Thoroughly mix all ingredients except cream and mushrooms. Place mushrooms in buttered 1-quart casserole, dot with butter mixture and pour on cream. Bake at 375 degrees 1 hour, uncovered, stirring once or twice.

Serves 4
Easy
May do ahead

Jane Dominick
CODY, WYOMING

Herb and Honey Onions

3 large sweet Spanish
onions, halved
1/4 cup melted butter or
margarine
2 Tablespoons wine vinegar
2 Tablespoons honey
1/2 teaspoon salt
1/2 teaspoon paprika
1/2 teaspoon dry mustard
1/4 teaspoons age

Place onion, cut-side-down, in pan or casserole. Mix remaining ingredients well and pour over onions. Cover and bake at 350 degrees 50 minutes, until tender. Dish may be prepared several hours ahead and refrigerated until baking time.

Serves 6
Easy
May do ahead

Mrs. Thomas V. Cinquina
St. Louis, Missouri

Spinach Italienne

"Makes spinach suitable for a banquet and inviting to a child."

2 pounds fresh spinach or
2 (10-ounce) packages
chopped frozen spinach
2 Tablespoons butter
1 clove garlic, optional
1 Tablespoon flour
1/2 cup half and half
Salt and freshly grated
pepper
Nutmeg
1/2 cup seedless raisins
1/2 cup pine nuts or slivered
almonds
Butter

Wilt washed spinach in the water that clings to it or undercook frozen spinach. Drain thoroughly and chop finely. Melt butter in an iron or earthenware casserole and swirl garlic in butter about 1 minute. Add spinach and stir in flour. When blended, add cream and season to taste with salt, pepper and nutmeg. Meanwhile, soak raisins in cold water at least 10 minutes and drain. Saute nuts lightly in butter. When nuts are golden brown, add raisins. Set aside and keep warm. At serving time, add raisins and nuts to hot spinach mixture.

Serves 4–6
Easy

Miriam Sample
Billings, Montana

Easy Spinach

4 Tablespoons butter
2 Tablespoons flour
2 Tablespoons grated onion
2 packages frozen chopped
   spinach, cooked and
   drained
6 eggs, beaten
1 cup grated Cheddar
   cheese
   Salt and pepper, to taste
1/2 cup Parmesan cheese

Melt butter in skillet, add flour and stir until smooth. Add onions and brown lightly. Add spinach, eggs, Cheddar, salt and pepper. Cook over medium heat at least 5 minutes, stirring so spinach will not stick to bottom of pan. Top with Parmesan.

Serves 4

Judith P. Schmidlapp
CODY, WYOMING

Prijshac (Serbian Spinach)

"Made for a picnic by a Polish girl with a Serbian mother."

1 pound spinach
3 eggs, well beaten
2 cups small curd cottage
   cheese
1/4 cup butter, cut in small
   chunks
1/4 teaspoon salt
4 ounces Colby or Tescott
   cheese, cut in 1/2-inch
   cubes
3 Tablespoons flour

Wash spinach carefully in cold water, then chop in bite-sized pieces. Wash again in clean water and drain. Place spinach in large mixing bowl. Mix in eggs, cottage cheese, butter, salt and Colby cheese and blend together with a serving fork. Sift flour over mixture and mix together 2–3 minutes. Turn mixture into greased dish and bake at 350 degrees 45–60 minutes until surface browns. Dish may be refrigerated and reheated.

Serves 8
Easy
May do ahead

Steven Lopata
CLAYTON, MISSOURI

Swiss Green Beans

"Makes every-day beans into a real taste treat."

2 Tablespoons butter or
  margarine
2 Tablespoons flour
1/4–1/2 teaspoon salt
1/8 teaspoon pepper
1 teaspoon sugar
1 teaspoon grated onion
1 cup sour cream
4 cups French-style
  green beans, cooked
  and drained
2 cups rice cereal,
  crushed
2 cups grated Swiss
  cheese

Melt butter and stir in flour, salt, pepper, sugar and onions. Gradually add sour cream, stirring constantly. Cook until thickened, stirring occasionally. Fold in beans and heat thoroughly. Pour into greased 1 1/2-quart casserole. Combine cereal and cheese and sprinkle over beans. Bake at 400 degrees about 20 minutes.

Serves 6

Mrs. Felix Bedlan
Fairbury, Nebraska

String Beans in Sour Cream and Tomato Sauce

1 pound fresh string
  beans, trimmed
2 cups thinly sliced
  onions
1 small green pepper,
  seeded and cut in
  1/2-inch pieces
4 Tablespoons butter
3 medium tomatoes,
  peeled, seeded and
  chopped
1 Tablespoon finely
  chopped fresh basil or
  1 1/2 teaspoons dried
1 egg
1 cup sour cream
1 teaspoon salt
  Freshly ground black
  pepper

Bring beans to a boil. Reduce heat and cook, uncovered, 8–10 minutes until tender. Drain and cool under running water and set aside. Saute onions and green pepper in butter 5–8 minutes until tender but not brown. Stir in tomatoes and basil and boil rapidly 1–2 minutes until most of the juices have evaporated. Stir in green beans and simmer until heated through. In a mixing bowl, beat together egg, sour cream, salt and pepper. Stir into vegetables. Transfer to serving bowl and serve at once.

Serves 6
Easy

Yvonne Nielson
Cody, Wyoming

String Beans with a Difference

4 small ripe tomatoes
2 cloves garlic, crushed
6 Tablespoons butter
3/4 teaspoon basil
2 packages frozen French-
style green beans
Scant teaspoon salt
1/4 teaspoon freshly ground
pepper

Cut tomatoes in half, remove pulp and seeds and cut shell in thin strips. In a small saucepan, saute garlic in butter 1 minute. Remove garlic and add basil. In separate pan, cook beans until barely tender, drain, add tomato strips, salt and pepper and just heat, no more than 1 minute. Stir in seasoned butter and serve.

Serves 8

Margot Belden Todd
CODY, WYOMING

Vera Cruz Tomatoes

1/4 cup chopped onion
2 Tablespoons bacon
drippings
8 ounces fresh spinach,
snipped
1/2 cup sour cream
3 slices bacon, cooked and
crumbled
Dash Tabasco
4 medium tomatoes
Salt
1/2 cup shredded mozzarella
cheese

Cook onions in drippings until tender. Stir in spinach and cook, covered, 3–5 minutes until tender. Remove from heat and stir in sour cream, bacon and Tabasco. Cut off tops of tomatoes, remove centers, leaving shells, invert and drain. Salt shells and fill with spinach mixture. Place on baking dish and bake at 375 degrees 20–25 minutes. Top with cheese and bake until melted.

Serves 4
Easy

Mrs. John R. Woods
ST. LOUIS, MISSOURI

Tomato Pudding

"A great success with beef."

4 cups tomato puree
1/2 teaspoon salt
1/8 teaspoon pepper
1 cup brown sugar
4 cups cubed bread, about
8 slices
1/3 cup melted butter

Bring tomato puree, salt, pepper and sugar to a boil. Place bread cubes in buttered 1 1/2-quart casserole and pour on melted butter, tossing lightly. Pour hot tomato mixture over cubes. Bake at 350 degrees about 45 minutes.

Serves 6
Easy

Miriam Sample
BILLINGS, MONTANA

Green Tomatoes Summers

"Use the first tomatoes in your garden or, if you live in the mountain West, the last."

6 green tomatoes
4 Tablespoons butter
2 cloves garlic, minced
1/2 loaf day-old garlic bread
   Seasoned salt
   Pepper
   Basil or dill

Wash tomatoes and slice thinly. Melt butter in a skillet and add garlic. Add tomato slices and sprinkle on seasonings. Using a food processor with a metal blade, grind bread and sprinkle generously over tomatoes. Cook over medium heat. Tomatoes should be warm but not soggy.

Serves 12
Easy

Mrs. George E. Summers
PALM BEACH, FLORIDA

Fresh Tomato Tart

CRUST:

2 cups flour
1/2 teaspoon salt
2 Tablespoons sugar
4 teaspoons baking powder
1/3 cup shortening
3/4 cup buttermilk

FILLING:

5 medium tomatoes
3/4 teaspoon salt
1/2 teaspoon dried basil
1/4 teaspoon pepper

TOPPING:

1 cup mayonnaise,
  preferably homemade
1 cup coarsely grated Swiss
  cheese
1 cup coarsely grated
  Cheddar cheese

Blend crust ingredients as for pastry. Cover and let rise slightly 30 minutes. Prepare filling by slipping tomato skins in boiling water. Cut tomatoes in 1-inch pieces and toss with seasonings. Combine topping ingredients. Grease 6 custard cups or individual souffle dishes. Press 1/3 cup dough in bottom and up sides of each. Bake at 450 degrees about 8 minutes until just beginning to brown. Dough will puff up and pull down slightly from the rim of the dish. Fill each with about 1/2 cup filling and mound about 1/2 cup topping on each. Reduce heat to 400 degrees and bake tarts about 15 minutes longer, until topping is lightly browned and puffy. Serve warm or cold.

Serves 6
Time-consuming

Yvonne Nielson
CODY, WYOMING

Turtle Beans

"Left-over beans make marvelous black bean soup."

1 pound black turtle beans
8 cups water
1 teaspoon sugar
1 teaspoon soda
4 ounces salt pork, cut in
   small cubes
1 large red pepper, finely
   chopped
2 large green peppers, finely
   chopped
3 Tablespoons olive oil
1 large onion, finely chopped
2 cloves garlic, crushed
1/2 cup solid pack tomatoes,
   finely chopped
1 teaspoon vinegar
1 teaspoon oregano
3 teaspoons salt
1/4 teaspoon Tabasco

Wash and sort beans carefully. Soak overnight in a large steel or enamel bowl with the water, sugar and soda. In a 4-quart pot, cook beans in soaking water with salt pork, red pepper and a green pepper. Cover and simmer 3 hours, stirring occasionally. Remove from heat and allow to stand overnight, again using steel or enamel container. Heat olive oil in cooking pot, saute onion, garlic and remaining pepper until onion is soft. Add beans and remaining ingredients. Simmer 1–2 hours, stirring occasionally. Add more water if mixture is too thick. When done, beans should be soft but not cooked to a mush. Remove a cup of beans, mash, and return to pot before serving. To speed the first cooking, cook the beans in a pressure cooker about 40 minutes.

Serves 10–12
May be frozen
Must do ahead

Margot Belden Todd
CODY, WYOMING

Deer Creek Zucchini

"Fresh garden herbs greatly enhance this dish."

2 medium onions, minced
2 Tablespoons butter or
   olive oil
2 pounds zucchini, washed
   and cubed
2 cups canned tomatoes
1/2 teaspoon salt
   Dash pepper
2 Tablespoons fresh basil,
   chopped
2 Tablespoons fresh oregano,
   chopped
2 Tablespoons parsley,
   chopped
1/2 cup grated sharp cheese

Saute onions in butter until golden. Add zucchini and cook over low heat 10 minutes, stirring frequently. Add tomatoes, salt, pepper and herbs and simmer 10 minutes longer. Place in greased casserole, cover with cheese and bake at 375 degrees about 30 minutes until cheese browns.

Serves 6
Easy

Hope Williams Read
CODY, WYOMING

Zucchini Pancakes

"Another good use for zucchini."

1 1/2 cups grated zucchini
2 Tablespoons grated
   onion
1/4 cup Parmesan cheese
1/4 cup flour
2 eggs
2 Tablespoons mayonnaise
1/4 teaspoon Italian
   seasoning
   Salt and pepper, to taste
   Oil

Pat extra water from zucchini between paper towels. Combine all ingredients except oil. Heat oil in skillet, pour in 1-inch rounds of batter and brown on both sides. Serve plain or with tomato sauce or sour cream.

Serves 4   *Dorothy Marchezak*
Easy   EXPORT, PENNSYLVANIA

Annette's Zucchini Casserole

4–6 zucchini, sliced or cut in
   1/2-inch cubes
2 cups sour cream
1/2 cup butter
1 teaspoon lemon pepper
1/4 cup Italian-style bread
   crumbs
1/4 cup grated Parmesan
   cheese

Cook zucchini in boiling water 2 minutes. Drain and place in 2-quart baking dish. Mix in sour cream. Slice butter and add with lemon pepper. Sprinkle bread crumbs and then cheese on top. Cover and bake at 375 degrees 35 minutes. Uncover and cook 10 minutes longer. Recipe may be doubled or tripled to serve a crowd.

Serves 8   *Mrs. Richard E. Brown*
Easy   LONG LAKE, MINNESOTA

Zucchini and Carrots

3 Tablespoons butter
2 cups diced carrots
2 pounds zucchini, cut in
   large cubes
2/3 cup heavy cream
1 teaspoon cornstarch
1/2 teaspoon salt
1/8 teaspoon pepper
2 Tablespoons snipped
   fresh, or 2 teaspoons dry,
   dill

Melt butter, add carrots and cook, covered, over low heat 5 minutes, stirring occasionally. Add zucchini and continue to cook approximately 10 minutes until tender but still crisp. Combine remaining ingredients and add to vegetables. Simmer briefly until thickened slightly.

Serves 4–6   *Laura Flanigan*
Easy   ENFIELD, NEW HAMPSHIRE

Vegetable Casserole

"A nice change for mixed vegetables."

1 package frozen green
  beans
1 package frozen lima
  beans
1 package frozen green
  peas
  Salt and pepper
1 cup heavy cream, stiffly
  beaten
1 cup mayonnaise
1/2 cup Parmesan cheese

Cook vegetables together 4 minutes, drain and season. Combine cream with mayonnaise and cheese for sauce. Put vegetables in casserole dish, top with sauce and bake at 350 degrees 15–20 minutes until brown on top.

Serves 8
Easy

Nan Thorne Fogle
BOULDER, COLORADO

Ratatouille

"I learned this recipe in France during my junior year of college."

1 large or 2 medium
  onions, sliced
6 or 8 cloves garlic, minced
1/2 cup olive oil
1 eggplant, sliced
3 zucchini, thinly sliced
6 fresh tomatoes, skinned
  and coarsely cubed or
  1 large can stewed
  tomatoes
2 green peppers, cut in
  circular slices
  Salt and pepper, to taste

Saute onions and garlic in oil until soft. In a casserole dish, make 3 alternating layers of eggplant, zucchini, tomatoes, green peppers, onions, garlic, salt and pepper. Place onions near top of each layer so flavor will seep throughout. Green pepper rounds make an attractive final layer. Bake at 350 degrees 45 minutes. Ratatouille may be served hot or cold.

Serves 8–10
Easy

Katie Peters
SANTA FE, NEW MEXICO

Mustard Sauce

"Great for any vegetable of the cabbage family."

1 cup sour cream
1 Tablespoon prepared
    mustard
1 Tablespoon minced onion
1/4 teaspoon salt
1/8 teaspoon pepper
1 Tablespoon chopped
    green onions

Combine all ingredients, mixing well. Cook and stir over low heat 5 minutes. To hold for an hour or so, keep warm in a double boiler over hot, but not boiling, water.

Serves 6–8
Easy
May do ahead

Rose Marie Julien
CODY, WYOMING

Hollandaise Sauce

7 egg yolks
2 Tablespoons cold water
1 cup clarified butter
    Juice of 1 lemon
    Seasoned salt

Beat yolks and water together in double boiler. Heat slowly and continue to beat until creamy. Remove from heat and cool slightly. Add melted butter 1 Tablespoon at a time. Add lemon juice and stir thoroughly. Adjust seasoning. Serve on or with vegetables, fish, steak or eggs. Any leftover sauce may be kept in the refrigerator and used later, as much as a week, by adding a few drops of boiling water and stirring.

Serves 8

Jane Stires
NEW YORK, NEW YORK

Curry Sauce for Vegetables

1 1/2 cups mayonnaise
3 Tablespoons lemon juice
3 Tablespoons honey
3 teaspoons curry powder
1 1/2 cups grated Cheddar
    cheese

Combine mayonnaise, lemon juice, honey and curry powder. Serve with vegetables. Serve cheese in separate bowl for topping.

Serves 4
Easy

Sue Ludewig
CODY, WYOMING

Pasta, Potatoes and Rice

George Montgomery's Spaghetti Sauce

"My jack rabbit and rattlesnake recipes are my best, but where do you get a jack or rattler in Beverly Hills these days?"

3 medium onions, diced
3 Tablespoons butter
2 green peppers, chopped
3 celery stalks, diced
2 sprigs fresh parsley
2 medium carrots, diced
4 pounds ground round
    Salt and pepper, to taste
1 (29-ounce) can tomato
    sauce
1 (12-ounce) can tomato
    paste

Saute onions in butter until light brown. Add peppers, celery, parsley and carrots. Simmer 5 minutes. Brown meat quickly in deep skillet. Season with salt and pepper. Add cooked vegetables, tomato sauce and tomato paste. Fill the 12-ounce can half full of water, pour over meat mixture, stir and simmer a half hour. Serve over spaghetti cooked al dente. Sprinkle with grated Parmesan cheese. Make sauce the day before if possible.

Serves 8–10
Easy   *George Montgomery*
May do ahead   LOS ANGELES, CALIFORNIA

Pesto alla Genovese

2 cups fresh basil leaves
1 cup fresh Italian parsley
1/2 cup grated Parmesan
    cheese
1/2 cup grated Romano cheese
1/2 cup blanched almonds
4 Tablespoons blanched
    pine nuts
12 blanched walnut halves
1 clove garlic
3 Tablespoons butter
1/2 Cup olive oil
    Linguine

Place all but pasta in blender or processor and blend until smooth. Cook pasta al dente. Fork pasta directly into bowl with pesto and toss well. Add 4 Tablespoons of water from pasta pot. Toss again. Note: blanching nuts helps remove their skins.

Serves 4   *K. T. Roes*
Easy   CODY, WYOMING

Linguine with Asparagus

2 pounds thin asparagus,
    cut in 1-inch pieces
3 Tablespoons grainy
    mustard
3 Tablespoons olive oil
2 large green onions,
    thinly sliced
1 small clove garlic,
    minced
1 1/2 teaspoons anchovy
    paste
    Pinch thyme
2 Tablespoons minced
    fresh parsley
1 pound linguine, cooked
    and drained
    Salt and freshly ground
    pepper, to taste

In a large pot of boiling salted water, cook the asparagus until tender but still bright green, about 3 minutes. Drain and rinse under cold running water. Drain well and set aside. In a small bowl, combine remaining ingredients except linguine. Mix well and set aside. In a serving bowl, toss the linguine with the dressing and the asparagus. Adjust seasoning. Serve warm or at room temperature. May be made 1 hour before serving.

Serves 4
Easy   *Robin Weiss*
May do ahead   CODY, WYOMING

Spinach Lasagne

3 (1-pound, 14-ounce)
    cans tomatoes
2 (15-ounce) cans tomato
    sauce
2 onions, chopped
3 cloves garlic, minced
2 teaspoons Italian
    seasoning
2 bay leaves
2 cups sliced mushrooms
2 packages frozen
    chopped spinach
3 or 4 eggs, beaten
1 pound ricotta or cottage
    cheese
1 (16-ounce) box lasagne
    noodles
2 cups Parmesan or
    mozzarella cheese

Combine first 6 ingredients for sauce and cook at least 3 hours or until reduced and quite thick. Add mushrooms during last 20 minutes of cooking. For spinach filling, cook spinach and press out liquid. Combine with eggs and ricotta. Cook noodles and drain. To assemble lasagne, start with a layer of sauce, then noodles, then spinach filling, then Parmesan. Continue, ending with a layer of sauce. Bake uncovered at 350 degrees 45–60 minutes. Wait at least 20 minutes before cutting. Recipe produces extra sauce which may be frozen.

Serves 8   *Michele Hemry*
May be frozen   CODY, WYOMING

"The Homesteaders" by W. H. D. Koerner. *Courtesy of Buffalo Bill Historical Center, Cody, WY; 24.77*

Spaghetti Carbonara

"This is one of my daughters' favorite suppers."

8–10 strips bacon, cooked and
    crumbled
2 eggs, slightly beaten
1 cup grated Parmesan
    cheese
1/4 cup cream
    Salt and pepper, to taste
1 (16-ounce) package
    spaghetti

Combine all but spaghetti. Cook pasta and drain. Toss with bacon mixture and serve immediately on a warmed platter or bowl.

Serves 4–6
Easy

Pamela Stockton
Cody, Wyoming

Pasta Primavera

"Everyone will love this, either hot or cold."

1 pound broccoli, cut in
    bite-sized pieces
2 small zucchinis, thinly
    sliced
8 ounces asparagus, cut in
    1-inch pieces
1 (16-ounce) package
    linguine
1 large clove garlic,
    chopped
1 basket cherry tomatoes,
    halved
1/4 cup olive oil
1/4 cup chopped fresh basil
    or 1 teaspoon dried
8 ounces mushrooms,
    thinly sliced
1/2 cup frozen peas
1/4 cup chopped parsley
1 1/2 teaspoons salt
1/4 teaspoon black pepper
1/4 teaspoon crushed red
    pepper
1/4 cup butter
3/4 cup heavy cream
2/3 cup freshly grated
    Parmesan cheese

Cook broccoli, zucchini and asparagus in boiling salted water until tender but still crisp. Drain and put in large bowl. Cook and drain linguine. Saute garlic and tomatoes in oil in large skillet 2 minutes. Stir in basil and mushrooms and cook 3 minutes. Stir in peas, parsley, salt, black pepper and red pepper, cooking 1 minute more. Add mixture to vegetables in large bowl. Melt butter in same skillet. Stir in cream and cheese. Cook over medium heat, stirring constantly until smooth. Add linguine and toss to coat. Stir in vegetables. Heat gently, just until hot.

Serves 10–12

Mrs. Leo N. Chase
JACKSON, WYOMING

Cream Cheese Pasta

"Good to take to a carry-in supper."

2 Tablespoons oil
1 pound ground meat
2 cloves garlic, crushed
  Salt and pepper, to taste
1 (16-ounce) can tomatoes
1 (15-ounce) can tomato
  sauce
1 medium package fine egg
  noodles
1 (8-ounce) carton sour
  cream
4 ounces cream cheese
3 green onions, chopped
8 ounces Cheddar cheese,
  grated

Put the oil in pan and add meat. Saute with garlic, salt and pepper. Add tomatoes and tomato sauce. Cook 5 minutes or until bubbles form. Boil noodles. Drain and mix in bowl with sour cream, cream cheese and green onions. Fill a 3-quart casserole with alternate layers of pasta, meat mixture and cheese. Bake at 350 degrees about 30 minutes or until bubbly.

Serves 8
May be frozen
May do ahead

Mrs. John F. Giles III
DALLAS, TEXAS

Gnocchi

"Good with roast lamb or ham."

2 cups cold water
3/4 cup sweet butter
2 cups flour
6 whole eggs
1 cup freshly grated
  Parmesan cheese
  Pinches salt, sugar and
  white pepper
  Pinch nutmeg
  Salt and pepper, to taste
2 cups light white sauce
  Grated Parmesan cheese
  Butter

Place cold water and butter in saucepan and bring to a boil. Add flour and stir vigorously with wooden spoon until thick and smooth. Remove from heat and add eggs, one at a time, stirring vigorously until well blended. Add 1/2 cup Parmesan and salt, sugar and white pepper. Beat well. Put in pastry bag with a large tube and pipe into boiling salted water until gnocchi float. Remove with slotted spoon and put on dry cloth. Cut into 1 to 1 1/2-inch long pieces and layer in a flat casserole. Add remaining cheese, nutmeg, salt and pepper to white sauce and pour onto gnocchi. Top with cheese and dots of butter. Bake at 350 degrees 35 minutes until lightly brown.

Serves 8–10

Margaret S. Coe
CODY, WYOMING

Chicken Cascia

2 cups chopped onion
2 Tablespoons oil
2 cups sliced mushrooms
1 pound small pasta shells
5 pounds chicken breasts,
  skinned, boned and cut
  in 3/4-inch cubes
1 chicken bouillon cube
1/4 teaspoon sage
1/8 teaspoon basil
1/2 teaspoon Beau Monde
  seasoning
1 teaspoon garlic salt
1 teaspoon cracked black
  pepper
3 cups milk or cream
3 Tablespoons butter
2 Tablespoons flour
2 ounces pimiento, optional

Slowly cook onions in oil in 12-inch frying pan over low heat until onions are translucent. Add mushrooms and stir until they are heated, not cooked. Remove from oil and set aside. Cook pasta al dente in 4 quarts boiling salted water. While pasta is cooking, cook chicken in oil in frying pan until chicken turns white. Add mushrooms, bouillon, spices and 1 cup milk. In a saucepan, melt butter, add flour and cook over low heat 2 to 3 minutes, stirring constantly. Mixture should bubble vigorously. Very slowly add some liquid from chicken to saucepan and continue to stir. Add more liquid and stir until smooth. Repeat until all liquid and remaining milk have been added. Return thickened sauce to chicken. Keep warm, stirring occasionally. Drain shells and combine with chicken sauce in a casserole. Garnish with pimiento strips, if desired, and serve piping hot with hot bread and green salad.

Serves 6
May be frozen

Steven Lopata
CLAYTON, MISSOURI

Spaghetti-Broccoli Casserole

1 bunch broccoli, flowerets
  and smallest stems
8 ounces spaghetti or
  spaghettini
2 Tablespoons olive oil
1 teaspoon finely minced
  garlic
4 small ripe tomatoes, cut
  in 1-inch cubes
  Freshly ground pepper, to
  taste
1/2 teaspoon dried hot red
  pepper flakes
1/2 cup heavy cream
1 teaspoon dried basil or
  1/2 cup chopped fresh
1 Tablespoon butter
1/3 cup grated Parmesan
  cheese

Steam flowerets and set aside. Cook spaghetti and drain. Heat oil in casserole and add garlic, cooking until wilted. Add tomatoes. Cook and stir 1 minute. Add broccoli and ground pepper. Add spaghetti to broccoli mixture. Add red pepper, cream, basil and butter. Bring mixture to near boil, toss briefly and serve. Top with cheese.

Serves 4–6

Mrs. George B. Drake, Jr.
CUTCHOGUE, NEW YORK

Lamb Pastitsio

1 Tablespoon olive oil
1/2 small onion, finely
    chopped
2 cloves garlic, minced
8 ounces lean ground lamb
3/4 cup tomato sauce
2 Tablespoons minced
    fresh parsley
1/4 teaspoon dried
    rosemary, crumbled
    Pinch cinnamon
    Salt and freshly ground
    pepper, to taste
2 Tablespoons butter
1 Tablespoon flour
3/4 cup milk
2 Tablespoons freshly
    grated Parmesan cheese
    Pinch freshly grated
    nutmeg
4 ounces ziti or other
    tubular pasta
1 egg, beaten
1/2 cup grated Swiss cheese

Heat oil in heavy skillet over medium heat. Add onion and garlic and stir until soft, about 5 minutes. Add lamb and stir until almost cooked. Drain off fat. Blend in tomato sauce, parsley, rosemary and cinnamon. Season with salt and pepper and set aside. Melt 1 Tablespoon butter in heavy, small saucepan over medium low heat. Blend in flour with wooden spoon and stir 3 minutes. Gradually add milk until sauce thickens and just comes to a boil, about 5 minutes. Remove sauce from heat, stir in Parmesan and nutmeg and set aside. Cook pasta in large pot of boiling, salted water until al dente, about 10 minutes. Drain well and return to pot. Mix in egg and remaining Tablespoon butter. Grease 1 shallow baking dish. Place half of pasta in the dish and cover with all of lamb. Sprinkle with half the cheese and top with remaining pasta. Spoon sauce over and sprinkle with remaining cheese. Dust lightly with nutmeg. Cover and refrigerate or bake at 375 degrees 55–60 minutes until puffy and golden. Bring to room temperature before baking refrigerated dish.

Serves 4
May do ahead

Rosemary Merriam
WASHINGTON, D.C.

Garlic Grits

"Good grits."

1 cup instant grits
4 1/2 cups boiling water
1 teaspoon salt
1 roll garlic cheese, cut
    in pieces (or 6 ounces
    grated Cheddar cheese
    and 2 cloves garlic,
    mashed)
1/2 cup butter, cut in pieces
2 eggs, slightly beaten
    Milk

Cook grits in water until thick, as instructed. Add salt, cheese and butter. Add enough milk to eggs to measure 1 cup. Add to grits and blend. Pour into greased casserole and bake at 350 degrees 45–60 minutes.

Serves 4–6
Easy

Margaret S. Coe
CODY, WYOMING

Papa's Saturday Night Potatoes

"This casserole was Papa's Saturday night specialty when the kids were growing up."

Butter
6 medium potatoes, grated
4 medium onions, grated
1/2 cup cream
Salt and pepper, to taste
Dash nutmeg

Combine ingredients and put in buttered casserole. Bake in very slow oven, about 200 degrees, approximately 4 hours.

Serves 6–8
Easy

Thyra Thomson
CHEYENNE, WYOMING

Patrician Potatoes

"Rich—but oh so delicious!"

1 (13.75-ounce) package instant potatoes
1 (8-ounce) package cream cheese, softened
1 small carton sour cream
1 Tablespoon grated onion
Salt and pepper, to taste
1/2 cup toasted almonds

Prepare potatoes, but with less water than usually used. Mix warm potatoes with cheese. Add all but almonds. Mix well and spoon into casserole. Refrigerate. Sprinkle with almonds and bake at 350 degrees 30 minutes. Garnish with generous chunks of butter and parsley.

Serves 8
Easy
Must do ahead

Helen Cashman
MINNEAPOLIS, MINNESOTA

Potato Pancakes

"Good for breakfast or brunch too."

3 pounds potatoes, peeled and grated
1 medium onion, minced
3 eggs, slightly beaten
Salt and pepper, to taste
1/2 cup dry bread crumbs
Oil

Drain potatoes slightly and add onions, eggs, salt, pepper and bread crumbs. Mix well. Drop by Tablespoons in hot oil and brown on both sides. They may be kept hot in the oven on a large tray but do not overlap them.

Serves 6
Easy

Mildred Auslander
SPRINGFIELD, NEW JERSEY

Powderhorn Potatoes

8 large potatoes
1 cup grated sharp Cheddar
  cheese
1/2 cup milk
2 cups sour cream
1 bunch green onions,
  chopped
  Salt and pepper, to taste
2 Tablespoons poppy seeds

"Wonderful served with wild game or beef."

Boil potatoes, drain, cool and grate. Mix remaining ingredients, except seeds, and add to potatoes. Place in an oiled casserole. Sprinkle with poppy seeds to give the "gunpowder" effect. Bake, covered, at 350 degrees 30 minutes, then brown lightly under broiler.

Serves 8–10
Easy

Sue Cogswell
CODY, WYOMING

Parmesan Potatoes

1/4 cup flour
1/4 cup Parmesan cheese
3/4 teaspoon salt
1/8 teaspoon pepper
6 large potatoes, peeled and
  cut lengthwise into fourths
1/3 cup butter

"A great break from plain potatoes."

Combine flour, cheese, salt and pepper in a plastic bag. Wet potatoes and shake in bag to coat them. Melt butter in flat baking dish, big enough to hold potatoes. Place potatoes in melted butter in a single layer. Bake at 375 degrees 1 hour, turning once. Serve with chopped parsley.

Serves 6–8
Easy

Debbie Wilson
PINEDALE, WYOMING

Sweet Potato Souffle

1 (1-pound, 3-ounce) can
  sweet potatoes
1/4 cup melted butter
1/2 teaspoon salt
2 Tablespoons brown sugar
1/2 cup hot milk
3 eggs, separated
1 teaspoon grated lemon
  rind
1/2 cup shredded coconut

"Attractive substitute for glazed yams with marshmallows."

Drain sweet potatoes and mash. Add butter, salt, brown sugar, milk and egg yolks, beating until light and fluffy. Beat egg whites until stiff and fold into mixture along with lemon rind and coconut. Put into an ungreased casserole and bake at 350–375 degrees 1 hour or until top is lightly browned. To cook frozen dish, bake at 350 degrees an hour and a half.

Serves 6
Easy
May be frozen

Pat Ridgway
TUCSON, ARIZONA

La Jolla Potatoes

4 medium potatoes, baked
  and chilled
1 ripe banana
4 Tablespoons butter
1 cup heavy cream
  Parmesan cheese

Peel potatoes and banana and slice thinly. Banana must be ripe but not overripe. Melt butter and stir into banana and potatoes. Heat cream just short of boiling and pour over the mixture. Sprinkle with cheese and heat at 325 degrees 15–20 minutes or until hot.

Serves 4–6
Easy

Yvonne Nielson
CODY, WYOMING

Rice with Sour Cream and Chiles

1 cup long-grain white rice
1 (4-ounce) can green
  chiles, drained and
  chopped
8 ounces Monterey Jack
  cheese, shredded
1 1/4 cups sour cream
  Salt and pepper, to taste
2 Tablespoons butter

Cook rice and combine with chiles, sour cream, and 3/4 of the cheese and season. Mix lightly but thoroughly. Place in 2-quart casserole, sprinkle top with remaining cheese and dot with butter. Bake, uncovered, at 350 degrees 30–45 minutes until golden brown on top. May be assembled early in the day and refrigerated until baking time.

Serves 6–8
May do ahead

Pamela Stockton
CODY, WYOMING

Rice Monterey

"Interesting way to serve rice."

1/2 cup chopped onion
3/4 cup chopped celery
2 Tablespoons olive oil
1/4 cup chopped nuts or
  sunflower seeds
2 1/2 cups cooked brown rice
  Salt and pepper, to taste
1 cup shredded Cheddar
  cheese

Saute onion and celery in olive oil until translucent. Add nuts and saute 1 minute. Add rice and cook until heated completely through, then add salt and pepper to taste. Serve topped with shredded cheese.

Serves 4
Easy

Sue Ludewig
CODY, WYOMING

Rice Pilaf

6 strips bacon, diced
1 large onion, diced
1/2 green pepper, diced
1 clove garlic, minced
2 cups white rice
1 (8-ounce) can sliced
    mushrooms, undrained
1 (10 1/2-ounce) can
    consomme
1/2 cup water

Fry bacon in large heavy skillet. When bacon is half done, add onion, pepper and garlic and brown gently together. Add rice, mushrooms with liquid, consomme and water. Cook over low heat, stirring occasionally. Add more water if necessary. Cook another 20–30 minutes until rice is done.

Serves 8
Easy

Katherine Sluka
WAPITI, WYOMING

Baked Rice

"Pleasant accompaniment for roasted chicken."

1 cup brown or wild rice
1/3 cup chopped onions or
    chives
1/2 cup diced celery
1 (10 1/2-ounce) can
    consomme, beef
    bouillon or chicken
    broth
1 2/3 cans water
1 teaspoon salt, optional
1/2 cup butter, cut in small
    pieces
1 cup ripe olives, sliced
1/2 cup grated Parmesan
    cheese

Mix first 6 ingredients in a greased, shallow casserole. Top with butter and bake at 350 degrees 45 minutes. Mix olives lightly into rice and top with cheese. Bake 15 minutes more.

Serves 8
Easy

Mrs. Phillip V. Carroll
CHARLES CITY, IOWA

Salads and Salad Dressings

Oriental Chicken Salad

Juice and grated rinds
  from 4 lemons
4 cloves garlic, minced
2 Tablespoons soy sauce
6 Tablespoons sesame oil
6 Tablespoons walnut or
  peanut oil
4 cups cooked and diced
  chicken
2 cups rice
1 medium green pepper,
  finely diced
3 medium carrots,
  julienned and blanched
1 pound snow peas,
  blanched, or 1 (10-ounce)
  package French-cut green
  beans, blanched until
  partly cooked
1 bunch green onions,
  very thinly sliced
1 1/2 cups slivered almonds,
  toasted
  Salt and freshly ground
  pepper, to taste

Combine juice and rinds with garlic, soy sauce and oils. Use to marinate chicken while cooking rice and preparing vegetables. Add hot rice, vegetables and almonds to chicken and season to taste. Chill and serve on a bed of lettuce leaves.

Serves 12
Must do ahead

Robin M. Weiss
CODY, WYOMING

More Than Chicken Salad

Combine marinade ingredients in a cruet and shake.

MARINADE:

2 Tablespoons lemon juice
1 teaspoon prepared
   mustard
1/4 cup oil
1/4 teaspoon salt
1/4 teaspoon pepper
1/4 teaspoon tarragon
1/4 teaspoon basil
1/4 teaspoon thyme
1/4 teaspoon marjoram

For salad, toss chicken with marinade and refrigerate 2 hours. Add remaining ingredients and toss to blend. Serve on lettuce bed or with tomato slices.

Serves 6
Must do ahead

Karla Carr
CODY, WYOMING

SALAD:

2 cups cooked and diced
   chicken
1 1/2 cups halved seedless
   green grapes
1 cup mayonnaise
1/2 cup chopped celery
1/2 cup slivered almonds,
   toasted
1 teaspoon lemon juice

Bev's Summer Steak

"Nice in the summer since the broiling can be done early in the day."

1 1/2 pounds beef sirloin
1 small jar sliced
   mushrooms
1 medium green pepper,
   sliced in rings
1/3 cup red wine vinegar
1/4 cup oil
1 teaspoon salt
1/2 teaspoon onion salt
1/2 teaspoon Worcestershire
   sauce
1/4 teaspoon pepper
1/4 teaspoon tarragon
2 cloves garlic, crushed
4 lettuce cups
   Cherry tomatoes, sliced

Trim off fat, then broil meat 3–4 inches from heat until medium-well done. Cool. Cut into 3/8-inch strips. Mix remaining ingredients except lettuce and tomatoes. Toss with meat in bowl, cover and refrigerate at least 3 hours. When ready to serve, lift meat and vegetables into lettuce cups using slotted spoon and decorate with tomatoes.

Serves 4
Easy
Must do ahead

Nancy Fees
CODY, WYOMING

Wildly Delicious Turkey Salad

SALAD:

6 ounces wild rice
4 ounces fresh
   mushrooms, sliced
1 cup fresh spinach, cut in
   strips
2 green onions, with tops,
   thinly sliced
2 cups cooked turkey,
   cubed

DRESSING:

1/4 cup oil
1/4 cup vinegar
2 teaspoons salt, optional
2 teaspoons sugar
   Cherry tomatoes,
   halved, optional

Cook rice according to directions in 2 1/3 cups water and cool. Add mushrooms, spinach, onions and turkey.

For dressing, mix all ingredients except tomatoes. Pour over rice mixture. Let stand overnight in refrigerator. Serve garnished with tomatoes.

Serves 6–8
Easy
Must do ahead

Katharine McMillan
INDIO, CALIFORNIA

Rice and Ham Salad

1 (10-ounce) package frozen
   green peas
2 cups cooked rice
3/4 cup mayonnaise
1 Tablespoon grated onion
1/2 cup diced dill pickle
1/2 cup diced cooked ham
8 ounces Cheddar cheese,
   cubed
   Dash paprika
   Olives

Cook peas and drain. Gently combine all ingredients but paprika and olives, folding in peas last. Sprinkle with paprika. Chill and serve on a bed of lettuce leaves, garnished with olives.

Serves 8   *Dorothy Marchezak*
Easy   EXPORT, PENNSYLVANIA

Supper Salad

"A hearty salad."

MEATBALLS:

1 pound ground beef
1/2 cup wheat germ, toasted
1/2 cup minced onion
1/4 cup ketchup
1 egg, slightly beaten
1 teaspoon chili powder
1 teaspoon dried marjoram
1/2 teaspoon cumin
1/4 teaspoon salt
1/4 teaspoon pepper

SALAD:

1 head lettuce, torn in large
   pieces
2 tomatoes, cut in wedges
1 green pepper, cut in thin
   strips
1/2 cup pitted black olives,
   sliced
1 green onion, sliced in
   1/2-inch pieces
1/2 cup Italian salad dressing

Combine beef, wheat germ, onion, ketchup, egg and seasonings and shape into 36 meatballs. Bake in shallow pan at 400 degrees 10–12 minutes.

Meanwhile, place lettuce in large salad bowl. Arrange tomatoes, green peppers and olives around sides. Place baked meatballs in center of salad. Sprinkle green onions on top and pour salad dressing over all. Meatballs may be shaped and refrigerated ahead of time. Kidney beans, avocado slices or tortilla chips may be added.

Serves 6   *Patricia Blatt*
Easy   CODY, WYOMING

Ziti Salad with Sausage

DRESSING:

1/3 cup red wine vinegar
1/2 teaspoon salt
1/4 teaspoon freshly ground
   pepper
1/8 teaspoon cayenne
1/4 teaspoon rosemary,
   crumbled
1/4 teaspoon oregano,
   crumbled
1/4 teaspoon basil, crumbled
1 1/3 cups olive oil, vegetable
   oil or a combination
1/4 cup freshly grated
   Parmesan cheese

SALAD:

12 ounces ziti or other
   tubular pasta
2 pounds salami or
   pepperoni, thinly sliced
1 pound zucchini, thinly
   sliced
4 medium tomatoes, cut
   in wedges
1 medium green bell
   pepper, coarsely chopped
1 cup minced fresh parsley
3 ounces pimiento,
   chopped
   Freshly grated Parmesan
   cheese, optional

Combine vinegar, seasonings and herbs in small bowl. Whisk in oil in slow, steady stream until well blended. Mix in Parmesan and set dressing aside.

Cook pasta al dente in 4–6 quarts boiling, salted water. Drain and rinse under cold water until cool. Drain again. Combine pasta and remaining ingredients, except Parmesan, in large bowl. Add half the dressing and toss. Add as much of the remaining dressing as necessary to coat salad thoroughly. Sprinkle with additional Parmesan, if desired, and serve.

Serves 8

Sandy Martin
GALLATIN GATEWAY, MONTANA

Salmon Mousse

1 envelope gelatin
2 Tablespoons lemon juice
1 small onion, sliced
1/2 cup boiling water
1/2 cup mayonnaise
1/2 teaspoon paprika
1/2 teaspoon dried dill,
   to taste
1 (1-pound) can pink salmon
1 cup heavy cream

In a blender, combine first 4 ingredients just until onion is pureed. Add next 4 ingredients and blend. Add cream, 1/3 cup at a time, and blend until smooth. Pour into oiled 1-quart mold and chill several hours until firm. To unmold, dip bottom and sides into warm water and turn onto a serving plate. Garnish with parsley.

Serves 8–12
Easy
Must do ahead

Mrs. Malcolm S. Mackay
ROSCOE, MONTANA

Spring Salad

1/2 pound spaghetti, cooked
1/4 cup olive oil
2–3 Tablespoons lemon juice
2–3 tomatoes, peeled and
   chopped
1 green pepper, chopped
4 green onions, chopped
1/2 cup black olives, sliced
   Handful parsley, minced
   Salt and pepper, to taste

Combine all ingredients and serve.

Serves 12
Easy

Harriet G. McGee
CODY, WYOMING

Terrine of Sole

TERRINE:

3 cups fresh spinach,
  washed and stemmed
3 pounds fresh or thawed
  frozen, boneless, skinless
  fillet of sole, pike, red
  snapper or cod, chunked
2 teaspoons salt
1 Tablespoon white pepper
  Whites of 2 large eggs
2 cups heavy cream

SAUCE:

1 Tablespoon butter
2 cups watercress leaves
1/8 teaspoon salt
  A few grains white pepper
1 cup heavy cream, whipped
  Dill sprigs
  Lemon slices

Boil spinach 2 minutes. Rinse with cold water and drain well. In food processor with steel blade, puree fish, salt, pepper and egg whites in 2 equal batches. Turn on and off until fish is finely chopped and forms a thick paste. For each batch, add 1 cup cream, 1/2 cup at a time, processing after each addition until just blended. (Over blending makes butter.) Scrape into large bowl. Squeeze spinach very dry. Put in processor with 1 1/2 cups fish mixture and process 15–25 seconds, until spinach is finely chopped. Spread 2 cups plain fish mixture in a greased, glass loaf dish. Layer the spinach mixture evenly on top, then remaining fish mixture. Cover with greased aluminum foil and set in a pan of water. Bake at 375 degrees 60 minutes. Remove and cool 1 1/2 hours, then refrigerate 4 hours.

For sauce, melt butter, add watercress and cook 30–50 seconds until wilted. Remove from heat and finely chop. Season. Just before serving, fold watercress mixture into whipped cream. To serve, drain all water from loaf pan, turn terrine onto a board and cut into 10 slices. Garnish with dill and lemon and serve with the sauce.

Serves 8–10
Time-consuming
Must do ahead

Yvonne Nielson
CODY, WYOMING

Shrimp Salad Mold

1 can cream of celery soup,
  undiluted and heated
1 envelope unflavored
  gelatin, dissolved in
  3 Tablespoons water
1 cup minced celery
1/2 cup minced onion
2 cans shrimp, drained
1 cup mayonnaise

Combine soup and gelatin. Mix in remaining ingredients and place in oiled 1-quart mold. Serve cold with mild crackers.

Serves 4–6
Easy
Must do ahead

Marie C. Parker
KINGSTON, NEW YORK

Everglades Club Egg Curry Ring

1 Tablespoon curry
    powder
2 cups chicken stock
2 Tablespoons unflavored
    gelatin, softened in a
    little water
3 hard-boiled eggs, sliced
1 1/2 cups mayonnaise
    Salt, to taste

Dissolve curry in boiling stock. When cool, stir in gelatin. Place eggs and mayonnaise in blender and blend well. Add gelatin mixture and salt. Pour into ring mold. Chill until firm. Unmold onto platter. Ring may be served with crab meat or chicken salad in center.

Serves 6–8   *Mrs. Byron Ramsing*
Must do ahead   CODY, WYOMING

Egg Ring

"A wonderful salad accompaniment."

2 envelopes unflavored
    gelatin
1 cup cold water
1 cup boiling water
3/4 cup minced parsley
2/3 cup minced green pepper
1 1/2 Tablespoons minced
    green onions
2 cups mayonnaise
1 cup cottage cheese
1 1/2 teaspoons salt
1/4 teaspoon pepper
1/2 teaspoon paprika
12 hard-boiled eggs, cooled
    and riced

Soak gelatin in cold water 15 minutes, then dissolve in boiling water and cool to tepid. Mix gelatin, chopped vegetables, mayonnaise, cottage cheese and seasonings. Mix in eggs. Pour into a buttered ring mold. Cover and chill overnight. To serve, unmold on a bed of salad greens and fill center with seafood or chicken salad. Use a large serving platter so mounds of filling may be placed around the outside of the ring. Serve with extra mayonnaise if using seafood.

Serves 12–16   *Margot Belden Todd*
Must do ahead   CODY, WYOMING

As I have not got Will Crawford's address, I wrote him what you said care "Everybody's Magazine" and if I hear from him will certainly go out to see him. Am having my troubles just now on a gun calender of a hunter coming around the edge of a log cabin and a big grizzly just rushing out of the door, the man is about to fire from the hip.

I have not done much modeling

15[W] 23 St, N.Y.
July 14, 1908

In the Kootney country.

Untitled—Illustrated letter to Charles M. Russell written by Philip R. Goodwin. *Courtesy of Buffalo Bill Historical Center, Cody, WY; 26.83.1*

Champagne Salad

"Sweet and crunchy."

3/4 cup sugar
8 ounces cream cheese, softened
10 ounces frozen strawberries, thawed
1 large can crushed pineapple, well drained
1–2 bananas, diced
9 ounces non-dairy whipped topping
1/2 cup chopped nuts

Cream sugar and cheese. Add remaining ingredients. Put in a 9 × 13-inch pan and freeze. Thaw 15 minutes before serving.

Serves 8
Easy
Must do ahead

Jewell Allen
RAWLINS, WYOMING

Cottage Cheese Pineapple Salad

1 (3-ounce) package lime gelatin
1 1/2 cups hot water
1/2 cup pineapple juice
1 cup cottage cheese
1 cup crushed pineapple
1 1/2 cups chopped celery
1/4 cup broken nut meats
1/4 cup sliced stuffed olives
1/4 teaspoon salt
1/2 cup mayonnaise
1 Tablespoon vinegar

Dissolve gelatin in hot water, add pineapple juice and cool. When slightly thickened, whip. Add remaining ingredients, mixing carefully. Pour into 3-quart mold and chill several hours or overnight.

Serves 12
Must do ahead

Ellen Waggoner
CODY, WYOMING

Avocado Cocktail

"Attractive served in a pretty cocktail or stemmed glass at the beginning of a meal."

COCKTAIL:

2 medium avocados
2 stalks celery, finely
    chopped
    Lemon juice, optional

DRESSING:

1 cup mayonnaise
4 Tablespoons lemon juice
6 Tablespoons chili sauce
2 hard-boiled eggs, chopped
    Watercress or parsley

Cut avocados in 1/2-inch cubes. Sprinkle with lemon juice if prepared ahead of time.

For dressing, combine mayonnaise, lemon juice, chili sauce and eggs. To assemble, place about 1 Tablespoon of celery in each serving glass, follow with a layer of avocado, and top generously with dressing. Garnish with sprigs of watercress or parsley.

Serves 4
Easy

Elizabeth Field
NEWCASTLE, WYOMING

Cauliflower Salad

"Colorful served in a glass bowl."

SALAD:

1 large head cauliflower,
    thinly sliced
1 can pitted ripe olives,
    sliced
1/2 cup coarsely chopped
    green pepper
1/2 cup coarsely chopped
    pimiento
1/2 cup chopped onion

DRESSING:

1/2 cup olive oil
3 Tablespoons lemon juice
3 Tablespoons white wine
    vinegar
2 Tablespoons salt
1/2 teaspoon sugar
1/4 teaspoon pepper

Combine salad ingredients in a bowl. Beat dressing ingredients with a mixer or whisk until blended. Pour over cauliflower mixture and refrigerate, covered, until well chilled, at least 4 hours and preferably overnight. Serve on salad greens or in a glass bowl.

Serves 8–10
Must do ahead

Mary Lou McDonald
GREENWICH, CONNECTICUT

Cauliflower Marinade

1 cauliflower, cut in
 bite-sized pieces
1/4 cup vinegar
1/2 cup oil
1/2 cup sliced stuffed olives
4 ounces bleu cheese,
 crumbled
1/4 cup chopped green onions

"Great for a picnic."

Combine all ingredients and marinate overnight.

Serves 8
Easy
Must do ahead

Lorraine Trythall
Cody, Wyoming

Celery Victor Hugo

"Different, attractive and flavorful."

8 celery hearts
2 cans chicken broth
1 cup vinegar
 Anchovy fillets
2 hard-boiled eggs, chopped

After trimming and cleaning, tie celery in 2 bunches. Cook in broth until just tender. Remove celery, cover with 2 cups of the broth and the vinegar and let stand overnight. Place on platter and garnish with anchovy and egg. Serve with Lorenzo or French dressing.

Serves 8
Easy
Must do ahead

Margaret S. Coe
Cody, Wyoming

Cole Slaw

"Healthful, new ingredients zip up an old favorite."

4 cups shredded cabbage
2 large carrots, grated
2 apples, grated
1/2 cup plain yogurt
1/2 cup mayonnaise
1 Tablespoon honey
3 Tablespoons vinegar
1/2 cup sliced red onion
 Salt and pepper, to taste

Combine all ingredients. Mix well. Cover and chill until serving time.

Serves 8
Easy
Must do ahead

Douglas Clark Sunderland
Cody, Wyoming

Charlemagne Salad with Hot Brie Dressing

SALAD:

1 medium head curly endive
1 medium head iceberg
lettuce
1 medium head Romaine
lettuce
Garlic croutons

DRESSING:

1 cup olive oil
1 teaspoon minced green
onions
2 teaspoons minced garlic
1/2 cup sherry wine vinegar
2 Tablespoons fresh lemon
juice
4 teaspoons Dijon mustard
10 ounces ripe Brie cheese,
rind removed and cut in
small pieces
Freshly ground pepper

"From the Charlemagne Restaurant in Aspen, Colorado."

Tear greens in bite-sized pieces and toss with croutons in large bowl. Warm olive oil in large skillet on low heat 10 minutes. Add green onions and garlic and cook until translucent, stirring occasionally. Blend in vinegar, lemon juice and mustard. Add Brie and stir until smooth. Season with pepper. Toss hot dressing with salad.

Serves 10
Easy

Robin Weiss
CODY, WYOMING

Furious Frank's Hearts of Palm Salad

SALAD:

1 can hearts of palm, sliced
1/8 cup sunflower seeds
2 heads Boston, bibb or red
  leaf lettuce

DRESSING:

1/3 cup olive oil
2 Tablespoons lemon juice
1 teaspoon sugar
1/2 teaspoon salt
1/2 teaspoon aromatic bitters
1/4 teaspoon paprika
2 Tablespoons sliced stuffed
  green olives
2 Tablespoons minced onion
2 Tablespoons finely
  chopped celery

Combine dressing ingredients. Shake vigorously and chill at least 2 hours. Toss hearts of palm with sunflower seeds and lettuce. Add dressing and serve.

Serves 8
Easy
Must do ahead

Nancy Fees
CODY, WYOMING

Pea Salad

2 pounds frozen peas
2 cups sour cream
2 cups chopped celery
1/2 cup chopped green onions
1 cup cashews
1 cup bacon bits

Mix peas, sour cream, celery and onions, cover and refrigerate overnight. Before serving, add cashews and bacon and toss.

Serves 6
Easy
Must do ahead

RoyAnn Bormuth
CODY, WYOMING

Layered Vegetable Salad

"Refreshing taste for a lawn garden party."

2–3 cups fresh spinach,
  chopped
1 teaspoon salt
1/4 teaspoon pepper
1 Tablespoon sugar
1 pound bacon, fried and
  crumbled
6 hard-boiled eggs, sliced
2–3 cups lettuce, shredded
1 (8-ounce) can water
  chestnuts, sliced
1 teaspoon salt
1/4 teaspoon pepper
1 Tablespoon sugar
1 (10-ounce) package frozen
  peas, thawed
1/2 cup sliced Bermuda
  onions or green onions
1 cup mayonnaise
1 cup Miracle Whip
1 cup Swiss cheese, grated

Sprinkle spinach over bottom of 2 1/2-quart flat casserole. Sprinkle salt, pepper and sugar over spinach. Top with bacon, eggs, lettuce, water chestnuts, remaining salt, pepper and sugar, peas and onions. Combine mayonnaise and Miracle Whip and spread over top. Sprinkle with Swiss cheese. Refrigerate at least 12 hours before serving.

Serves 16
Easy   *Mrs. C. V. Whitney*
Must do ahead   SARATOGA SPRINGS, NEW YORK

New Potato Salad

"Using unpeeled potatoes gives a favorite dish a new look."

2 pounds new potatoes
1 medium onion, chopped
1 small green pepper,
    chopped
3/4 cup chopped celery
1 Tablespoon chopped
    parsley
3/4 cup mayonnaise
2 Tablespoons oil
2 1/2 Tablespoons vinegar
1 teaspoon salt
1/2 teaspoon dill seed

Boil new potatoes in salted water only until tender. Drain and cool. When cool, cut in 1/2-inch cubes. Place in bowl with onions, green pepper, celery and parsley. Mix together mayonnaise, oil, vinegar, salt and dill seed and pour over the vegetables. Mix thoroughly and chill at least 3 hours before serving.

Serves 6
Easy
Must do ahead

Mrs. Steven C. Motsinger
STATE ROAD, NORTH CAROLINA

Potato Salad

1/2 cup Italian salad dressing
7 medium potatoes,
    cooked in jackets,
    peeled and sliced
3/4 cup sliced radishes
1/3 cup sliced onions
1 cup mayonnaise
1/2 cup sour cream
1/2 teaspoon horseradish
1 teaspoon Dijon mustard
6 slices cooked bacon,
    crumbled

Pour dressing over warm potatoes. Chill 2 hours and add radishes and onions. Combine mayonnaise, sour cream, horseradish and mustard and fold into potatoes. Top with bacon.

Serves 8
Easy
Must do ahead

William D. Weiss
CODY, WYOMING

Lychee Nut Salad

SALAD:

1/3 cup Roquefort cheese
1 1/2 Tablespoons unsalted
  butter
4–6 drops Worcestershire
  sauce
1 (11-ounce) can lychee
  nuts, drained, or
  16 lychee nuts

DRESSING:

2 Tablespoons olive oil
2 Tablespoons cider
  vinegar
1 Tablespoon red wine
  Salt and freshly ground
  pepper, to taste

Bibb lettuce
Sliced avocados

Thoroughly mix cheese, butter and Worcestershire. Stuff lychees with the cheese mixture. Wrap tightly and refrigerate overnight.

For dressing, mix oil, vinegar, wine and seasonings. To serve, arrange stuffed lychees on bed of lettuce, drizzle with dressing and surround with avocado slices.

Serves 4–6
Easy   *John Sinai*
Must do ahead   SAN FRANCISCO, CALIFORNIA

Marinated Mushrooms

2 pounds small to
  medium mushrooms
1 package Good Seasons
  Italian dressing mix
1/2 cup white vinegar
2 Tablespoons water
1 1/3 cups salad oil
1/2 teaspoon dry mustard
  Juice of 1 small lemon
1 Tablespoon
  Worcestershire sauce
1 teaspoon seasoning salt
1 teaspoon pepper
  Small handfuls of celery,
  onion and parsley, finely
  chopped

"Excellent as an accompaniment to buffet luncheons or dinners."

Clean and trim mushrooms and rinse with cold water. Parboil in 3/4 inch of water 1–2 minutes. Spread on paper towel and pat dry. In large bowl, mix dressing with vinegar, water and oil. Add remaining ingredients. Toss and add mushrooms. Store 4–5 days in tightly covered container in refrigerator. Shake once a day. Keeps indefinitely.

Yields 1 pint   *Norma Strand*
Must do ahead   CODY, WYOMING

Simple Day-Ahead Salad

*Flowerettes from large
bunch fresh broccoli*
1 can water chestnuts
1 pound mushrooms, sliced
*1 can sliced black olives,
optional*
*1 package dry zesty
Italian dressing mix
Italian dressing
Cherry tomatoes, halved,
or sliced red onions*

Place all vegetables but tomatoes in a shallow bowl.
Sprinkle on package of dressing, then pour on enough
liquid dressing to cover. Toss and refrigerate 4 hours or
overnight. Just before serving, toss again and add either
tomatoes or onions for color.

Serves 6–8
Easy
Must do ahead

Margaret O'B. Smith
Somers, New York

Spinach Salad with Bacon and Apple

"A different taste for spinach."

SALAD:

*1 pound fresh spinach,
washed and stemmed*
5 slices bacon
1/3 cup sliced almonds
*3 green onions, thinly
sliced, using some green
parts*
*1 unpeeled red Delicious
apple, cored and chopped*

DRESSING:

*2 Tablespoons bacon fat
Oil*
*3 Tablespoons tarragon
vinegar*
1 teaspoon sugar
1/2 teaspoon dry mustard
1/8 teaspoon salt
1/8 teaspoon pepper

Prepare spinach ahead of time so it is cold and crisp. Cut
bacon in 1-inch pieces and cook until crisp. Drain, reserving 2 Tablespoons fat. Mix spinach with remaining
salad ingredients in large bowl. Combine bacon fat with
enough oil to make 1/3 cup and blend with remaining ingredients for dressing. Pour over spinach mixture, toss
lightly and serve.

Serves 4–6
Easy

Beverly J. Robertson
Cody, Wyoming

Spinach Salad

1 package fresh spinach,
 snipped in small pieces
1 can bean sprouts, drained
5 strips bacon, cooked and
 crumbled
2 hard-boiled eggs, finely
 chopped
1 cup oil
3/4 cup sugar
1 onion, grated
1/3 cup ketchup
1 teaspoon Worcestershire
 sauce
1/4 cup vinegar

Place spinach and sprouts in large bowl. Top with bacon and egg. Mix remaining ingredients for dressing and serve on the side.

Serves 8
Easy

Lois Miller
Cody, Wyoming

Spinach Salad with Chutney Dressing

SALAD:

1 pound fresh spinach,
 washed
6 mushrooms, sliced
1 cup sliced water chestnuts
6 slices bacon, cooked and
 crumbled
3/4 cup bean sprouts
1/2 cup shredded Gruyere
 cheese
1/4 cup thinly sliced red onion

Combine salad ingredients in large bowl. For dressing, mix first 5 ingredients in blender, slowly adding oil. Pour over salad. Dressing may be refrigerated and then allowed to stand at room temperature 30 minutes before using.

Serves 6
Easy

Adelaide D. Valentine
Denver, Colorado

DRESSING:

1/4 cup wine vinegar
3 Tablespoons chutney
1 clove garlic, crushed
2 Tablespoons grainy
 mustard
2 teaspoons sugar
1/2 cup oil

Herbed Tomatoes

6 medium ripe tomatoes,
   peeled
2/3 cup oil
1/4 cup vinegar
1/4 cup snipped parsley
1/4 cup sliced green onions
1 teaspoon salt
1/4 teaspoon freshly ground
   pepper
2 teaspoons snipped fresh
   thyme or marjoram
   leaves, or 1/2 teaspoon
   dried herbs
1 clove garlic, minced

Place tomatoes in deep bowl. Combine remaining ingredients in a jar and shake well. Pour over tomatoes, cover and chill several hours or overnight, occasionally spooning dressing over tomatoes. At serving time, spoon dressing over tomatoes again, then transfer to serving platter.

Serves 6
Easy   *Katharine McMillan Roberts*
Must do ahead   NORTHAMPTON, MASSACHUSETTS

Tipi Tomatoes and Onions

"A summer picnic tradition in northern Michigan."

1 red onion, sliced
2 large tomatoes, sliced
1/4 cup crumbled bleu cheese
1/2 cup olive oil
2 Tablespoons lemon juice
Dash freshly ground pepper
1/2 teaspoon sugar
Dash paprika
Lettuce leaves

Layer onion and tomato slices in a glass bowl. Combine remaining ingredients except lettuce, mixing well, and pour over onion and tomatoes. Chill 24 hours and serve on lettuce leaves.

Serves 4–5
Easy   *William D. Weiss*
Must do ahead   CODY, WYOMING

Cognac Dressing

"Excellent with shrimp."

2 Tablespoons horseradish
Juice of 1/2 lemon
Few drops Worcestershire sauce
1/2 cup ketchup
Drop Tabasco
1 cup mayonnaise
2 ounces cognac
Salt and pepper, to taste
More lemon juice, if desired

Blend first 5 ingredients well, then gradually blend in mayonnaise. Stir in cognac and season to taste, adding more lemon juice if desired. Allow to rest several hours before using.

Yields 2 1/4 cups
Easy
Must do ahead

William E. Weiss
CODY, WYOMING

Anne's Salad Dressing

"Super on any tossed salad."

1 small onion, finely chopped
1 cup mayonnaise
1/3 cup oil
1/4 cup ketchup
2 Tablespoons sugar
2 Tablespoons vinegar
1 teaspoon prepared mustard
1/2 teaspoon salt
1/4 teaspoon celery seed
1/2 teaspoon paprika
Dash freshly ground pepper
1 cup crumbled bleu cheese

Blend all ingredients except cheese in blender or food processor until smooth. By hand, gently fold in cheese. Chill.

Yields 2 cups
Easy
May do ahead

Anne C. Hayes
CODY, WYOMING

John's Salad Dressing

1 cup oil, part or all
    olive oil (may include
    2 Tablespoons walnut
    oil)
1 1/2–2 ounces tarragon red
    vinegar
1 egg yolk, beaten
    Pinch salt
1 teaspoon Dijon
    mustard
    Dash Worcestershire
    sauce
3/4 teaspoon fines herbes
    Pinch sugar

Blend thoroughly with a whisk or mixer. Serve over greens that have been seasoned with MSG and freshly ground black pepper. Variations: use dill weed instead of fines herbes; use a tiny bit of curry and mustard and 1 Tablespoon mayonnaise instead of egg yolk; or add chopped green onions to greens. For a fresh grapefruit salad, use chopped fresh mint in place of fines herbes.

Yields 1 cup
Easy   *John Sinai*
May do ahead   SAN FRANCISCO, CALIFORNIA

Mayfair Dressing

"The secret house dressing of the Mayfair Hotel, St. Louis, Missouri."

1 medium onion
1 clove garlic
1 heaping teaspoon MSG
1 heaping teaspoon
    pepper
2 teaspoons prepared
    mustard or 1 teaspoon
    dry mustard
1 can anchovies
1 1/2 cups oil
2 eggs

Put first 6 ingredients and 1/2 cup oil in blender and mix until smooth. Add eggs and blend. Add remaining oil and blend. If too thick, add a Tablespoon of hot water. Dressing is best if refrigerated a day before using. It may also be used as a dip.

Yields 2 cups
Easy   *Ginna Roes*
Must do ahead   CODY, WYOMING

French Tomato Dressing

1/2 cup sugar
1/2 cup vinegar
1/2 cup oil
  2 Tablespoon finely grated
    onion
  1 teaspoon salt
  1 can tomato soup,
    undiluted
1/3 teaspoon pepper

Mix all ingredients in blender. Chill.

Yields 2 3/4 cups
Easy
Must do ahead

Mrs. Atlee W. Davis
BARTOW, FLORIDA

Green Goddess Salad Dressing

"Delightful tang."

  2 cloves garlic
  4 ounces anchovy paste
  4 Tablespoons fresh lemon
    juice
  5 ounces tarragon vinegar
  2 cups sour cream
  4 cups mayonnaise
    Salt and freshly ground
    pepper, to taste
1/2 cup chopped green onions,
    including light green stems
  1 cup chopped parsley

Combine first 7 ingredients in food processor and blend until smooth, using steel blade. Add onions and parsley. Using quick on-and-off pulses, continue chopping until onions and parsley are finely chopped and distributed throughout.

Yields 1 1/2 quarts
Easy

Margaret S. Coe
CODY, WYOMING

Poppy Seed Dressing

1 1/2 cups sugar
   2 teaspoons dry mustard
   2 teaspoons salt
1/2 cup wine vinegar
   2 cups oil
   1 small onion, grated
    Scant 1/4 cup poppy
    seeds

Combine first 4 ingredients, then slowly whisk oil into mixture. Place in a jar with onion and seeds and shake well. Add extra Tablespoon of vinegar if necessary. This is excellent on salad of avocado slices alternated with grapefruit segments on a bed of lettuce.

Yields 1 quart
Easy

Margaret S. Coe
CODY, WYOMING

Russian Dressing

   1 cup oil
1/2 cup cider vinegar
   1 medium onion, finely
    chopped
3/4 cup sugar or less, to taste
   1 Tablespoon
    Worcestershire sauce
1/3 cup ketchup

Combine all ingredients in blender. Store in tightly covered jar in refrigerator. Dressing will keep up to 2 weeks.

Serves 12–15
Easy
May do ahead

Gloria Cottle
CODY, WYOMING

Sour Cream Dressing

1 cup sour cream
1 cup mayonnaise
1 Tablespoon sugar
  Dash Tabasco
  Garlic salt, to taste
4 ounces bleu cheese,
  crumbled

Combine all ingredients and blend well. Prepare a day ahead and refrigerate.

Yields 2 cups
Easy
Must do ahead

Barbara M. Hassrick
WALPOLE, NEW HAMPSHIRE

Sweet and Sharp Vinaigrette Salad Dressing

"For a favorite tossed salad."

1/4 cup white wine or
    tarragon vinegar
2 Tablespoons Dijon
    mustard
1/4 teaspoon salt
1/8 teaspoon freshly ground
    pepper
1 1/2 Tablespoons sugar
1 Tablespoon Italian
    seasoning
2–3 cloves garlic, minced or
    pressed
1/2 cup olive oil

Combine all ingredients except olive oil and stir well. Whisk in the oil gradually until mixture thickens and emulsifies. This recipe may be multiplied. However, once past double, subsequent additions of garlic should be reduced by half and sugar to a Tablespoon.

Yields 1 cup
Easy
May do ahead

Dick Ludewig
CODY, WYOMING

"La Cantina de Las Palomas" by Edward Borein. *Courtesy of Buffalo Bill Historical Center, Cody, WY; Gift of Mrs. William K. Laughlin; 25.62*

Mexican Foods

Hot Bean Dip

16 ounces cream cheese, softened
2 (10-ounce) cans bean dip
20 drops Tabasco
2 cups sour cream
1 cup sliced green onions
1 package taco seasoning
Salt, to taste
8 ounces Cheddar cheese, grated
8 ounces Monterey Jack cheese, grated

Beat first 7 ingredients together, adding 1 at a time. Layer half in 9 × 13-inch baking dish, then layer with half of each cheese. Top with remaining bean mixture, then the remaining cheeses. Bake at 350 degrees 20 minutes.

Serves 15–20 *La Rae Daniels*
Easy HUNTINGTON BEACH, CALIFORNIA

Chihuahua Dip

"Excellent hot or cold."

1 (16-ounce) can refried beans
2 or 3 avocados, chopped
1 cup sour cream
1 cup mayonnaise
1 package taco seasoning
3 tomatoes, seeded and chopped
1 bunch green onions, chopped
1 pound Cheddar cheese, grated

Cover bottom of 8 × 10-inch baking pan with beans. Mix together avocados, sour cream, mayonnaise and seasoning for second layer. Top with additional layers of tomatoes, onions and cheese. Bake at 350 degrees 30 minutes. Serve with chips.

Serves 12 *Dede Wells*
Easy CINCINNATI, OHIO

Chile Con Queso

"A party favorite in Cody."

2 Tablespoons butter
1/4 cup minced onion
1 (8 1/4-ounce) can
  tomatoes, finely chopped,
  juice reserved
1 (4-ounce) can green chiles,
  drained and finely chopped
1/4 teaspoon salt
2 pounds Monterey Jack
  cheese, cubed
1/4 cup heavy cream

Melt butter in skillet and saute onions until tender. Add tomatoes, chiles and salt. Simmer 15 minutes, stirring occasionally. Add cheese and stir until melted. Add cream and simmer 2 minutes, stirring constantly. Remove from heat and let stand 15 minutes. Serve in chafing dish with corn chips.

Serves 6–8
Easy

Margaret S. Coe
CODY, WYOMING

Guacamole Pie

1 large avocado, mashed
  Salt
1 Tablespoon lemon juice
1 cup sour cream
1 package taco seasoning
1/4 cup grated Monterey Jack
  or Cheddar cheese
1/4 cup grated onion
1/4 cup sliced black olives
1 tomato, seeded and
  chopped
  Tabasco, to taste

Mix avocado with salt and lemon juice. Mix sour cream and seasoning. Layer avocado mixture, sour cream mixture and remaining ingredients in order. Serve with chips.

Serves 12
Easy
Must do ahead

Polly Uihlein
MILWAUKEE, WISCONSIN

Quesadillas

"This appetizer can be made open face by omitting the top tortilla. Either way, they're great!"

SALSA:

1 small can tomato sauce
1 small can hot jalapeno relish

QUESADILLAS:

4 (12-inch) flour tortillas
1 cup shredded Cheddar cheese

Combine tomato sauce with relish and boil in saucepan about 5 minutes. Spread a tortilla with about 2 Tablespoons salsa. Top with 1/4–1/2 cup cheese and cover with another tortilla. Make a second quesadilla and place both on a baking sheet. Broil 4–6 inches from heat until lightly browned and cheese begins to melt. Turn and repeat. Remove, cut in pie-shaped sections and serve hot. Use other fillings such as black olives, onions and avocado. Salsa may also be used as a hot dip with tortilla chips.

Serves 4–8
Easy

James Herman
CODY, WYOMING

Super Nachos

1/2 cup chopped onion
1 Tablespoon butter or oil
1 pound lean ground beef
1 teaspoon seasoned salt
1 large can refried beans
1 (4-ounce) can diced green chiles
1/2 pound Monterey Jack cheese, grated
1/2 pound sharp Cheddar cheese, grated
1 can black olives, chopped
1/2 cup chopped green onions
1 cup sour cream, at room temperature
3/4–1 cup pureed avocado
3/4–1 cup hot taco or enchilada sauce, heated
Tortillas or tortilla chips, heated

Saute onions in butter until lightly browned. Add beef and salt and cook, stirring, several minutes. In lightly oiled, 9 × 13-inch baking dish, layer beans, beef mixture, chiles and cheeses. Bake at 400 degrees 20–25 minutes until beans are hot and cheese melts. Remove and top with olives and green onions. In the center of the dish, make a strip by layering sour cream, avocado and sauce. Serve at once on tortillas or with chips.

Serves 6–8

Polly Parsons
ROUGH AND READY, CALIFORNIA

Empanadas

"A great hit at the Frontier Festival."

8 ounces ground spicy
 sausage
1 teaspoon chili powder
1/2 teaspoon ground cumin
1/2 teaspoon garlic powder
1/2 teaspoon coriander
1 (10-ounce) package frozen
 patty shells, thawed

Brown meat and drain. Add spices. Roll dough to 1/16-inch thickness and cut in 3-inch rounds. Put 2 teaspoons filling on each circle. Fold in half. Crimp edges with fork and prick tops. Place on ungreased baking sheet. Bake at 400 degrees 20 minutes. May be frozen and reheated at 400 degrees 8 minutes. Serve with salsa (see index).

Serves 8–10
May be frozen

Temptations
CODY, WYOMING

Baked Empanadas

PASTRY:

2 cups flour
2 teaspoons baking powder
1/2 teaspoon salt
2 Tablespoons lard
1 egg
1/2 cup milk

Sift dry pastry ingredients and cut in lard. Beat egg with milk and add. Mix and roll out in small circles.

FILLING:

3 Tablespoons lard
1 Tablespoon paprika
2 large onions, chopped
1 pound beef, cubed
 Cumin
 Salt
 Red pepper
2 hard-boiled eggs, chopped
 Raisins
 Olives

For filling, heat lard and add paprika. Remove from heat and let stand for a moment. Pour over onions and meat. Add spices, to taste. Allow to cool completely and divide among pastry circles. Add eggs, raisins and olives. Fold over pastry and seal. Bake at 400–450 degrees 20 minutes and serve with salsa. (See index.)

Serves 4
Easy
May be frozen

Henry Gardiner
BOZEMAN, MONTANA

Green Chile Pie

1 large can green chiles
1 1/2 cups grated Cheddar
  cheese
1 1/2 cups grated Monterey
  Jack cheese
2 Tablespoons minced
  onion
1/4 teaspoon salt
1/4 teaspoon black pepper
1/2 teaspoon chili powder
5 eggs, well beaten

Grease an 8 × 8-inch pan and line with chiles as for pie crust. Mix all but eggs and sprinkle over chiles. Pour in eggs and bake at 375 degrees 20–25 minutes until eggs are cooked and top is light brown. Let cool 7–10 minutes until set. Cut in small pieces and serve as an appetizer or a main course.

Serves 4
Easy

Gladys Byers
CODY, WYOMING

Anticuchos Perianos

"Served in Lima, Peru, as a traditional hors d'oeuvre and also during Fiesta Week in San Antonio, Texas, a lavish, four-night affair held on the grounds of the historic La Villita."

MARINADE:

1 cup red wine vinegar
3 cups water
2 or 3 serrano or jalapeno
  peppers
Salt
Whole black peppercorns
1/2–1 teaspoon garlic salt or
  2 or 3 cloves garlic
Big pinch oregano
Big pinch cumin

1–2 pounds beef sirloin,
  cut in 1-inch cubes
1/4 cup bacon fat

Mix marinade ingredients in blender. Place beef in shallow pan, pour in marinade and toss well. Marinate 24 hours. String beef onto wooden or metal skewers. Add bacon fat to remaining marinade and use to baste. The bacon fat adds extra flavor and helps smoke the meat. Grill over hot coals.

Serves 6–8
Easy
Must do ahead

Roberta Byrd
DALLAS, TEXAS

Avocado Soup Casa Miguel

4 ounces lean bacon
1 medium onion, diced
12 large lettuce leaves
1 large avocado, peeled
   and diced
5 cups chicken stock
3 1/2 cups tomato juice
1 Tablespoon sugar
2 teaspoons
   Worcestershire sauce
1/4 teaspoon Tabasco
1/8 teaspoon chili powder

In a large heavy saucepan, saute bacon until crisp. Remove and reserve. Pour off all but 2 Tablespoons fat and saute onions until translucent. Add remaining ingredients, cover and simmer over low heat 25 minutes. Puree a portion at a time. (Do not use metal blade.) Adjust seasoning and sprinkle crumbled bacon on top.

Serves 6–8
Easy

William E. Weiss
CODY, WYOMING

Gazpacho de Madrid

"I was given this recipe, traditionally served on warm summer evenings, when living with a Spanish family in Madrid."

3 large or 4 medium
   peeled ripe tomatoes
1/2 medium green pepper
1/2 medium cucumber
1/3 medium onion
2 cloves garlic or 1
   teaspoon dried minced
3 Tablespoons red wine
   vinegar
2 Tablespoons olive oil
1 Tablespoon salt
1 pound French or Italian
   bread, crusts removed
   and soaked in water

Puree all ingredients but bread until smooth. Add part of the bread and puree again. Add remaining bread and puree. Pour into a bowl or tureen. It should be quite thick, like cake batter. Thin with water to desired consistency, chill a day and adjust seasoning. Prepare cubed fresh bread, sliced cucumber and chopped onions, green pepper and tomatoes and pass at the table or use to garnish individual servings.

Serves 8
Must do ahead

Gina Guy
PORTLAND, OREGON

Black Bean Soup

1 pound black turtle beans
6 cups water
1 pork chop
1 green pepper, chopped
1 medium onion, chopped
1 chorizo sausage
3 ounces salt pork
3 cloves garlic, crushed
2 bay leaves
4 Tablespoons oil
2 Tablespoons vinegar
1 teaspoon sugar, optional
　Salt and pepper to taste

Rinse beans well and place in large pot with water. Remove bone from pork chop and add to beans, reserving meat. Add half the green pepper and onions and whole sausage. Bring to a boil and cook 1 hour. Remove sausage, slice 1/8-inch thick and return to pot. Cube reserved meat and salt pork. Saute with remaining green pepper and onions, garlic and bay leaves in oil and vinegar. When onions are transparent, add to beans. Add sugar and cook until beans are tender. Adjust seasoning.

Serves 6

Whole Foods Trading Company
CODY, WYOMING

Pozole Blanco

"A golden hominy soup that is a great first course."

POZOLE:

1 pound boneless lean
　pork, cut in 1-inch cubes
6 chicken thighs
1/2 medium onion, halved
2 cloves garlic
2 teaspoons salt, to taste
2 peppercorns
6 cups water
1 (1-pound, 3-ounce) can
　golden hominy

GARNISHES:

3 or 4 limes, halved
1/2 medium onion, chopped
1/2 head lettuce, shredded
　Sliced radishes
　Sliced avocado
2 Tablespoons dried
　oregano
　Salsa Fresca

Put pork and chicken in separate, large saucepans. Divide onions, garlic, salt, peppercorns and water between each pan. Bring to a boil and skim foam. Cover and simmer pork 1 hour and chicken 45 minutes. Meanwhile, prepare garnishes and salsa. Remove pork and chicken with slotted spoon and place in Dutch oven. Strain broth and add to meats. Drain and rinse hominy and add. Bring to a boil, reduce heat, cover and simmer 30 minutes. Adjust seasoning. Serve with garnishes and Salsa Fresca (see index).

Serves 6–8

Sandra M. Foxley
ENGLEWOOD, COLORADO

Texas Chili

"Chili con carne, as we know it, was probably first served in San Antonio,"

2 medium green peppers, seeded and finely chopped
5 stalks celery, finely chopped
2 medium onions, finely chopped
6 cloves garlic, finely chopped
2 fresh jalapenos, stemmed, seeded and finely chopped
3 Tablespoons oil
10 Tablespoons dried ground red chili powder
1 (4–5 pound) beef brisket with some fat remaining, cut in 1/2–3/4-inch cubes or coarsely ground
1 (12-ounce) can stewed tomatoes
2 Tablespoons cumin
1 Tablespoon oregano
1 quart water
2 Tablespoons freshly ground black pepper
Salt, to taste

Saute green peppers, celery, onions, garlic and jalapenos in oil in large stew pot 5–6 minutes until soft and translucent. Add chili powder and cook another 3–4 minutes. In small batches, add meat and saute until lightly browned. Add tomatoes, cumin, oregano and water and blend thoroughly. Stir in pepper and salt and simmer over low heat, uncovered, 2 1/2 hours. Add water as necessary to maintain consistency of a hearty soup. Serve with chopped onions and fresh jalapenos on the side or sprinkled over the top.

Serves 10

Larry Sheerin
SAN ANTONIO, TEXAS

Bueno Bread

"Easy, quick and delicious."

1 loaf French bread
3 cups grated Monterey Jack cheese
1 (4-ounce) can chopped green chiles
1 cup mayonnaise
2 drops Tabasco

Slice loaf horizontally. Mix remaining ingredients and spread on bread. Bake at 350 degrees 20–30 minutes. Cut in slices to serve.

Serves 8

Mrs. R. W. Martin, Jr.
BOZEMAN, MONTANA

Chile-Cheese Corn Bread

"The sausage makes the difference."

8 ounces chorizo, casing
   removed and chopped,
   or pepperoni
2 cups flour
1 1/2 cups yellow cornmeal
1/3 cup sugar
2 Tablespoons baking
   powder
1 1/2 teaspoons salt
2 eggs
1 cup milk
1/2 cup oil
1/2 cup sour cream
1 1/2 cups shredded Cheddar
   cheese
1 (4-ounce) can chopped
   green chiles, drained

In a 10-inch skillet, cook chorizo over medium-low heat until lightly browned, stirring occasionally (do not cook pepperoni). Remove chorizo with slotted spoon and drain on paper towel. Grease 9 × 3-inch springform pan. Mix dry ingredients in large bowl. In medium bowl, beat eggs, milk, oil and sour cream with whisk or fork until smooth. With fork, stir into flour mixture until just blended. Stir in chorizo, cheese and chiles. Spoon batter into pan and bake at 375 degrees 45 minutes until golden and tester comes out clean. To serve, carefully loosen from side of pan, remove ring and slice.

Serves 14

Trapper's Cabin Ranch
GALLATIN GATEWAY, MONTANA

Indian Corn Bread

2 cups chopped onions
1/4 cup butter
1 cup sour cream
1 cup shredded Cheddar
   cheese
1 1/2 cups self-rising corn
   meal or corn meal with
   1/2 teaspoon baking
   powder
2 Tablespoons sugar,
   optional
1/4 teaspoon dill weed
2 eggs, beaten
1 (8 3/4-ounce) can
   cream-style corn
1/4 cup milk
1/4 cup oil
Dash hot sauce

Saute onions in butter until tender. Remove from heat, stir in sour cream and 1/2 cup cheese and set aside. Combine cornmeal, sugar and dill and set aside. Stir together eggs, corn, milk, oil and hot sauce. Add to cornmeal mixture, stirring well. Spoon into lightly greased, 9-inch square pan. Spread sour cream mixture over batter and sprinkle with remaining cheese. Bake at 375 degrees 30–35 minutes. Cool slightly and cut in 3-inch squares.

Serves 8

Pamela Benziger
CODY, WYOMING

John Wayne's Chile-Cheese Souffle

"This recipe was given to me by 'The Duke' when he visited the Buffalo Bill Historical Center in Cody in 1976."

1 pound Monterey Jack
cheese, grated
1 pound Cheddar cheese,
grated
2 (4-ounce) cans green
chiles, drained, seeded
and diced
4 eggs, separated
1 Tablespoon flour
2/3 cup evaporated milk
1/2 teaspoon salt
1/8 teaspoon pepper
2 medium tomatoes,
sliced and halved

Mix cheeses and chiles and place in buttered, shallow 2-quart baking dish. Beat egg yolks slightly, then mix with flour, milk and seasonings. Beat whites until soft peaks form, then fold into yolk mixture. Spread evenly over cheese layer in baking dish. Make an overlapping border around the edge of the dish with tomatoes, pushing slices halfway into mixture. Bake at 325 degrees 30–40 minutes.

Serves 6

Margot Belden Todd
CODY, WYOMING

Chile Relleno Casserole

1 (4-ounce) can green
chiles, chopped
1/2–1 pound Cheddar cheese,
grated
1/2–1 pound Swiss cheese,
grated
1 pound ground beef,
browned
4 eggs, separated
1 (13-ounce) can
evaporated milk
6 Tablespoons flour
Salt and pepper, to taste

Layer chiles and cheeses in large, deep casserole and add beef. Beat egg whites until stiff. Beat yolks, fold into whites with milk, flour, salt and pepper and pour over beef. Bake at 350 degrees 60 minutes until firm. Jalapeno cheese may be substituted for the milder cheeses.

Serves 6–8
Easy

Elkhorn Ranch
GALLATIN GATEWAY, MONTANA

Huevos Ricardo

8 ounces Velveeta cheese
8 ounces salsa picante
1/4 teaspoon coriander
1/2 teaspoon cumin
1/2 teaspoon oregano
4 English muffins, split and buttered
8 large eggs
12 ounces cream cheese, softened
8 ounces sour cream
Paprika
Sliced black olives

Melt cheese in double-boiler insert over simmering water. Add salsa. Grind together coriander, cumin and oregano or use ground seasonings and add to sauce. Reduce heat and keep warm. Grill muffins and keep warm. Poach eggs. Spread muffins liberally with cream cheese, leaving a slight indentation in centers. Place one egg on each muffin, top with sauce, add dollop of sour cream, sprinkle lightly with paprika and top with olives. Serve at once with chorizo, refried beans and salsa on the side. Note: to avoid overcooking and make other preparations less hurried, poached eggs may be removed from cooking water and slipped into a bowl of very warm water to which 12 Tablespoons of white vinegar have been added.

Serves 4–8

Dick Ludewig
Cody, Wyoming

Fiesta Enchiladas

2 pounds lean ground beef
1 large onion, chopped
1 (10-ounce) package frozen chopped spinach, thawed and drained
1 teaspoon cumin
1 teaspoon pepper
1/2 cup grated Parmesan cheese
2 (10-ounce) cans tomato soup
1 (10-ounce) can enchilada sauce
1/2 cup tomato sauce
1/2 cup green chile salsa
12 corn tortillas
2 cups grated Monterey Jack cheese

Brown beef until crumbly and drain fat. Add onions, spinach, cumin, pepper and Parmesan. In separate pan, combine soup and enchilada sauce and simmer 10 minutes. Combine tomato sauce and salsa in separate bowl. Dip tortilla into soup-enchilada mixture, fill with 1/2 cup meat and add 1 Tablespoon salsa mixture. Place seam-side-down in 3-quart casserole. Repeat and sprinkle with remaining cheese. Bake at 350 degrees 30 minutes. Serve topped with sour cream, sliced black olives and green onions.

Serves 6

Trapper's Cabin Ranch
Gallatin Gateway, Montana

Chicken Enchiladas

2 medium onions,
  chopped
1 clove garlic, chopped
4 Tablespoons olive oil
1 1/2 cups diced green chiles
5 ripe tomatoes, skinned
  and chopped
  Pinch oregano
8 ounces grated Cheddar
  cheese
2 cups sour cream
1 pound chicken meat,
  cooked, shredded and
  cooled
12 tortillas

Saute onions and garlic in oil. Add chiles, tomatoes and oregano. Cover and cook over low heat until thick. Combine cheese, sour cream, and chicken. Dip tortillas in chile mixture, fill with chicken mixture, roll, place in flat casserole and cover with remaining sauce. Bake at 350 degrees 15 minutes. Serve on bed of lettuce with garnishes of avocado slices, olives, sour cream or refried beans.

Serves 6

Robin Weiss
CODY, WYOMING

Crab Meat Enchiladas

1 cup cooked crab meat,
  flaked
6 green onions, chopped
2 green chiles, chopped,
  or a 4-ounce can
2 cups grated Monterey
  Jack cheese
1/2 cup tomato sauce
1/2 cup taco sauce
8 corn tortillas
1/2 cup chopped green olives

Combine crab, onions and chiles with 1 cup cheese. Combine tomato and taco sauces. Dip tortillas in sauce mixture. Divide meat mixture among tortillas and roll. Place in baking dish and top with remaining cheese and olives. Bake at 350 degrees 20 minutes until cheese melts. Serve topped with sour cream.

Serves 4

Temptations
CODY, WYOMING

King Ranch Casserole

"This came from Sug Hedgpeth and is a favorite standby."

1 (3–4 pound) chicken or
　equivalent in breasts
　and thighs
2 Tablespoons butter
1 medium onion, chopped
1 can cream of mushroom
　soup
1 can cream of chicken
　soup
1 can tomatoes with green
　chiles
1 Tablespoon chili powder
1 teaspoon oregano
1 package corn tortillas,
　cut in pieces
　Grated sharp Cheddar
　cheese

Boil, bone and dice chicken, reserving 1 cup stock. Melt butter in skillet and saute onions until tender. Add soup, tomatoes, chili powder, oregano and reserved stock and simmer. In buttered, deep casserole, layer half portions of chicken, tortillas, sauce and cheese. Repeat layers. Bake at 325 degrees 45–60 minutes until cheese melts.

Serves 6–8

Margaret S. Coe
Cody, Wyoming

Mole de Pollo

1 slice dry bread
2 Tablespoons raisins
1/2 ounce unsweetened
　chocolate
3 Tablespoons almonds
2 Tablespoons minced
　onion
1 medium green pepper
1 large tomato
1 clove garlic
3 Tablespoons flour
1 Tablespoon ground red
　chile
1/4 teaspoon cinnamon
1/4 teaspoon cloves
2 1/2 cups chicken stock
4 pounds cooked chicken,
　cubed

Grind first 8 ingredients in food processor. Stir in flour and spices. Add stock and mix well. Cook until thick, add chicken and cook 30 minutes more. Serve with beans and warmed tortillas.

Serves 6
Easy

How Kola Ranch
Cody, Wyoming

Arroz con Jocoqui y Pollo

1 large broiling chicken,
  cut up
Celery
Onion
Salt and pepper
5–6 cups cooked rice
3 cups sour cream
2 cans peeled green chiles,
  drained and sliced
1 pound Monterey Jack or
  sharp Cheddar cheese,
  sliced in strips
1/2 cup grated Cheddar
  cheese
Paprika

Cook chicken, in water to cover, with celery, onion and seasonings until tender. Cool in broth and reserve broth. In a buttered, deep, 4–6-quart casserole, layer rice, sour cream, chiles, cheese and chicken. Repeat, ending with a layer of rice. Sprinkle layers with a little broth. Bake at 350 degrees 30 minutes. Top with grated Cheddar, sprinkle with paprika and cook until cheese is golden and bubbly. Note: may also be served, omitting the chicken, as a side dish for meat, fish or broiled chicken.

Serves 6–8

Mrs. Charles B. Arnold
ALBUQUERQUE, NEW MEXICO

Jalapeno Chicken

"This is a favorite from Sunset magazine."

6 medium jalapeno peppers
2 Tablespoons oil
1 medium onion, chopped
1 clove garlic, minced
1/4 teaspoon cumin
1 (10 3/4-ounce) can
  condensed cream of
  chicken soup
1 (10-ounce) package frozen
  chopped spinach
1/2 teaspoon salt
2 pounds cooked chicken,
  diced
2 cups sour cream
1 (8-ounce) package corn
  chips
8 ounces Monterey Jack
  cheese, shredded
Paprika

Reserve 1 pepper for garnish. Seed and dice remaining peppers. Heat oil in 10-inch skillet over medium heat and cook peppers, onion and garlic until tender, stirring occasionally. Stir in cumin and cook 1 minute. Stir in soup, spinach and salt. Bring to a boil over high heat, breaking up spinach with a fork. Reduce heat to low, cover and simmer until spinach is cooked. Stir in chicken and sour cream and heat thoroughly. Remove from heat. In a 2-quart casserole, layer 1/3 corn chips, 1/3 cheese and 1/2 chicken mixture. Repeat layers, ending with cheese. Bake at 350 degrees 30 minutes until mixture is heated. Sprinkle with paprika and garnish with reserved pepper, halved or cut in thin strips.

Serves 8

Robin Weiss
CODY, WYOMING

Chimichangas

FILLING:

2 Tablespoons oil or bacon
   drippings
2 pounds lean beef, cut in
   1-inch cubes
1 medium onion, finely
   diced
1/2 cup mild salsa
1 teaspoon salt
1/2 teaspoon pepper
1 clove garlic, mashed
1–2 cups water

TORTILLAS:

2 cups all-purpose flour
2 teaspoons baking powder
1 teaspoon salt
2–3 teaspoons margarine
   About 1 cup warm milk
   Beaten egg
   Oil

Heat oil in large, heavy-bottomed pot. Brown meat, add onions and cook until translucent. Add salsa, salt, pepper, garlic and 1 cup water. Cover and simmer, adding enough water to keep meat covered. Cook about 2 hours until meat is tender. Remove from heat, cool and reserve liquid. Shred meat and return to liquid. Cook over medium heat until liquid is reduced and meat is still moist.

To make tortillas, mix dry ingredients and work in margarine. Slowly add enough milk to form a soft dough. Knead gently a few minutes, cover and let rest 10 minutes. Divide dough into 6 equal parts. Roll in 10-inch circles. Cook in hot, oiled skillet. Cook one side until top begins to bubble, flip and cook other side briefly. Keep cooked tortillas warm. If made ahead, keep tightly wrapped.

To assemble, divide filling into 6 parts and fill tortillas. Roll up and brush edges with egg. Heat 2 inches of oil and fry until golden brown. Drain well and serve immediately with salsa and garnishes of guacamole, sour cream, shredded lettuce, chopped tomatoes, minced green onion and black olives.

Serves 6
Time-consuming
May do partly ahead

Frances Clymer
CODY, WYOMING

Simple Chimichangas

"The name speaks for itself!"

1 pound boneless pork,
  cut in 1-inch cubes
2 cups water
2 Tablespoons vinegar
1 (4-ounce) can green chiles
1 clove garlic, minced
1/4 teaspoon cumin
1/4 teaspoon oregano
1/4 cup butter
4 flour tortillas
4 slices pineapple
2 bananas
3–4 cups shredded Romaine
  lettuce
2 radishes, sliced
1 cup grated Monterey Jack
  cheese
1 cup sour cream
1 cup salsa

Place pork in 2 or 3-quart pan, cover and cook 10 minutes. Remove cover and brown meat. Add water and simmer, covered, 1 1/2 hours. Uncover and slowly boil away liquid. Add vinegar, chiles, garlic and spices. Cool and shred meat. Melt butter in 10-inch frying pan, brush tortillas with butter, fill with meat, roll and place on baking pan, seam-side-down. Bake at 500 degrees 8 minutes. Saute pineapple in remaining butter. Add bananas, turning once, and remove from heat. Place chimichanga on bed of lettuce and garnish with fruit, radishes, cheese, sour cream and salsa.

Serves 4

Margot Belden Todd
CODY, WYOMING

Tamales

1 large package corn husks
1 (4-pound) pork roast
1 (4-pound) beef roast
2 cloves garlic, minced
2 small cans sliced black
  olives
1 cup raisins
2 large cans enchilada
  sauce
5 pounds masa harina

Soak corn husks 2–3 hours in sink. Cover meats with water and boil gently until tender. Cool and shred with fork. Reserve broth. Add garlic, olives, raisins and sauce. Mix well and simmer 15 minutes. Mix masa according to package directions, using reserved broth in place of water. Spread masa mixture on corn husks, place large spoonful of meat mixture in center of masa and fold up tightly. Place seam-sidedown on rack in large steamer and steam about 2 hours until masa is no longer sticky or doughy.

Serves 12
Time-consuming
Must do ahead

Pamela Stockton
CODY, WYOMING

California Avocado Meat Loaf

1 pound ground beef
5 Tablespoons chopped
  onion
1/3 cup cracker crumbs
1/4 cup chili sauce
1 Tablespoon
  Worcestershire sauce
1/4 teaspoon pepper
1 teaspoon salt
1 egg, beaten
4 ounces Velveeta cheese,
  quartered
2 avocados, peeled and
  halved
1 cup bread crumbs
  Lemon juice, optional

Combine first 8 ingredients and divide mixture into 8 parts. Make each into a flat circle on waxed paper and make a depression in the center of each. Place a piece of cheese in the cavity of each avocado half. Put avocados onto 4 beef circles, invert remaining circles on top, then seal well to look like balls. Sprinkle with bread crumbs and bake at 375 degrees 20 minutes. During preparation, lemon juice may be sprinkled on avocado halves to prevent discoloration.

Serves 4
Easy

Mary McMillan
CODY, WYOMING

Tacos para Sopear

1 onion, chopped
2 Tablespoons oil
1/2 cup chopped green
  pepper
3 large cloves garlic,
  minced
1 pound lean ground beef
1 (1-pound) can plum
  tomatoes, chopped
2/3 cup chopped green olives
  with pimientos
1/2 cup corn
1/3 cup raisins
2 Tablespoons brown sugar
1 1/2 Tablespoons vinegar
1 Tablespoon beef broth
  concentrate
3 Tablespoons chili powder
1 teaspoon cumin
3 drops Tabasco
12 corn taco shells, heated

Cook onions in oil until tender. Add green pepper and garlic. Add beef and cook until brown. Add tomatoes with juice, olives, corn, raisins, sugar, vinegar, broth and spices. Cook 5–10 minutes, stirring, until excess liquid evaporates. Spoon into taco shells and garnish with shredded lettuce and grated Monterey Jack cheese.

Serves 6

How Kola Ranch
CODY, WYOMING

Mexican Crepes

CREPE BATTER:

3 eggs
1/2 cup flour
1 cup yellow cornmeal
2 1/4 cups milk
1 1/2 Tablespoons oil
1/2 teaspoon chili powder
1/4 teaspoon salt
1/4 teaspoon butter or
   margarine

FILLING:

3/4 pound lean ground beef
1 large onion, chopped
1 clove garlic, minced
1 (15-ounce) can chili
   without beans
1 (8-ounce) can tomato
   sauce
1 (4-ounce) can diced
   green chiles
1 (2 3/4-ounce) can sliced
   ripe olives, drained
1 1/2 cups grated Cheddar
   cheese

For crepes, blend all ingredients but butter until smooth. In a 6 or 7-inch shallow pan, melt butter over medium heat and swirl to coat sides. Pour in 2 Tablespoons batter quickly, tilting pan so batter flows evenly over bottom. Cook until edges are lightly browned. Flip and cook other side. Stir batter before repeating. If made ahead, wrap airtight and chill up to a week. Before separating, let warm to room temperature.

For filling, cook beef, onions and garlic in skillet over medium heat, stirring, until meat is brown. Drain fat. Stir in chili, sauce, chiles and olives. Stir and simmer 5 minutes. Remove from heat, cool and stir in 1/2 cheese. Place about 1/4 cup of filling in each crepe, roll up and place seam-side-down in greased 10 × 15-inch baking pan. Cover and chill or freeze. Bake at 375 degrees 10 minutes or frozen dish 20 minutes. Sprinkle with remaining cheese and cook 5 more minutes. Serve with sour cream, sliced green onions and salsa.

Serves 6–8
May be frozen
May do ahead

Ralph Stewart
BILLINGS, MONTANA

Shrimp San Carlos

"A colorful Mexican dish. The ingredients are easily found in the Southwest and California."

3 dozen cooked shrimp
1/2 cup lime juice
2 tomatoes, minced
1 small onion, minced
3 or 4 jalapeno, serrano or any
   fresh hot peppers
3 Tablespoons fresh
   coriander leaves
   Salt and pepper, to taste

Combine all ingredients and chill. Serve with pieces of melba toast or on rounds of fresh jicama. If served on plates, diced avocados may be added.

Serves 6
Easy

Laurie Pew
TUCSON, ARIZONA

Ceviche Mirador

"An excellent first course for summer."

3 pounds sea bass, turbot
   fillets or other white
   flaky fish, skinned,
   boned and cubed
3/4–1 cup fresh lemon juice
2 large tomatoes, skinned
   and finely chopped
1 1/2 cups finely sliced green
   onions
1 clove garlic, minced
1 small jar green olives
   with pimientos, finely
   chopped
4 small hot jalapeno or
   serrano peppers, finely
   chopped
1 teaspoon crushed
   oregano
1/2 cup minced parsley
1/2 teaspoon salt
2 Tablespoons wine
   vinegar
3 Tablespoons olive oil

Put fish in a large glass jar with lemon juice. Cover jar tightly and refrigerate overnight, turning and shaking occasionally. (The marinating process produces a fish that looks and tastes cooked.) The next day, drain off juice and reserve half. Combine remaining ingredients with fish and reserved juice. Put into large glass bowl or jar and cover tightly. Refrigerate 24 hours, stirring occasionally to mix thoroughly. Serve in large bowl garnished with lettuce leaves, in individual glass serving cups with lettuce or watercress or on fried tortillas.

Serves 10–12
Must do ahead

Margot Belden Todd
CODY, WYOMING

Marshall's Guacamole

2 avocados, peeled and
   quartered
1/2 teaspoon salt
3 Tablespoons oil
1/4 teaspoon garlic powder
1 Tablespoon finely diced
   onion
1/4 teaspoon black pepper
3/4 cup finely diced
   tomato, fresh or canned
2 teaspoons lemon juice
1/2 teaspoon Tabasco or hot
   sauce

Dice and mash avocados with a stiff fork. Add remaining ingredients and mix with a fork.

Serves 4–6

Jane Dominick
CODY, WYOMING

Salsa Fresca

"Sabrosa with many Mexican dishes, especially pozole."

4 small tomatoes, peeled
  and chopped
1 cup finely chopped onion
1 jalapeno pepper, seeded
  and finely chopped
2 Tablespoons oil
1 teaspoon vinegar
1 teaspoon lime juice
1/2 teaspoon dried oregano,
  crushed
1/2 teaspoon salt

In a medium bowl, combine tomatoes, onions and pepper. Add remaining ingredients and mix well. Let stand 2 hours to blend flavors, but no more than 24 hours if refrigerated. Serve at room temperature. Add another pepper for extra zip.

Yields 2 cups
Easy
Must do ahead

Sandra M. Foxley
ENGLEWOOD, COLORADO

Salsa Cruda

2 large tomatoes, cut and
  seeded
1/4 cup green onions
1 jalapeno pepper
1 clove garlic
Juice of 1 lime
1/4 cup coriander leaves,
  preferably fresh
1 teaspoon oregano
Salt and pepper, to taste

Puree all ingredients. Use as an accompaniment to Mexican dishes. Remove seeds from jalapeno for a milder sauce.

Yields 1 1/2 cups
Easy

Robin Weiss
CODY, WYOMING

Mexican Almond Cookies

"Melt-in-your-mouth cookies."

1 cup whole almonds,
   blanched and lightly
   toasted
1/2 pound confectioners' sugar
3/4 cup vegetable shortening
   6 Tablespoons unsalted
   butter
   1 teaspoon vanilla
1/2 teaspoon almond extract
   2 cups cake flour
1/4 teaspoon salt
   Confectioners' sugar

Finely grind almonds in processor and, with machine running, add sugar, shortening and butter for 10 seconds. Blend in extracts, add flour and salt and blend until smooth. Flour hands lightly. Roll dough into teaspoon-sized balls and arrange on ungreased baking sheets. Bake at 375 degrees about 15 minutes. Transfer to wire racks and dust lightly with confectioners' sugar. Store in airtight containers.

Yields 6 dozen
May be frozen

Mrs. Paul Lyons
SYOSSET, NEW YORK

Spanish Flan

3/4 cup sugar
   1 teaspoon water
   1 can sweetened condensed
   milk
   7 Tablespoons water or
   3 Tablespoons rum and
   4 Tablespoons water
2–3 drops vanilla
   3 eggs
1/3 cup slivered almonds,
   toasted

In a straight-sided, 1-quart, double-boiler insert, combine sugar and 1 teaspoon water. Cook directly over medium heat until sugar caramelizes, stirring occasionally. Remove from heat and swirl caramel in pan to coat sides evenly. Set aside. Combine milk, water and vanilla and blend briefly. Add eggs, 1 at a time, then pour into caramel. Place over boiling water, cover and cook 1 1/2-2 hours until flan is set. Cool in pot and refrigerate several hours before serving. To serve, invert on serving dish and top with almonds.

Serves 6
Must do ahead

Margot Belden Todd
CODY, WYOMING

Pastel de Pecana (Honey Pecan Cake)

CAKE:

4 eggs, separated
1/2 cup unsalted butter,
    melted and cooled
1/2 teaspoon vanilla
2/3 cup sugar
Pinch salt
2/3 cup pecans, finely ground
1/3 cup flour

GLAZE:

2 Tablespoons butter
1/2 cup honey

"Simply scrumptious."

Lightly butter and flour an 8 or 9-inch cake pan. In small bowl, beat egg yolks, butter and vanilla. Add 1/2 sugar and beat until thick and creamy. Beat egg whites and salt until frothy in large bowl. Continue to beat, adding remaining sugar, 2 Tablespoons at a time, until stiff peaks form. Fold 1/3 whites into yolk mixture, then fold yolk mixture into whites. Combine pecans and flour and sift into egg mixture, 1/3 at a time, folding after each addition. Pour into pan and bake at 350 degrees 30 minutes for 8-inch pan and at 325 degrees for 25 minutes for 9-inch pan. Remove from oven, let stand 10 minutes, turn out onto rack and let cool 1 hour.

For glaze, melt butter, add honey and boil 3–4 minutes. Cool and pour over cake. Use hot knife to cut cake. Serve warm and topped with ice cream.

Serves 6–8
Must do ahead

La Comida
CODY, WYOMING

Game Dishes

Braised Bear Steak

"Very tender, not greasy."

3/4 cup flour
   Salt and pepper, to taste
1 teaspoon thyme
4 pounds bear steak
1 cup sliced onion
4 Tablespoons bacon fat
1 1/2 cups beef broth
1 cup dry red wine
2 Tablespoons tomato
   paste

Pound the flour and seasonings into the steak with the edge of a plate or meat pounder. Brown onions in bacon fat. Add meat and brown well. Add part of the broth and wine and bring to a boil. Cook briskly 5 minutes. Turn the steak, reduce the heat and cover the pan. Simmer 1–1 1/2 hours, adding more liquid if necessary. When the steak is tender, remove it to a hot platter. To the pan juices, add tomato paste and additional liquid if needed to make a smooth sauce. Adjust seasoning and pour over steak.

Serves 8

Four Bear Ranch
CODY, WYOMING

Buffalo Steaks

3 pounds buffalo loin or
   rib steaks, 3/4–1 inch
   thick
3 Tablespoons melted
   butter
   Salt
   Pepper
   Paprika

Trim off excess fat. Brush steaks with half the melted butter. Sprinkle with seasonings. Grill over charcoal 3–4 minutes on each side; basting with remaining butter and seasonings. Steaks may also be pan-broiled in a heavy skillet. Do not overcook. Steaks may be marinated several hours before broiling if desired with Dennis Day Marinade (see index).

Serves 6
Easy

American Buffalo Association
CODY, WYOMING

Buffalo Parmesan

1 1/2 pounds buffalo round
    steak
1 egg, beaten
1/3 cup Parmesan cheese
1/3 cup fine bread crumbs
1/3 cup olive oil
1 medium onion, minced
1 teaspoon salt
1/4 teaspoon pepper
1/2 teaspoon marjoram or
    oregano
1 (6-ounce) can tomato
    paste
2 cups hot water
8 ounces mozzarella
    cheese, sliced
1–1 1/2 pounds cooked
    spaghetti
    Parmesan, Romano
    and mozzarella
    cheeses, grated

Pound steak to tenderize and cut in serving pieces. Dip meat in egg and roll in mixture of Parmesan and bread crumbs. Heat oil over medium heat in a heavy skillet and brown meat on both sides until golden brown. Set aside. In the same skillet, cook onion over low heat until soft and stir in spices. Add tomato paste and gradually add hot water, stirring constantly. Boil gently 5 minutes. Place meat in a deep casserole and top with the mozzarella. Pour half the sauce over meat and cheese and top with spaghetti. Add remaining sauce and an additional sprinkling of cheeses. Bake at 350 degrees 30 minutes. Game meat may also be used.

Serves 4

Barbara A. Smith
REXBURG, IDAHO

Buffalo Roast in Brown Bag

"Brown-bag roasting produces tender, juicy meat.

1 (3–4 pound) buffalo
    roast
1/2 teaspoon salt
1/2 teaspoon paprika
1/4 teaspoon lemon
    pepper

Rub roast with mixed seasonings and place in a shallow roasting pan. Slide the pan into a large, heavy brown bag. Seal open end by folding and securing with paper clips. Bake at 350 degrees 36-38 minutes per pound or until meat thermometer registers 160 degrees, for medium. Let roast stand at room temperature 20–30 minutes before carving. Make gravy as for roast beef. Buffalo is best if not overcooked.

Serves 6–8
Easy

American Buffalo Association
CODY, WYOMING

Buffalo Stew

"Flavor improves if stew is kept a day in refrigerator."

6 pounds buffalo steak,
cut in 2-inch chunks
10 Tablespoons butter or
margarine
4 large onions, thinly
sliced
1/2 cup flour
1 (12-ounce) can beer
1 (10 1/2-ounce) can beef
broth, undiluted
1 teaspoon chopped garlic
1 Tablespoon vinegar
1 teaspoon sugar
1 teaspoon thyme
1 bay leaf
Salt and pepper, to taste

Brown buffalo on all sides in 4 Tablespoons butter in a large, preferably cast-iron, casserole. It may be easier to do in 3 or 4 batches, since meat browns best in a single layer. Remove and saute onions in 2 Tablespoons butter until lightly browned. Set onions aside. Add the final 4 Tablespoons butter to the pan along with the flour and mix to a paste. Add beer and broth gradually, beating with a whisk until sauce is thick and smooth. Add remaining ingredients and the meat and onions. Mix gently together. Bring to a boil. Cover and bake at 275 degrees 3–8 hours until tender.

Serves 6–8

Lynne Bama
WAPITI, WYOMING

Wapiti Tamale Pie

"Great for cookouts."

2 cups yellow corn meal
2 cups boiling water
1 teaspoon salt
1 1/2 pounds ground elk
3/4 pounds bulk pork
sausage, broken up
with a fork
1/2 cup chopped onion
1 teaspoon garlic powder,
optional
2 teaspoons chili powder
3 (16-ounce) cans pinto
beans
1 (16-ounce) can tomatoes
1 cup Cheddar cheese,
grated

For mush, combine corn meal, water and salt and boil until very thick, stirring frequently. Cook elk, sausage and onions in heavy skillet until meat is browned and onions soft. Drain off excess fat. Mix together garlic powder, chili powder, pinto beans and tomatoes and add to meat mixture. Line sides and bottom of a 4 quart baking dish with mush. Fill with meat mixture and cover top with mush. Sprinkle with cheese and bake, uncovered, at 350 degrees 1 hour.

Serves 10–12

Inez King
CODY, WYOMING

Hunter's Stew

1 1/2 pounds elk or venison
    back strap or rump
    roast, cubed
  1/2 cup flour
    Salt and pepper, to taste
    2 Tablespoons oil
    1 cup coarsely chopped
    onion
    1 clove garlic, minced
    1 teaspoon salt
  1/2 teaspoon pepper
  3/4 cup dry red wine
    2 cups water
    1 beef bouillon cube
    2 cups carrots, cut in
    1-inch slices
    1 cup celery stalks, cut
    in 1-inch slices
    1 cup fresh cranberries
    1 teaspoon sugar
    1 Tablespoon steak sauce
    2 teaspoons Hungarian
    paprika
    4 juniper berries, optional
    2 whole cloves
    1 bay leaf
    1 Tablespoon cornstarch

"A complete meal served with corn bread and a spinach salad."

Dredge meat in seasoned flour and brown in hot oil in a Dutch oven with onion and garlic. When brown, add salt, pepper, wine, water and bouillon and bring to a boil. Cover and simmer 1 1/4 hours. Add remaining ingredients except cornstarch. Cover and simmer another 45 minutes until vegetables are tender. If necessary, thicken with cornstarch mixed with a little cold water.

Serves 6
Must do ahead

Mrs. Paul Koeppe
FORT WORTH, TEXAS

Venison Piquante

"A different way to serve venison."

2 pounds trimmed venison
   About 1/3 cup flour
1/2 teaspoon salt
1/4 teaspoon pepper
1/2 cup butter
1/2 teaspoon caraway seeds
1 medium onion, finely
   chopped
   Juice of 1/2 lemon
2 cups sour cream
2 beef bouillon cubes,
   crushed
1/2 cup beef broth, optional

Cut venison in 2-inch cubes. Dredge in mixture of flour, salt and pepper. Melt butter in a heavy skillet and brown meat on all sides. Add remaining ingredients, stirring well to mix. Cover and cook slowly 1 1/2 hours. Add beef broth if needed. Serve with wild rice.

Serves 6

Ralph Stewart
BILLINGS, MONTANA

Venison Stew

"Specialty of Auguste Zimmerman, former chef at the Waldorf and New York Athletic Club."

8 ounces salt pork, diced
3 pounds venison shoulder
   or brisket, cubed
1 stalk celery
3 onions, chopped
1 carrot, sliced
3 Tablespoons flour
   Salt and freshly ground
   black pepper, to taste
3 cups broth made from
   bones and meat scraps
1 bay leaf
   Juice of 1/2 lemon
2 whole cloves
1/2 cup dry red wine

Saute salt pork in a large heavy skillet until lightly browned. Add venison and brown quickly on all sides. Add celery, onions and carrots and cook until wilted. Sprinkle with flour and cook, stirring, 2 minutes. Add remaining ingredients except wine and bring to a boil. Cover and simmer gently about 1 hour or until meat is tender. Stir in wine and cook 15 minutes longer.

Serves 6

William E. Weiss
CODY, WYOMING

Barbecued Venison Kabobs

"Cook indoors or outdoors."

1 (10 1/2-ounce) can
  condensed tomato soup
1 small clove garlic,
  minced
1/4 cup olive oil
2 Tablespoons wine vinegar
1 Tablespoon sugar
1/2 teaspoon salt
1/8 teaspoon oregano
1/8 teaspoon thyme
1 pound venison, cut in
  1 1/2-inch cubes
  Green pepper, chunked
1 medium onion, cut in
  1/2-inch slices

Blend first 8 ingredients. Add venison and stir until well coated. Cover and place in refrigerator 4 hours. On 4 skewers, alternate venison, green pepper and onion. Brush kabobs with marinade and broil about 3 inches from heat in oven or place 4–5 inches from coals on an outdoor grill. Baste kabobs with marinade and turn every 3–4 minutes. Serve immediately or keep war in the oven.

Serves 4
Easy
Must do ahead

Marlene Raasch
POWELL, WYOMING

Greek Stew

"Very tasty with minimal effort to prepare."

3 pounds game meat,
  cubed
4 Tablespoons butter
2 cups dry red wine
2 cups beef broth or stock
6 ounces tomato paste
1/4 cup red wine vinegar
2 Tablespoons brown
  sugar
1 1/2 teaspoons cumin
1 teaspoon minced garlic
1/2 teaspoon allspice
1 bay leaf
18 small onions
8 ounces mushrooms
  Salt and pepper, to taste

Saute meat briefly in melted butter. Add all ingredients except onions and mushrooms. Simmer 1 1/2 hours. Blanch onions in boiling water 1 minute. Add to stew and simmer 30 minutes. Saute mushrooms and add to stew. Adjust seasoning. Serve with noodles.

Serves 6
Easy

Douglas Clark Sunderland
CODY, WYOMING

Shirley Gatewood's Salami

"Keeps very well in refrigerator, up to three weeks."

5 pounds ground game
    meat
5 heaping teaspoons
    curing or popcorn salt
3 teaspoons mustard seed
2 3/4 teaspoons garlic powder
2 3/4 teaspoons very coarse
    pepper
2 teaspoons liquid smoke
2 3/4 teaspoons celery seed
    Coarsely ground pepper

Mix all ingredients but final pepper, put into an airtight container and refrigerate overnight. Allow mixture to return to room temperature and stir well once a day for 3 days. On the fourth day, mix and form into 3 × 6-inch rolls, pressing out air. Roll each in pepper to coat. Bake at 140 degrees 8 hours on broiler pan, turning a quarter turn every 2 hours. Cool completely and roll each in waxed paper and then in foil.

Easy
May be frozen
Must do ahead

Shirley Gatewood
ADDY, WASHINGTON

Barbecue Sauce for Game

3 Tablespoons bacon fat
1 Tablespoon brown sugar
1 teaspoon salt
1 teaspoon pepper
1 teaspoon cumin seed
1/2 teaspoon chili powder
1 large onion, chopped
1/2 green pepper, chopped
3/4 teaspoon celery salt
2 (6-ounce) cans tomato
    paste
2 cups water
1 Tablespoon lemon juice

Mix all ingredients and simmer 15 minutes. Use as a baste or pour over 4 pounds browned meat and bake in a covered pan at 350 degrees 1 hour for a Texas style barbecue.

Yields 4 cups
Easy

Babe Martoglio
CODY, WYOMING

Wild Goose Cassoulet

4 cups navy beans
6 cups water
4 ounces Italian salami,
    cubed
1 cup dry white wine
4 tomatoes, peeled, seeded
    and chopped
4 large onions, diced
4 peppercorns
2 teaspoons chopped parsley
1/4 teaspoon rosemary
2 cloves garlic, minced
1 bay leaf
1 (8-pound) goose
    Salt
    Pepper
1/2 cup olive oil
2 cups dry white wine
6 garlic sausages
1 cup bread crumbs

Soak navy beans in water to cover for at least 10 hours. Drain beans, discarding any that float, and put them in a large earthenware casserole. Add salami, white wine, tomatoes, onions, peppercorns, parsley, rosemary, garlic, bay leaf and enough water to cover the mixture. Cover casserole tightly and bake at 200–225 degrees 6 hours, adding more water if necessary. Clean a goose and cut it into 10 or 12 pieces. Rub each piece with salt and pepper. Heat olive oil in a large skillet until sizzling hot, add the pieces of goose and brown them lightly on all sides. Reduce heat, add wine and simmer, covered, 30 minutes. Stir the goose meat and the sauce carefully into the casserole. In another skillet saute sausages until they are well browned, reserve the fat and stir the sausage carefully into the casserole. Cover dish and bake at 250 degrees 1 1/2 hours. Saute bread crumbs in the reserved sausage fat and sprinkle them over the top of the cassoulet. Bake 10 minutes more, uncovered, until the bread crumbs are browned.

Serves 10–12
Time-consuming
Must do ahead

William E. Weiss
CODY, WYOMING

Mallard a l'Orange

1 cup orange juice
3 ounces curacao or white
    wine
2–3 Tablespoons butter
    Salt
    Pepper
1 duck
1 apple, peeled and cubed
4 stalks celery, sliced

Heat and stir juice, liqueur, butter and seasonings for a basting sauce. Stuff duck with apple and celery. Pour sauce over duck and bake at 375 degrees 10–12 minutes. Remove and baste again. Broil until brown, about 8 minutes. Turn, baste, and brown an additional 2 minutes.

Serves 1–2

Salli Allen
CODY, WYOMING

Bunchy's Goose

"A really tender wild goose."

1 wild goose, drawn,
  plucked, washed and dried
1 recipe appropriate stuffing,
  optional
  Juice and rind of 1 orange
2 teaspoons grated fresh
  ginger
1/3 cup honey
1 teaspoon marjaram
1 teaspoon Worcestershire
  sauce
1/4 cup soy sauce
1/4 teaspoon onion salt
1 can beef consomme
1 can chicken consomme

Stuff goose, if desired. Roast, breast down and uncovered, at 450 degrees 25 minutes. Mix remaining ingredients for marinade and pour over goose. Cover and reduce heat to 275 degrees and roast 4 hours. Don't peek!

Serves 4–6

Dorothy H. Dines
DENVER, COLORADO

Sauce for Roast Breast of Canvasback

"Enhances the flavor of any game bird."

1 cup currant jelly
1/3 cup butter
1/4 cup lime juice
1 Tablespoon dry mustard
3 Tablespoons grated orange
  rind
3 Tablespoons grated lemon
  rind
1/3 cup sherry

Melt jelly and butter, add remaining ingredients except sherry, and heat well. Heat sherry, blending it in at the last.

Yields 2 cups
Easy

William E. Weiss
CODY, WYOMING

Roast Saddle of Hare

"A pleasant change from fried rabbit."

2 saddles of hare
1–1 1/2 jars Dijon mustard
1/2 cup butter, melted
1 1/2 cups heavy cream
Salt and pepper
4 egg yolks
1/4 cup cognac
1/8 teaspoon lemon juice

Spread saddles with a layer of mustard 1/4-inch thick. Let them stand, covered, in the refrigerator several hours. Place the saddles in a deep casserole that will just hold them. Spoon melted butter over saddles and roast at 300 degrees, basting from time to time with 1/2 cup cream. After 1 1/2 hours, add another 1/2 cup cream and salt and pepper to taste. Roast another 30 minutes or until tender. Remove meat to hot platter. Mix the remaining 1/2 cup cream with egg yolks and blend into the sauce. Stir until smooth and thickened, but do not boil. Adjust seasoning. Add cognac and lemon juice.

Serves 4
Easy
Must do ahead

William E. Weiss
CODY, WYOMING

Flaming Hare

8 green onions, thinly
    sliced
8 ounces mushrooms,
    sliced
1/4 cup butter
2 rabbits, cut up
Flour
1/2 cup brandy
2 cups chicken broth
Salt and pepper
6 slices bacon
2 cups heavy cream
1/4 cup horseradish

Saute green onions and mushrooms in butter 5 minutes in heavy skillet and set aside. Dredge rabbit pieces lightly with flour and brown lightly in skillet, about 15 minutes. Pour some brandy into a ladle and pour the rest over the rabbits. Warm brandy in ladle and light it, then flame the rabbits. When flame dies, add broth, salt and pepper. Add mushrooms and onions. Put bacon over meat and bake, uncovered, at 375 degrees 45 minutes. Baste often. Stir cream and horseradish into pan juices and roast 15 minutes longer.

Serves 6–8

Douglas Clark Sunderland
CODY, WYOMING

ALEXANDER PIPE.

"Weapons of War" by Alexander Pope. *Courtesy of Buffalo Bill Historical Center, Cody, WY; 201.69*

Pheasant and Snow Peas

"Pheasant with an oriental touch."

2 whole pheasant breasts
2 teaspoons cornstarch
1 egg white
1 Tablespoon sake or sherry
    Salt and pepper, to taste
4 ounces fresh snow peas
4 Tablespoons peanut oil
4 ounces fresh mushrooms,
    sliced
1/2 teaspoon salt, optional
2 slices fresh ginger root,
    peeled
1 teaspoon cornstarch
    dissolved in 1 Tablespoon
    water

Bone and slice pheasant into pieces about 2 inches long and 1 inch wide. In a large mixing bowl combine pheasant and cornstarch, tossing them until each piece is lightly coated. Add egg white, wine, salt and pepper and mix thoroughly. Snap off tips of snow peas and remove strings. Heat a 12-inch wok or skillet over high heat 30 seconds. Pour in 1 Tablespoon oil and heat another 30 seconds. Add mushrooms, snow peas and remaining salt. Stir-fry over moderate heat about 2 minutes. Transfer vegetables to platter and set aside. Add 3 Tablespoons oil to pan and heat 30 seconds. Drop in ginger slices, cook 30 seconds, then remove and discard them. Add pheasant and fry for 2 minutes. Return vegetables to pan, add corn starch mixture and cook, stirring constantly, until ingredients are coated with a light, clear glaze. Transfer to heated platter and serve with rice.

Serves 2

Shirley Wilkerson
CODY, WYOMING

Pheasant Soup

1 pheasant
4 Tablespoons butter
4 Tablespoons minced lean
    ham
1 onion, sliced
4 Tablespoons flour
1 bouquet garni
6 cups chicken stock
2 teaspoons ketchup
1/4 teaspoon celery salt
1/4 teaspoon pepper
1 Tablespoon finely chopped
    truffles or dried
    mushrooms
1/2 cup sherry
1/2 cup cream

Roast the pheasant until nearly done. Remove and shred breast meat. Melt butter and saute ham and onion until light brown. Add flour and brown slightly. Add bouquet garni, stock, ketchup, celery salt, pepper and quartered bird carcass together with the shredded meat and truffles. Simmer 1 hour and skim well. Remove carcass and bouquet garni, add the sherry and cream and cook 5 minutes.

Serves 4

William E. Weiss
CODY, WYOMING

Rolling Rock Pheasant Crepes

"An elegant luncheon dish with a salad."

MIREPOIX:

1/3 cup each finely diced
    carrots, celery and onion
2 Tablespoons butter
2 juniper berries
1/8 teaspoon crushed pepper
1 bay leaf
    Pinch rosemary
1 young pheasant, ready to
    roast
    Several strips bacon

SAUCE, PART I:

1 Tablespoon flour
1 cup pheasant or chicken
    broth
1/3 cup dry red wine

SAUCE, PART II:

2 shallots, minced
2 Tablespoons butter
8 medium mushrooms,
    chopped
    Salt, to taste
    Freshly ground pepper,
    to taste
2 Tablespoons cognac

CREPES:

1 cup sifted flour
3/4 cup milk
3 eggs
    Dashes salt, white pepper
    and nutmeg
    Butter

BEARNAISE GLACAGE:

1/3 cup Bearnaise sauce
1/3 cup dry white wine
1/3 cup whipped cream
2 egg yolks, slightly beaten
1 cup whipped cream
1/2 cup grated Parmesan
    cheese

For mirepoix, saute vegetables in butter with berries and seasonings until lightly browned, about 5 minutes. Coat outside of pheasant with mirepoix and place several strips of bacon over breast. Roast at 350 degrees, uncovered, 40–45 minutes. Remove from oven, cool and place in a bowl. To drippings in roasting pan, add Sauce Part I ingredients for brown gravy. Set aside.

For Sauce Part II, saute vegetables 3 minutes in butter, then add to gravy. Adjust seasoning and add cognac. Remove all meat from cooled pheasant, dice, and add to prepared sauce. (If making a day ahead, refrigerate and reheat gently before filling crepes.)

For crepes, stir milk into flour until smooth. Add eggs, one at a time, and stir until very smooth. Stir in seasonings. Heat small crepe pan, add a scant 1/4 teaspoon butter. When pan is just smoking, pour in 1 1/2–2 Tablespoons batter, just enough to cover the bottom of pan. Cook crepes until just golden, 1–2 minutes on each side. Make 12 and place them between paper towels to keep moist.

For glacage, combine Bernaise sauce, wine and cream.

To assemble dish, divide pheasant mixture among crepes and roll. Lay them side by side on the bottom of a buttered earthenware casserole in a single layer. Cover with half the glacage and glaze. To remaining glacage, add egg yolks and 1 cup whipped cream. Mix well and pour over the crepes. Sprinkle with Parmesan. Glaze again in 375-degree oven or under broiler.

Serves 4
Time-consuming
May do ahead

Robin Martin
OYSTER BAY, NEW YORK

Roast Baby Pheasant with Sauce Perigourdine

4 baby pheasants (1 1/2
    pounds each), cleaned
    and trussed
4 lardons
2 Tablespoons oil
2 stalks celery, diced
2 medium carrots, peeled
    and diced
1 medium onion, peeled
    and diced
2 bay leaves
    Pinch rosemary
1 cup chicken broth
4 teaspoons diced truffle
2 Tablespoons sherry
2 Tablespoons cognac
1 teaspoon chopped green
    onion

Cover the breast of each pheasant with a lardon. In a large saute pan, heat oil and add the diced vegetables, bay leaves and rosemary. Lay the pheasants on top of the vegetables and bake at 350 degrees about 40 minutes, basting occasionally with broth. When the birds are cooked, remove them to a serving dish and keep warm, reserving the cooking juices. Combine remaining ingredients in a small saucepan and boil a few minutes until the liquid is reduced by about half. Strain the cooking juices from the baking pan and pour into the truffle mixture. Simmer over low heat about 15 minutes. When ready to serve, pour the sauce over pheasants. Serve with wild rice and braised celery.

Serves 4

"21" Club
NEW YORK, NEW YORK

Pheasant with Sauerkraut

"One of the most pleasant marriages of flavors and a spectacular dish."

5–6 pounds fresh sauerkraut
1 pound salt pork, thinly
    sliced
2 cloves garlic, minced
1 teaspoon pepper
18 juniper berries
2 pheasants
1 lemon
2 onions
4 cloves
4 sprigs parsley
5 Tablespoons butter
5 Tablespoons oil
    Salt and pepper, to taste
2 1/2 cups chicken stock
2 garlic sausages

Thoroughly wash and drain sauerkraut. Line an 8-quart braising pan with salt pork. Put half the sauerkraut on the pork and add garlic, pepper and 12 berries. Rub the insides of the pheasants with a cut lemon. In each cavity place an onion studded with 2 cloves and a couple sprigs of parsley. Truss the birds. Heat butter and oil in a 12-inch skillet and brown the birds on all sides. Transfer the birds to the bed of sauerkraut and cover them with the rest of the sauerkraut. Add remaining berries and chicken stock and adjust seasoning. Bring the mixture to a boil, cover the pan tightly, and cook at 300 degrees 1 1/2 hours. or until the birds are tender, adding garlic sausages half way through cooking time. To serve, arrange the sauerkraut in a bed or mound on a large hot platter and place the pheasants on top. Garnish platter with sliced sausages. Add a border of boiled potatoes if desired.

Serves 4
Time-consuming

William E. Weiss
CODY, WYOMING

Pheasant Jubilee

"Easy and fun to do."

2 pheasants, quartered
1/2 cup seasoned flour
1/3 cup butter
1 onion, chopped
1/4 cup brown sugar
1/4 cup seedless raisins
3/4 cup chili sauce
1 Tablespoon Worcestershire
  sauce
1/2 cup bing cherries, drained
1/2 cup sherry

Roll pheasant in flour. Brown in butter and remove to casserole. Brown onions and add to casserole. Make sauce of brown sugar, raisins, chili sauce and Worcestershire. Pour over pheasant. Cook, covered, at 325 degrees 1 1/2 hours. Meanwhile, soak cherries in sherry. Add cherries and sherry mixture and bake, uncovered, 15 minutes.

Serves 6–8

Robin Martin
OYSTER BAY, NEW YORK

Wild Turkey

1 wild turkey
  Dry red wine, enough to
  cover turkey
8 ounces highly spiced pork
  sausage
1/2 cup chopped onion
  Pinch sage
1/2 cup sliced mushrooms
2 cups bread crumbs
1 apple, chopped
1/4 cup sherry
  Salt and pepper
  Cheesecloth
  Melted butter

Marinate turkey in wine 2 days in refrigerator. Stuff bird with sausage, onion, sage, mushrooms, bread crumbs, apple and sherry. Truss. Rub exterior of bird with salt and pepper. Dip 3 single thicknesses of cheesecloth in warm melted butter. Wrap entire bird with cloth, one thickness at a time. Wrap securely in foil. Place in oven, breast-side-up. Cook at 300–350 degrees 5–6 hours. Remove foil and brown bird 20 minutes before serving.

Serves 6
Must do ahead

4 Bear Ranch
CODY, WYOMING

German Potato Stuffing

"Unusual and delicious as stuffing for wild duck or goose."

4 potatoes, peeled and cut in
  1-inch cubes
1 onion, finely chopped
1 cup celery, sliced
  Salt
  Pepper
  Pinch poultry seasoning
1 Tablespoon parsley flakes
1 cup heavy cream

Combine potatoes, onion and celery. Add seasonings and mix with heavy cream. enough to make a soupy consistency. Spoon into cavity, using as much of the cream as cavity will hold. Prepare and bake extra dressing on the side, if desired.

Yields enough for
1 goose or 2 ducks
Easy

Helen Hornby
LIVINGSTON, MONTANA

Camp Cooking

Don Stroud's Chili

2 pounds diced beef or
  game meat
1 pound pork, ground or
  diced
2 large onions, chopped
3 cloves garlic, minced
1 teaspoon oregano
1 1/2 Tablespoons cumin
1 Tablespoon coriander
4–6 ounces chili powder
2 (14 1/2-ounce) cans
  tomatoes
2 (7-ounce) cans diced
  green chiles
1 (10 3/4-ounce) can beef
  broth
2 cans hot water
1 Tablespoon salt
4 (15-ounce) cans pinto
  beans

Brown meats. Add onions, garlic and spices. Stir. Add tomatoes and chiles and stir again. Add remaining ingredients and cook at least 1 hour, stirring occasionally.

Serves 15
Easy   *Trisha Stanton*
May be frozen   Albuquerque, New Mexico

Easy Bean Soup

1 (15-ounce) can
  ranch-style beans
1 (14-ounce) can beef
  broth
1 (8-ounce) can stewed
  tomatoes
1 teaspoon instant minced
  onion

Puree beans, broth and tomatoes until smooth. Pour into saucepan, add onion and bring to a boil. Simmer, uncovered, 15 minutes.

Yields 4 cups   *Carolyn Depue*
Easy   Wickenburg, Arizona

Sourdough Starter and Pancakes

"First ya git yer starter goin'. Then treat it right and keep it growin'."

STARTER:

1 1/4 teaspoons dry yeast
2 cups flour
2 Tablespoons sugar
2 1/2 cups water

For starter, beat all ingredients together. Cover with a cloth and let stand in a warm place 2–3 days. When bubbling and lively, it is ready to use.

PANCAKES:

2 cups starter
About 2 cups flour
Water
1 teaspoon salt
1/3 cup sugar
1 egg
1 teaspoon soda

For pancakes, mix starter with enough flour to make a firm ball. If packing into the mountains, transport in that form. Upon arrival at camp, add enough water to make a thin batter. Add salt and sugar and keep in a warm place until the next morning. When ready to prepare breakfast, remove 2 cups batter and reserve for starter. To remaining batter, add egg and soda and beat well. Cook on a griddle or iron skillet.

Must do ahead
Easy

Mrs. Ellen Waggoner
CODY, WYOMING

Rancher's Omelet

"Good any time of day."

6 slices bacon, diced
2 Tablespoons chopped onion
1 cup diced potatoes
6 eggs, beaten
1/2 teaspoon salt
2 Tablespoons fresh minced or equivalent dried parsley
Dash Tabasco
2 Tablespoons milk

Fry bacon and drain. Saute onions in bacon fat until soft. Add potatoes and cook until brown. Add eggs and seasonings. Add milk and cook until firm.

Serves 2–3
Easy

Marlene Raasch
POWELL, WYOMING

Sierra Mountain Scrambled Eggs

"A hearty camp breakfast to start off the day."

2 Tablespoons bacon fat or
  butter
4 eggs, beaten
1/2 cup corn or peas, optional
1/4 teaspoon pepper
1/4 teaspoon Spike or
  similar seasoning
1 cup grated Cheddar or
  Swiss cheese

Heat fat in a frying pan. Add eggs and corn. Stir in spices and cheese. Stir mixture frequently until cheese melts and ingredients are well mixed. Cook until eggs are done.

Serves 2
Easy

Warren N. Sargent, Jr.
VISALIA, CALIFORNIA

Hot Cocoa Mix

"Perfect for packing into the mountains."

1 (8-quart) box instant
  nonfat dry milk
1 (6-ounce) jar powdered
  nondairy coffee creamer
1 pound confectioners'
  sugar, sifted
1 pound presweetened
  cocoa powder

Mix all ingredients together and store in a tightly covered container. To use, add 1/4 cup mix to 3/4 cup hot water.

Yields 60 cups
Easy

Candy Felts
CODY, WYOMING

Toasty Nut Granola

"Great as a snack or breakfast cereal."

6 cups regular oatmeal
1 cup chopped nuts
3/4 cup wheat germ
1/2 cup brown sugar, firmly
  packed
1/2 cup shredded coconut
1/2 cup sesame seeds
1/2 cup oil
1/2 cup honey
1 1/2 teaspoons vanilla

Toast oatmeal in a 9 × 13-inch pan at 350 degrees 10 minutes. Combine remaining ingredients and add oatmeal. Bake in 2 batches at 350 degrees 20–25 minutes. Stir when cool and store in refrigerator.

Yields 9 cups
Easy

Susan Blaisdell Coe
RED BANK, NEW JERSEY

Beef Burgundy

"Winner of the 1982 Frontier Festival Camp Cook-Off."

5 pounds beef, cubed
1/2 cup oil
1/4 cup flour
3 cloves garlic
4 cups dry red wine
3 cups beef broth
2 stalks celery, chopped
2 carrots, sliced
4 sprigs parsley, minced
1 pound bacon
1 cup sliced onions
8 ounces mushrooms,
  sliced

In a Dutch oven, brown beef in oil, drain and set aside. Add flour and cook until foamy. Stir in garlic, wine and broth and bring to a boil. Add celery, carrots and parsley and simmer 2 hours. Saute bacon until crisp and crumble. Saute onions and mushrooms in bacon fat. Add bacon and mushrooms to meat mixture. Season to taste and serve over crisp hashed brown potatoes.

Serves 10

Barb Egan
CODY, WYOMING

Lentils and Sausage

12 ounces lentils
4 1/2 cups boiling water
2 teaspoons seasoned salt
2 cloves garlic, mashed
3/4–1 pound link sausage,
  cut in 1-inch chunks
1 onion, sliced
2 large carrots, thinly
  sliced
8 ounces tomato sauce
3 Tablespoons vinegar

Wash lentils, then place in a 4-quart Dutch oven with water, salt and garlic. Cover and cook over moderate heat 45 minutes. Brown sausage and add to lentils. Saute onion until limp and add with carrots. After 45 minutes, stir in tomato sauce and vinegar. Cook uncovered 20 minutes. Best if prepared 2 days before serving.

Serves 6
Easy
May be frozen

Douglas Clark Sunderland
CODY, WYOMING

Dick's Green Chile Stew

3 pounds pork shoulder,
  fat and bone removed,
  fat reserved
1/3 cup flour
3 medium onions,
  coarsely chopped
4 medium cloves garlic,
  minced
2 (16-ounce) cans whole
  green chiles, drained
  and seeded
2 (16-ounce) cans whole
  tomatoes, with liquid,
  chopped
1 (6-ounce) can tomato
  paste
1 (6-ounce) can tomato
  puree
3 cups water
2 1/2 teaspoons salt
1/2 teaspoonsoregano
1/2 teaspoon cumin
1/2 teaspoon coriander

In a heavy skillet, render pork fat over medium high heat and remove fat scraps from skillet. Cut pork in 1/2-inch cubes. Coat meat with flour by shaking in a paper sack. Shake off excess flour and add cubes to hot skillet a few at a time, stirring to brown evenly. Remove meat to 5-quart Dutch oven or other large heavy pot. Repeat until all cubes have been browned. Add onions and garlic to skillet and saute, stirring occasionally, until onions are limp. Add to pot with pork. Slice green chiles in 2-inch pieces and add to pot with remaining ingredients. Bring to a boil. Reduce heat and simmer, uncovered, 30 minutes. Adjust seasoning and simmer another 30 minutes. Note: this may be too hot for novices so start with half the green chiles and, when adjusting seasoning, add more as desired.

Serves 8　　　　　　　　　　　*Dick Ludewig*
Easy　　　　　　　　　　　CODY, WYOMING

Rock Salt Roast

"Roast will be medium rare with a light salt rime."

5 pounds ice cream rock
  salt
1 (4–5 pound) roast

Pour 2 inches of rock salt into a domed Dutch oven. Place roast on the salt. Fill oven with rock salt so the roast is surrounded by 2–3 inches of salt. Place in hot coals 45–60 minutes, depending on the size of the roast.

Serves 6　　　　　　　　　　　*John Horton*
Easy　　　　　　　　　　　CODY, WYOMING

Chicken Cacciatore alla Paolo

"An easy camp dish."

1 chicken, cut up
1 large yellow onion, diced
4 cloves garlic, crushed
2–3 Tablespoons olive oil
1 (28-ounce) can tomatoes
1 (6-ounce) can tomato
   paste
1 Tablespoon oregano
1 Tablespoon basil
1 (4 ounce) can mushrooms,
   drained

In a Dutch oven over an open fire, brown chicken, onion and garlic in oil. Stir and turn frequently until chicken is browned and onions are translucent. Add tomatoes and cut them up in the pan. Add all other ingredients except mushrooms. Move oven from hot part of the fire and simmer, uncovered, 45 minutes. Add mushrooms just before serving. Serve with rice.

Serves 4
Easy

Paul Hoffman
CODY, WYOMING

Dutch Oven Trout

"A nice change from fried trout on pack trips."

6 medium trout, cleaned
   Juice of 1 lemon
1 teaspoon salt
1 clove garlic, minced
1 cup dry white wine
2 Tablespoons minced onion
2 Tablespoons dry bread
   crumbs
4 Tablespoons melted butter

Wash and dry trout. Rub the outside of the fish with lemon juice and sprinkle with salt. Place garlic in the bottom of a Dutch oven and arrange trout in a single layer. Add wine, sprinkle with onion and crumbs and spoon on the butter. Set oven on coals and cover lid with another layer of coals. Bake about 30 minutes.

Serves 5
Easy

Elizabeth Woolsey
WILSON, WYOMING

Barbecue Sauce

"Gives a zesty lift to campfire cooking."

1/2 cup corn syrup
1/2 cup ketchup
1/2 cup finely chopped onion
1/4 cup cider vinegar
1/4 cup prepared mustard
1/4 cup Worcestershire sauce

In a saucepan, combine all ingredients. Bring to a boil, stirring frequently. Reduce heat and simmer 15 minutes to thicken.

Serves 6
Easy
Must do ahead

Dee Potter
CODY, WYOMING

Willie Milligan

"Best in a Dutch oven on an open fire."

1 (31-ounce) can pork and
   beans
1 pound hot dogs
3 cooked potatoes
1 cup maple syrup
8 ounces Cheddar cheese
   grated

Combine first 4 ingredients and simmer. When ready to serve, sprinkle cheese on top and allow to melt.

Serves 8
Easy

Elkhorn Ranch
GALLATIN GATEWAY, MONTANA

Pack Trip Beans

"Handy when fresh meat runs out and trout is not available."

1 can lima beans, drained
1 can kidney beans, drained
1 can navy beans, drained
1 clove garlic
3 Tablespoons bacon fat
3 onions, chopped
3 Tablespoons brown sugar
1/2 cup ketchup
3 Tablespoons vinegar
1 teaspoon salt
1 teaspoon dry mustard
1/4 teaspoon black pepper

Put all ingredients in a Dutch oven and mix well. Cover and cook over coals about 1 hour, then cook uncovered an additional 15 minutes.

Serves 6
Easy

Elizabeth Woolsey
WILSON, WYOMING

Alice Fales' Chuck Wagon Baked Beans

"Very good with hamburgers or steak."

1 (1-pound, 15-ounce) can
  Campbell's Beans
1/4 cup dark molasses
1/4 teaspoon ginger
1/8 teaspoon pepper
1/4 teaspoon salt
1/2 cup chopped onion
3 slices bacon, cut in pieces

Mix all ingredients except bacon in a bean pot or Dutch oven. Place bacon on top and bake, covered, about 2 hours in a bed of coals or at 350 degrees in a conventional oven.

Serves 4
Easy

Mrs. Arnold H. Rohlfing
DARIEN, CONNECTICUT

Baked Chanterelles

"Check a mushroom book if you're not absolutely sure. The right ones are a forest delight."

1 1/2 cups butter
  2 teaspoons onion, finely
    chopped
  1 clove garlic, minced
3/4 teaspoon dry sherry
1/2 teaspoon rosemary
1/2 teaspoon salt
1/2 teaspoon pepper
4–8 cups mushrooms

Melt butter in a Dutch oven and stir in all ingredients but mushrooms. Add mushrooms and stir until they are well covered. Cook over light coals 30 minutes until the mushrooms have absorbed the butter.

Easy

Elizabeth Woolsey
WILSON, WYOMING

Skillet Potatoes

1/2 cup butter
  2 pounds baking potatoes,
    peeled and thinly sliced
  1 teaspoon salt
1/4 teaspoon pepper
1/2 cup sliced onions

Melt 4 Tablespoons butter in iron skillet until bubbly. Arrange about 1/3 of the potatoes in a circular, overlapping layer in the hot butter. Sprinkle with salt and pepper, top with onions and dot with 2 Tablespoons butter. Repeat layers, ending with dots of remaining butter. Cook over high heat 5 minutes. Cover skillet tightly with heavy foil and bake at 350 degrees 30 minutes. Remove foil cover and bake 5 more minutes, then invert on a hot platter to serve. If camp cooking, use a Dutch oven.

Serves 6
Easy

Margot Belden Todd
CODY, WYOMING

Dutch Oven Potatoes

"Even Father Murphy would rave about these."

1 pound thick-sliced bacon
2 large onions, diced
1 green pepper, diced,
 optional
8–10 potatoes, sliced
1 can flat beer
1 pound Cheddar cheese,
 grated

Cook bacon in Dutch oven, remove and crumble. In grease, lightly brown onions and pepper. Add potatoes and beer and stir occasionally until cooked. Sprinkle with bacon and cheese. Replace lid and cook until cheese melts.

Serves 8
Easy

Merlin Olsen
SAN MARINO, CALIFORNIA

Mock Baked Potatoes

"An easy way to bake potatoes in camp."

Large baking potatoes,
1 per person
Foil

Wrap potatoes tightly in foil. Fill a large Dutch oven with water and bring to a boil. Put potatoes in the water and cook about 1 hour until soft but not mushy. The Dutch oven can be removed from the fire and potatoes allowed to stand until the rest of the meal is ready.

Easy

Marty S. Coe
CODY, WYOMING

Potato Casserole

"No boring peeling."

1 (32-ounce) package
 frozen hashed brown
 potatoes
1/2 cup butter, melted
1 teaspoon salt
1/4 teaspoon pepper
1/2 cup chopped onion
1 can cream of chicken
 soup
8 ounces sour cream
10 ounces Velveeta cheese
2 cups crushed corn flakes
1/4 cup melted butter

Thaw potatoes. Mix with next 7 ingredients. For topping, combine corn flakes and butter and sprinkle over potato mixture. Bake 1 hour in a Dutch oven in a bed of coals or in a conventional oven at 350 degrees 1 hour.

Serves 12
Easy

Dee Potter
CODY, WYOMING

Bear Sign

1/2 cup sourdough starter
  (see index)
1 cup milk
2 cups flour
3 Tablespoons butter,
  melted
1 egg, well beaten
1 teaspoon soda
1/2 cup brown sugar
1/4 teaspoon nutmeg
1/4 teaspoon cinnamon
  Oil

Mix starter, milk and flour and let rise, then add remaining ingredients. Flatten dough to 1/2-inch thick and cut in rounds with a can, drinking glass or cutter. Let rise 30 minutes. Deep fat fry until puffed and light brown.

Serves 10–15
Easy

Barb Egan
CODY, WYOMING

Sourdough Pie Crust

1/2 cup sourdough starter
  (see index)
1 1/4 cups flour
1/2 teaspoon salt
1/2 teaspoon baking soda
2 Tablespoons shortening,
  softened
4 Tablespoons cold water

Knead together first 5 ingredients. Add water. Cover and let rise 30 minutes. Roll out and place in a pie tin. Bake on a rack in a Dutch oven over an open fire. For an unfilled shell, bake about 8 minutes. For a filled crust, allow about 1 hour.

Yields one 9-inch pie crust
Easy
May be frozen

Barb Egan
CODY, WYOMING

Grandma's Doughnuts

"A descendant of Calamity Jane made these over an open fire in a Dutch oven."

1 cup sugar
1/2 cup butter, softened
1 cup milk, slightly
  warmed
3 eggs, slightly beaten
1 Tablespoon baking
  powder
About 3 1/2 cups flour
Lard
Confectioners' sugar

Cream sugar and butter. Add milk and eggs and mix well. Add baking powder and 2 cups flour. Mix lightly. Turn out on a floured board and lightly knead in remaining flour until a soft dough is formed. Roll dough 1/4-inch thick and cut with a doughnut cutter. Fry in hot lard until brown. Roll in confectioners' sugar while still warm. Note: doughnuts should be fried in smoking hot fat in an iron skillet or Dutch oven. Doughnuts will first drop to the bottom of the pan, but should float to the top in a moment. If dough does not rise, the fat is not hot enough and the doughnuts will be soaked in grease.

Yields 30

Rose Borner White
CODY, WYOMING

Apple Crisp

"Wonderful dessert for pack trips."

8–10 large green pie apples,
  peeled and sliced
2 Tablespoons cinnamon
1/2 cup butter
3/4 cup brown sugar
1/2 cup flour
3 packages instant apple
  and cinnamon oatmeal
1/2 cup water

Put apples in large cast iron skillet or Dutch oven. Combine cinnamon, butter, sugar, flour and oatmeal. Mix until crumbly and sprinkle over apples. Pour on water and cover with a lid. Bank coals around the sides of oven and place a few coals on top. It is not necessary to bury the pan completely. Cook 40 minutes, adding coals when needed. Serve with whipped topping.

Serves 12–15
Easy

Marty S. Coe
CODY, WYOMING

Hamburger Jerky

1 pound ground beef
1 teaspoon salt
1 teaspoon MSG
1/4–1/2 teaspoon barbecue
 sauce
3/4 teaspoon water
1/2 teaspoon liquid smoke
 Pinch garlic salt

Mix together and press into loaf pan lined with foil. Let stand 30 minutes at room temperature. Bake at 200 degrees 3 hours. Freeze 2 hours before slicing in thin strips.

Yields 1 pound
Easy
Must do ahead

LaDonna Zall
RALSTON, WYOMING

Cowboy in a Blanket

"Good to take along in a saddlebag."

2 loaves bread dough,
 frozen or homemade

FILLING:

2 cups cooked chicken,
 ham, beef, corned
 beef or turkey
4–5 Tablespoons
 appropriate gravy,
 soup, or other liquid
1/4 cup chopped onion
1/4 cup chopped green
 pepper
1/4 cup chopped celery
1/4 cup sprouts
 Salt and pepper,
 to taste
 Dash soy sauce
1 egg, beaten
 Sesame, caraway or
 poppy seeds

Thaw frozen dough or prepare homemade dough. Roll out 1 loaf into a 12 × 18-inch rectangle 1/2-inch thick. Cut into eight 6 × 6-inch pieces. Mix chopped meat with all ingredients except egg and seeds. Place 2 Tablespoons filling on each square of dough, keeping mixture away from the edges. Dampen edges with beaten egg and pinch together. Brush tops of squares with egg and sprinkle seeds lightly over them. Arrange on greased baking sheet, gently flatten each square and cover. Let rise in a warm place about 45 minutes. Repeat the procedure with the second loaf. When rising is complete, bake at 350 degrees 20–25 minutes. Cool. Refrigerate in plastic bags.

Serves 16
Must do ahead

Sharon McNicol
CODY, WYOMING

Cooking for a Crowd

Big Apple Cheese Ball

"Great snack for kids or pretty for guests."

4 cups grated sharp Cheddar
    cheese
3 ounces cream cheese,
    softened
1/2 cup apple cider
1 teaspoon Worcestershire
    sauce
1 teaspoon dry mustard
1/2 teaspoon onion salt
1/4 teaspoon cayenne
2 teaspoons caraway seeds
    Paprika
1 cinnamon stick

Combine first 8 ingredients, beat until smooth and refrigerate 2–3 hours. Form into shape of an apple, roll sides in paprika and insert cinnamon stick for stem. Refrigerate until serving time. Serve as a spread with crackers and assorted red and golden Delicious apple wedges.

Serves 40–50
Easy
Must do ahead

Mrs. Dale Fisher
EL DORADO, ARKANSAS

Curry Cheese Ring

"It keeps almost indefinitely, but is so good that it usually disappears quickly."

1 pound sharp Cheddar
    cheese, grated
8 ounces Monterey Jack
    cheese, grated
4 ounces bleu or Roquefort
    cheese, crumbled
1/4 cup dry sherry
1/2 cup mayonnaise
1/4 teaspoon curry, to taste
1/2 teaspoon freshly grated
    lemon rind

Heat cheeses in double-boiler insert or in glass or ceramic bowl in microwave until just creamy. Mix in sherry and mayonnaise, add curry and lemon rind and pour into 4-cup ring mold. Chill slightly and serve at room temperature on platter with grapes or berries in the center or surrounded with sliced apples and crackers.

Serves 30
Easy
Must do ahead

Gina Guy
PORTLAND, OREGON

Hot Cheese Dip

"Best when done slowly in a crock pot, this dip is a hit at parties and goes fast."

1 pound lean ground beef
1 onion, diced
1 green pepper, diced
   Salt and pepper, to taste
1 package taco seasoning
3/4 cup water
2 pounds Velveeta cheese,
   sliced
8 ounces Monterey Jack
   cheese with jalapeno
   peppers, sliced
1 pound Monterey Jack
   cheese, sliced
1 (8-ounce) jar picante
   sauce, to taste

Brown beef, onions and pepper. Add salt and pepper and drain. Add taco seasoning and water, simmer 10 minutes and set aside. Place cheeses in crock pot set on low temperature. Add picante sauce, starting with less than entire jar. When cheeses begin to melt, add beef mixture. The entire process takes about 2 1/2 hours.

Serves 20

Monica Hill
CODY, WYOMING

Quiche Lorraine Tarts

Pastry for 2 double pie
   crusts
4 eggs, beaten
2 cups heavy cream
1/2 teaspoon salt
2 teaspoons sugar
   Pinch nutmeg
   Pinch pepper
1 medium onion, thinly
   sliced
   Butter
6 slices bacon, cooked and
   crumbled
4 ounces Swiss cheese
   shredded
   Nutmeg

Line muffin tins with pastry. Beat together next 6 ingredients. Saute onions in butter. Sprinkle bottoms of tarts with bacon, then cheese and finally onions. Fill each 3/4 full with egg mixture. Sprinkle lightly with nutmeg. Bake at 400 degrees 10 minutes. Reduce heat to 350 degrees and bake 10 minutes longer.

Yields 55
Time-consuming
May be frozen

Marilyn Montville
CODY, WYOMING

Drunken Hot Dogs

2 pounds hot dogs
2 cups bourbon
2 cups brown sugar
2 cups ketchup

"Bourbon fumes can be strong and may blow open oven door, so stand back!"

Cut hot dogs in bite-sized pieces. Mix bourbon, sugar and ketchup, then mix in meat. Put into 4-quart casserole and bake at 350 degrees 45–60 minutes, stirring occasionally.

Serves 20
Easy

Anne C. Hayes
CODY, WYOMING

Heart Mountain Meatballs

MEATBALLS:

1 finger-sized piece good
  suet, minced
1 pound lean sirloin,
  ground
1 pound lean pork, ground
3 slices stale bread,
  shredded
2 eggs, slightly beaten
1/4 cup minced onion
3/4 teaspoon cornstarch
2 teaspoons soy sauce
1/4 teaspoon freshly ground
  pepper
1/8 teaspoon allspice
1 1/4 teaspoons salt
1 teaspoon Kitchen
  Bouquet
1/4 cup evaporated milk
1/4 cup oil

Mix suet with meats, then work in remaining ingredients except oil, using hands to ensure a good mix. Chill several hours, then form into teaspoon-sized balls. Heat oil in large, heavy skillet, add meatballs, about 18 at a time, and brown well all sides about 5 minutes. Remove with a slotted spoon to a bowl.

For sauce, add flour to juices left in skillet and cook until golden brown, stirring constantly. Slowly stir in broth and stir until smooth and thick. Stir in wine, add meatballs, cover tightly and simmer 30 minutes, stirring occasionally. Add more broth if needed. Serve in chafing dish with toothpicks.

Yields 100 small meatballs
May be frozen
Must do ahead

Karen Gibbons
CODY, WYOMING

SAUCE:

3 Tablespoons flour
2 cups beef broth or
  2 bouillon cubes in
  2 cups water
1 cup dry red wine or
  1 can mushroom soup

Beef Vegetable Soup

"A tasty, hearty soup, good for a cold night."

1 (1-pound, 12-ounce) can
  tomatoes
6 cups water
2 pounds boneless chuck,
  cut in 1-inch cubes
2 teaspoons salt
1 teaspoon pepper
1 cup sliced celery and
  leaves
1/4 cup chopped parsley
2 cups coarsely chopped
  cabbage
1 bay leaf
1/2 cup barley
2 (18-ounce) cans V-8 juice
1 package frozen cut green
  beans
2 cups sliced carrots
1 1/2 cups sliced onion
1 teaspoon Worcestershire
  sauce
2 beef bouillon cubes
1 cup grated Parmesan
  cheese

Drain tomatoes, set aside and place juice into kettle. Add 4 cups water and next 7 ingredients. Cover and simmer 1 hour. Discard celery, parsley and bay leaf. Add 1 cup water and barley and cook 30 minutes covered. Cook 1 hour, uncovered. Add reserved tomatoes, next 6 ingredients and 1 cup water. Simmer 45 minutes, uncovered. Serve sprinkled with cheese.

Serves 16
Easy

Temptations
CODY, WYOMING

Chili California Style

8 ounces pinto beans
5 cups canned tomatoes
1 pound green pepper,
chopped
2 1/8 cups chopped white
onion
1 1/2 Tablespoons oil
2 cloves garlic, crushed
1/2 cup chopped parsley
1/2 cup butter
2 1/2 pounds coarsely ground
beef
1 pound ground lean pork
1/3 cup chili powder
2 teaspoons salt
1 1/2 teaspoons ground black
pepper
1 1/2 teaspoons cumin
1 1/2 teaspoons MSG,
optional

Wash beans, then simmer until tender and add tomatoes. Saute green pepper and onions in oil. Add garlic and parsley. Melt butter, saute meats and add to onion mixture. Stir in seasonings and add to beans. Simmer 2 hours, stirring occasionally, and skim fat. Top each serving with 1 teaspoon chopped white onion and accompany with saltine crackers.

Serves 12
Must do ahead

Mrs. John McKillop
Ventura, California

Excellent Buns

"This dough may be used for fruit-filled buns, cinnamon rolls or doughnuts."

1 1/3 Tablespoons sugar
6 cups warm water
2 packages yeast
8 eggs
1 cup sugar
2 cups oil
1 Tablespoon salt
19–20 cups flour

Dissolve sugar in 1 1/3 cups water. Sprinkle in yeast and let stand 15 minutes. Beat together remaining water, eggs, sugar, oil and salt and mix in yeast. Add enough flour to make a soft dough and let rise 1 1/2 hours. Form into buns, butter or oil well and let rise until doubled. Bake at 350 degrees 15–20 minutes.

Yields approximately 12 dozen
Easy

Angie Lalonde
Winnipeg, Canada

Honey Buns

"A breakfast treat for a crowd."

4 loaves frozen white bread
  dough
1 cup honey
2 cups margarine

The night before serving, take bread from freezer, slit plastic bag, cover with dampened towel and leave in draft-free place. A half hour before breakfast time, heat deep-fat fryer to 425 degrees. Cut dough in strips about index-finger size. Handling lightly, drop into hot fat and brown each side. Warm honey and margarine, mix well and drop in strips, coating well. Remove to warm dish with slotted spoon. Serve at once or keep covered and warm.

Serves 30
Easy
Must do ahead

Lazy L&B Ranch
DUBOIS, WYOMING

Deluxe Buttermilk Hot Cakes

"I have made this recipe for 85–90 riders on the Big Horn Mountain Roundup Trail Ride"

4 cups flour
4 teaspoons baking powder
8 Tablespoons sugar
12 Tablespoons graham flour
1 teaspoon soda
  About 1 cup warm
  buttermilk
8 eggs
8 Tablespoons melted butter

Mix together dry ingredients except soda. Stir soda into 1 cup buttermilk, beat well into dry mixture, then beat in eggs and butter. Add enough additional buttermilk to make a very thin batter. Bake on medium-hot griddle. When bubbles appear, turn and brown other side. Serve at once. Pancakes should resemble crepes.

Serves 16
Easy

Kelly Howie
BIG HORN, WYOMING

Barbecued Beef Supreme

10 pounds chuck roast
5 onions, chopped
1 cup vinegar
2 teaspoons pepper
2 Tablespoons dry mustard
2/3 cup Worcestershire sauce
2/3 cup brown sugar
2 Tablespoons salt
4 cans tomato soup

Trim excess fat from meat, cut in bite-sized pieces and place in roasting pan. Combine remaining ingredients and pour over meat. Cover tightly and roast at 350 degrees 5–6 hours, stirring every hour. Serve on buns or in pocket bread.

Serves 20
Easy

Mrs. William D. Weiss
CODY, WYOMING

California Casserole

8 pounds ground beef
4 onions, chopped
4 cloves garlic, minced
1 package taco seasoning
2 cups tomato sauce
1 teaspoon sugar
4 (4-ounce) cans chopped
  green chiles
4 cups sliced black olives
8 cups small curd cottage
  cheese
4 eggs
2 pounds Monterey Jack
  cheese, sliced
1 (10-ounce) bag tortilla
  chips
4 cups grated Cheddar
  cheese
2 cups chopped green onions
2 cups sour cream

Brown meat in batches, adding onions and garlic to last batch. Return meat to pan. Add taco seasoning, tomato sauce, sugar, chiles and 1/2 olives and simmer over low heat 15 minutes. Beat cottage cheese with eggs and set aside. Spread 1/3 meat mixture in 12-quart casserole. Cover with layers of 1/2 Monterey Jack, cottage cheese mixture and chips. Repeat, ending with final layer of meat. Top with Cheddar and bake at 350 degrees 30 minutes. Serve with remaining olives, green onions and sour cream. Casserole may be assembled in advance, refrigerated and returned to room temperature before baking.

Serves 24
May do ahead

Temptations
CODY, WYOMING

Asado al Palo (Lamb Roast)

"Worth the effort."

1 lamb, 6–9 months old

**SALMUERA, SAUCE
FOR BASTING:**

1/2 cup salt
3 large cloves garlic, crushed
2 Tablespoons black pepper
2 teaspoons Tabasco
1/4 cup lemon juice
1/4 cup wine vinegar
Hot water

Kill lamb. Pelt and dress the carcass, leaving the kidneys in place, encased in 1/4–3/4 inches fat. Split the pelvic bone and brisket, but leave the lamb whole. Cut the legs off at the knees and hocks. Hang overnight in a cool, fly-proof place. (All of this could be done by a butcher.)

The next day, prepare a sprinkler bottle for basting. Use a 1-liter wine or soft drink bottle, equipped with a sprinkler head with 3 or 4 grooves sliced down the sides of the cork to allow a small amount of the sauce to escape as the bottle is shaken over the lamb. Fill the bottle with all the sauce ingredients but water to within 2 inches of the head, then top with hot water. Shake well until salt dissolves.

About 5 hours before the meal, start a large fire on level ground in a circular space about 4 1/2 feet in diameter. Start skewering the lamb 4 hours before the meal. Use a 3/4-inch steel rod, 7 feet long, sharpened on one end, with another 1/2-inch rod, 2 feet long, welded to it. The weld should be 6 inches from the top of the long rod. The second rod should have 1/2-inch diameter hooks fashioned on each end.

It takes 2 people to skewer the lamb. A heavy butcher table is ideal. One person spreads the rib cage at the sternum, pulling outwards in opposite directions with each hand. Using a heavy, sharp knife, the second person scores the ribs on both sides close to the backbone, cracking the ribs along the scoring lines as heavy pressure is applied on each set of ribs. Jam the pointed end of the skewer through the carcass, starting next to the tail and pointing the skewer directly down the backbone. It is difficult to penetrate the pelvis. One person must keep the carcass from sliding off the table, while the other person inserts the skewer. Sometimes the end of the skewer must be tapped with a heavy hammer to get it through the bone. Once through the pelvis, the skewer should be guided through the meat along the backbone until it protrudes where the backbone curves at the neck, which will probably require more hammering. Slide the carcass up the skewer until each hind leg can be wired to the hooks on the perpendicular rod. Next, spread the ribs flat by driving a 2-foot rod (either green willow or 1/2-inch steel) between the fourth and fifth ribs, counting from the tail. Insert the rod from the inside of the rib cage and continue over the backbone (on the top side of the animal when he was alive). Re-insert on the other side of the rib cage. Wire the rod to the ribs on each side if they appear to be slipping.

Carve each ham (back leg) so that 2 portions of the meat form large flaps, one to hang down and the other to stick up above the ham. This ensures that the thick meat will cook thoroughly. The flaps are held in place by driving sharpened, peeled green sticks through each flap and into the meat remaining on the hams.

To prepare the front shoulders, cut partway through the joint about the knee and break the joint back toward the tail. Then, slice around and under each shoulder blade along the ribs and backbone and loosen enough so that each shoulder blade hangs down beside the neck. Connect the upper leg to the shoulder on each side with another short piece of wire. Weave a peeled green stick through the shoulders and over the main metal shaft to hold the shoulders perpendicular to the fire.

To cook, drive the pointed end of the 7-foot rod about 18-inches into the ground at approximately a 45 degree angle over the fire. It helps to drive a shorter, preliminary stake into the ground before the fire is started. The firewood and coals should be spread in a semicircle beneath the uppermost part of the lamb (the hams attached to the crossbar). The lower portions will cook from reflected heat. A few coals may have to be raked under the lowest portions of the roast. Cook approximately 1 1/4 hours on the underside first, basting liberally every 15 minutes, until the fat on the backside begins to liquify. Rotate and cook another 45–60 minutes. Rotate once more and cook approximately 5 minutes to reheat front. Remove from fire to serve.

Serves 40
Allow 1/2 day for preparation

Marshall Dominick
Cody, Wyoming

Kentucky Style Ham

1 (15–16 pound) salt-cured
    smoked ham
1 large onion, sliced
1 orange, sliced
1 lemon, sliced
3 or 4 bay leaves
1 Tablespoon cloves

Scrub ham well with a brush and scrape clean. Soak overnight, skin-side-up, in plenty of water so salt drops to bottom. The next day, drain ham, place in large pot and cover with fresh water. Add remaining ingredients and simmer 20 minutes per pound. When bone pulls loose in the back, ham is done. Let cool in the water.

Serves 30
Easy
Must do ahead

Mrs. C. V. Whitney
Saratoga Springs, New York

Hot Turkey Salad

"May be adjusted for a crowd or a family."

Cooked meat from
12–13 pound turkey,
cubed
12 cups chopped celery
3 cups blanched almonds,
chopped
2 cups chopped green
pepper
3/4 cup chopped pimiento
3/4 cup finely chopped
onion
2 Tablespoons salt
3/4 cup lemon juice
3 cups mayonnaise
1 1/2 pounds Swiss or
Cheddar cheese, sliced
1 1/2 cups butter, melted
6 cups cracker crumbs

Combine first 9 ingredients in large bowl. Spoon into 3 greased 13 × 9 1/2-inch pans. Top with cheese. Combine butter and crumbs and sprinkle evenly over tops. Bake at 350 degrees about 45 minutes. Serve at once.

Serves 48

Beverly J. Robertson
CODY, WYOMING

Seafood Spaghetti

1 cup chopped celery
1 cup chopped onion
1/2 cup chopped green pepper
Butter
8 Tablespoons butter
8 Tablespoons flour
4 cups milk
1/2 teaspoon salt
1/2 teaspoon pepper
Sherry, to taste
1 (10 3/4-ounce) can
tomato soup
8 ounces sharp Cheddar
cheese, grated
1 quart oysters, drained
1 pound fresh crab meat
3 pounds fresh shrimp,
cooked and cleaned
1 pound vermicelli, cooked

Saute celery, onions and green pepper in a little butter until tender and set aside. Melt 8 Tablespoons butter and gradually stir in flour and milk. Season with salt, pepper and sherry and add to celery mixture with soup and 3/4 of the cheese. Stir in seafood. Fold in vermicelli, place in buttered casserole and top with remaining cheese. Bake at 350 degrees 45 minutes.

Serves 15–20
Easy
May be frozen

Mrs. Henry T. V. Miller
MEMPHIS, TENNESSEE

Carrots Parmesan

20 large carrots
1 teaspoon salt
1 teaspoon sugar
1 medium white onion,
   grated
3 cups heavy cream
1 1/2 cups Parmesan cheese,
   grated
1 teaspoon salt, to taste
1/2 teaspoon white pepper
1 cup pecan or walnut
   halves

Parboil carrots with salt and sugar. Scrape off skin, then grate carrots. Mix with onions, cream, cheese and seasonings. Put into 3-quart buttered casserole, top with nuts and bake at 350 degrees about 35 minutes.

Serves 18–20

Margot Belden Todd
CODY, WYOMING

Surprise Beans

"A staple at my parents' home during Cheyenne Frontier Days."

1 cup chopped onion
2 medium apples, peeled,
   cored, seeded and
   chopped
2 medium green peppers,
   seeded and chopped
6 slices bacon, cooked and
   crumbled, fat reserved
3 teaspoons curry powder
4 (1-pound) cans red
   kidney beans, drained
   and washed
2 (1-pound) cans whole
   tomatoes, half the liquid
   reserved
2 cups dark brown sugar
   Parmesan cheese

Saute onions, apples and peppers in bacon fat until onion is golden and apples and peppers are soft. Combine with curry, beans, tomatoes, reserved tomato liquid and sugar. Place in 2 1/2–3-quart casserole and top with cheese. Bake at 350 degrees 1 hour.

Serves 16–20
Easy
May be frozen

Gina Guy
PORTLAND, OREGON

Game Dinner Grits

"Always a hit with wild game."

6 eggs
1 1/2 cups milk
12 cups water
3 teaspoons salt
3 cups quick grits
1 cup butter
2 (6-ounce) garlic cheese
  rolls
2 (4-ounce) cans chopped
  green chiles
6 cloves garlic, minced
24 ounces sharp Cheddar
  cheese, grated

Stir eggs and milk into a bowl and set aside. Combine water and salt in 8-quart pot and bring to a boil. Stir in grits. Return to a boil and cook 5 minutes. Stir in remaining ingredients and pour into 2 greased, 3-quart casseroles. Bake at 350 degrees 1 hour. Let stand 15 minutes before serving.

Serves 35–40
Easy
May do ahead

Mrs. Samuel W. Smith
HOUSTON, TEXAS

Strawberry Nut Salad

2–3 bananas, sliced
2 (10-ounce)packages
  frozen strawberries
1 (1-pound, 4-ounce) can
  crushed pineapple,
  drained
1 cup chopped nuts
2 (3-ounce) packages
  strawberry gelatin
1 cup boiling water
2 cups sour cream

Combine fruits and nuts and mix well. Dissolve gelatin in water and fold in fruit mixture. Pour half into 13 × 9-inch glass dish and refrigerate until firm. Spread a layer of sour cream and add remaining fruit mixture. Chill until firm.

Serves 16–20
Must do ahead

Melba Coley
CODY, WYOMING

Chocolate Delight

1 package graham cracker
  crust mix
8 ounces cream cheese,
  softened
1 cup confectioners' sugar
1 cup non-dairy whipped
  topping
1 package vanilla instant
  pudding
1 package chocolate instant
  pudding
3 cups milk

Make crust according to directions and place in 9 × 13 × 2-inch pan. Bake at 350 degrees a few minutes. Mix cream cheese, sugar and whipped topping and pour over crust. Mix puddings and milk and pour over cheese layer. Dot with additional whipped topping. Chill.

Serves 24
Easy
Must do ahead

Amy McMillan
Cody, Wyoming

Buster Bar Delight

1 package Oreo cookies
1/2 cup margarine
1/2 gallon vanilla ice cream,
  softened
1 small jar hot fudge sauce
1 (12-ounce) can salted
  blanched peanuts
9 ounces non-dairy whipped
  topping

Crush cookies and mix with margarine. Press all but 1 cup into 9 × 13-inch pan. Spread ice cream on crust and freeze until firm. Pour fudge sauce over ice cream. Spread with peanuts and then whipped topping. Sprinkle remaining cup of cookie mixture on top and return to freezer. Freeze at least 1 1/2 hours.

Serves 24
Easy
Must do ahead

Amy McMillan
Cody, Wyoming

Buffalo Chip Cookies

1 cup vegetable shortening
  or butter, softened
1 cup margarine, softened
2 cups brown sugar
2 cups sugar
4 eggs
2 teaspoons vanilla
4 cups flour
2 teaspoons baking soda
2 teaspoons baking powder
2 cups oatmeal
2 cups corn flakes
1 cup chopped pecans
1 cup shredded coconut
12 ounces chocolate chips

Beat shortenings, sugar, eggs and vanilla at medium speed. Sift flour, baking soda, and baking powder and work into first mixture by hand until well incorporated. Stir in remaining ingredients. Drop by Tablespoonfuls on ungreased baking sheets. Bake at 350 degrees 8–12 minutes.

Yields 14 dozen
Easy

Roberta Byrd
DALLAS, TEXAS

Rum Balls Wyoming Style

"Watch it. You'll eat too many."

4 cups confectioners' sugar
2 cups cocoa
6 cups chopped pecans
1/2 teaspoon salt
8 Tablespoons white corn
  syrup
1 cup rum
1 scant cup bourbon
  Confectioners' sugar

Mix sugar, cocoa, pecans and salt in large mixing bowl. Add all but last ingredient. Mix until gooey but not soupy, adding more bourbon if necessary. Roll in confectioners' sugar and shape into small balls or form into long rolls for slices. Refrigerate until hard.

Serves 20
Easy

Gladys Byers
CODY, WYOMING

"The Life I Love" by Irving Bacon. *Courtesy of Buffalo Bill Historical Center, Cody, WY; Bequest in memory of the Houx and Newell Families; 15.64*

Sheet Cake

CAKE:

1 cup water
1 cup butter
3–4 Tablespoons cocoa
2 cups flour
2 cups sugar
1/2 cup buttermilk
1 teaspoon soda
2 eggs
1 teaspoon vanilla

Boil water, butter and cocoa and add to flour and sugar. Add buttermilk, soda, eggs and vanilla. Mix well. Bake in 11 × 15 × 1-inch jelly roll pan at 400 degrees 20 minutes.

For frosting, boil sugar, margarine and milk 30 seconds. Remove from heat and add chocolate chips and vanilla. Stir to thicken.

Serves 24
Easy

Candy Felts
CODY, WYOMING

FROSTING:

1 1/2 cups sugar
6 Tablespoons margarine
6 Tablespoons milk
1/2–3/4 cup chocolate chips
1 teaspoon vanilla

Apricot Slush

2 cups sugar
8 cups water
12 ounces orange juice
concentrate
12 ounces lemonade
concentrate
1 fifth apricot brandy
Ginger ale

Dissolve sugar in 2 cups boiling water. Add remaining water and other ingredients and put in freezer container. When frozen, serve in a glass with ginger ale.

Serves 20
Easy
Must do ahead

Dorothy Marchezak
EXPORT, PENNSYLVANIA

Ethelena's Punch

"A snap to mix in a hurry."

1 (46-ounce) can pineapple
   juice
1 (6-ounce) can frozen
   lemonade, thawed
1 (24-ounce) bottle
   lemon-lime soda

Combine ingredients. If desired, another batch may be frozen as ice cubes to prevent dilution of mixture from melting ice.

Yields 2 1/4 quarts
Easy

Katharine McMillan
INDIO, CALIFORNIA

May Wine Punch

1 small handful dried
   Waldmeister
4 cups cognac
1 1/2 cups sugar
4 cups water
4 cups lemon juice
8 cups Jamaica rum
4 ounces peach brandy
   Fresh strawberries

Soak Waldmeister in cognac in covered glass jar overnight. Shake sugar into punch bowl and dissolve in water. Strain Waldmeister from cognac and add with lemon juice, rum and brandy. Put large piece of ice in punch bowl and allow mixture to brew about 2 hours, stirring occasionally. Float fresh strawberries on the top and serve. (Dried Waldmeister is available at Ye Olde Herbal Shoppe, 8 Beekman, New York City.)

Yields 5 quarts
Easy
Must do ahead

Mrs. Charles B. Arnold
ALBUQUERQUE, NEW MEXICO

Slush Fruit Punch

"Great on a summer day."

7 bananas, peeled
7 oranges, peeled and
  sectioned
1 (16-ounce) can frozen
  orange juice, thawed
1 (46-ounce) can unsweetened
  pineapple juice
6 cups unsweetened apple
  juice
  Ginger ale or 7-Up, to taste

Mash bananas with shredding blade of food processor or mash with fork, keeping texture mushy. Process oranges with slicing blade. Change to plastic mixing blade, add some juice and mix 2–3 seconds. Mix with remaining juices in large bowl. Ladle the mixture into small plastic bowls or grapefruit or orange cups and freeze. When mixture is at slushy stage, mix again with a fork to distribute fruit evenly. Remove from freezer about 30 minutes before serving and add ginger ale.

Serves 25–35
Easy
Must do ahead

Katharine McMillan
Indio, California

Southern Egg Nog

12 egg yolks
 1 cup sugar
 4 cups milk
 1 fifth rum
 4 cups heavy cream, whipped
   Nutmeg

Beat yolks until light. Beat in sugar until thick. Stir in milk and rum. Chill 3 hours and pour into punch bowl. Fold in cream. Chill 1 hour. Dust with nutmeg.

Serves 24
Easy
Must do ahead

Roberta Byrd
Dallas, Texas

Sparkling Citrus Punch

2 cups fresh strawberries or
  1 cup whole frozen
1 (6-ounce) can frozen
  orange juice, thawed
1 (6-ounce) can frozen
  limeade, thawed
1 (6-ounce) can frozen
  lemonade, thawed
1 (28-ounce) bottle ginger ale
1 (28-ounce) bottle club soda
  Lime slices

Arrange berries in a single layer on baking pan. Freeze until solid, uncovered, then store in a plastic bag in freezer until serving time. Combine juices in large bowl or pitcher. Cover and chill until very cold. Just before adding ginger ale and soda, stir juices to blend. Pour punch into punch bowl and float lime slices and berries on top. May make ice ring of equal parts orange juice and ginger ale. For special occasions, substitute champagne for ginger ale.

Yields 3 quarts
Easy   *Mrs. C. V. Whitney*
Must do ahead   SARATOGA SPRINGS, NEW YORK

Spiced Tea

2/3 cup sugar
  4 whole cloves
  2 cinnamon sticks
  3 cups water
  2 Tablespoons loose tea
2/3 cup orange juice
1/3 cup lemon juice
  Ice water, to taste

"Wonderful with a summer luncheon."

Mix sugar, spices and water. Boil 5 minutes. Strain and pour over tea. Allow to stand 3 minutes. Strain again. Add juices and ice water.

Yields 2 quarts   *Mrs. C. V. Whitney*
Easy   SARATOGA SPRINGS, NEW YORK

Yummy Bourbon Dessert

48 almond macaroons or
    Amaretti (Italian
    macaroons)
1 cup bourbon
2 cups butter, softened
2 cups sugar
1 dozen eggs, separated
4 (1-ounce) squares
    unsweetened chocolate,
    melted
1 teaspoon vanilla
1 cup chopped pecans
2 dozen ladyfingers, split
1 1/2 cups heavy cream,
    whipped
    Chocolate curls, optional

Soak macaroons in bourbon. Cream butter and sugar together until fluffy. Beat egg yolks until light and blend into creamed mixture. Beat chocolate into butter mixture and add vanilla and pecans. Whip egg whites until stiff but not dry and fold into chocolate mixture. Line sides and bottom of 10-inch springform pan with ladyfingers. Alternate layers of chocolate mixture and macaroons in pan and chill overnight. Remove ring before serving and decorate with whipped cream and chocolate curls.

Serves 16
Must do ahead

Missy Hoster
Jackson, Mississippi

Balloons

"Disgustingly wonderful."

BALLOONS:

1 cup water
1/4 cup butter
1 cup flour
4 eggs, slightly beaten
    Hot oil

HOT BUTTERSCOTCH SAUCE:

2 Tablespoons butter
1 cup brown sugar
1/2 cup half and half

In a heavy saucepan, bring water to a boil and add butter. Add flour all at once and stir three minutes. Remove from heat and cool slightly. Using a 1/4-cup measure, add eggs to flour mixture and beat after each addition, then beat entire mixture 5 minutes. Drop by teaspoonfuls into hot oil in deep fryer and cook about 8 minutes or until they puff up and brown lightly.

For sauce, melt butter, add sugar and cream and boil gently 5 minutes. Serve balloons with sauce.

Serves 8

Linn Howard
Cody, Wyoming

Hazlenut Meringues with Raspberry Sauce

"From The Cordon Bleu Cookery School in London."

MERINGUES:

4 egg whites
1 1/4 cups superfine sugar
1 teaspoon vanilla
1/2 teaspoon vinegar
4 1/2 ounces hazelnuts,
    browned, skinned and
    finely ground
5 ounces heavy cream,
    whipped
    Confectioners' sugar

RASPBERRY SAUCE:

8 ounces raspberries
1/3 cup confectioners' sugar

Prepare two 8-inch cake pans by rubbing sides with butter, dusting with flour and lining bottoms with parchment paper. Beat whites until stiff, then gradually beat in sugar. Continue beating until very stiff, adding vanilla and vinegar. Fold in hazelnuts. Pour into cake pans and bake at 375 degrees 30–40 minutes. Turn onto cooling racks and peel off parchment. When cool, layer meringues with whipped cream and dust tops with confectioners' sugar.

For sauce, rub the raspberries through a nylon or stainless-steel strainer and beat in sugar, a little at a time, enough to thicken. Serve sauce separately.

Serves 6
Time-consuming

Diana M. Senior
CHICAGO, ILLINOIS

Sherry Almond Cream and Custard Sauce

CREAM:

1 Tablespoon gelatin
1/4 cup cold water
1 cup boiling water
1 1/4 cups sugar
6 egg whites, at room
temperature
1/2 teaspoon almond extract
1/3 cup sherry
1 cup sliced almonds,
toasted

CUSTARD SAUCE:

2 cups milk
6 egg yolks
1/8 teaspoon salt
1/4 cup sugar
1 cup heavy cream,
whipped
1/2 teaspoon vanilla
1/4 cup sherry

Soak gelatin in cold water 10 minutes. Add boiling water, stir until completely dissolved and add sugar, stirring well. Chill mixture until beginning to set, then beat until frothy. Beat egg whites until stiff. Fold gelatin mixture, almond extract and sherry into whites. Pour into melon mold, alternating layers of the mixture with almonds. Chill overnight.

For sauce, scald milk in double-boiler insert. Beat yolks slightly with salt and sugar. Slowly pour scalded milk into yolks, beating well. Return mixture to insert and cook until mixture coats a spoon. Cool. Fold in whipped cream, vanilla and sherry.

Serves 10–12
Easy
Must do ahead

Margot Belden Todd
CODY, WYOMING

Easy Chocolate Cheesecake

CRUST:

1 cup flour
1/2 cup margarine
1 1/2 cups finely chopped
pecans

FILLING:

1 1/2 cups non-dairy whipped
topping
1 cup confectioners' sugar
8 ounces cream cheese,
softened
1 large plus 1 small
package instant
chocolate pudding
4 cups milk

TOPPING:

1 1/2 cups non-dairy whipped
topping
1/2 cup grated chocolate

Mix crust ingredients well and press into a 9 × 13-inch baking pan. Bake at 350 degrees 15–20 minutes and cool.

Whip topping with sugar and cheese and spread over crust. Mix puddings with milk and add.

Cover with whipped topping and garnish with grated chocolate. Chill an hour or so.

Serves 8
Easy   *Marlene Farrell*
Must do ahead   DENVER, COLORADO

Cheesecake

"A real New York-style cheesecake."

CRUST:

1 1/4 cups graham cracker
        crumbs
1/4 cup sugar
1/3 cup butter or margarine

FILLING:

8 eggs
2 cups sugar
1 teaspoon vanilla
5 (8-ounce) packages
    cream cheese, softened
    and cut in quarters
1 cup heavy cream
3 Tablespoons flour

For crust, combine crumbs and sugar in small bowl. Melt butter and add to crumbs, mixing until thoroughly blended. Press into bottom of 10-inch springform pan and bake at 350 degrees 8 minutes.

For filling, cream together eggs, sugar and vanilla until light and fluffy. Add cream cheese slowly, beating well after each quarter, until as smooth as possible (small lumps are acceptable). Slowly add cream and flour, mix well and pour into crust. Bake at 500 degrees 10 minutes, then at 300 degrees 60 minutes more.

Serves 8–10

Mrs. Stephen C. Motsinger
STATE ROAD, NORTH CAROLINA

Caramel Cheesecake Custard

2/3 cup caramel sauce
8 ounces cream cheese,
    softened
1/2 cup sugar
1 teaspoon vanilla
6 eggs
2 cups milk

Pour sauce into buttered pan, 9 inches square and 1 1/2–2 inches deep. In a large bowl, beat cheese until smooth. Beat in sugar and vanilla, add eggs, 1 at a time, and beat until smooth at medium speed. Blend in milk at a very low speed. Carefully pour over top of caramel mixture. Put pan in center of a large pan filled with 1/2–3/4 inch boiling water. Bake at 350 degrees 50 minutes until center is set. Cool on rack, loosen from pan and invert onto rimmed serving dish. Chill.

Serves 8
Easy
Must do ahead

Mrs. Arne G. Sandberg
CODY, WYOMING

My English Plum Pudding

PUDDING:

    1 cup flour
    1 teaspoon soda
    1 teaspoon salt
    1 teaspoon cinnamon
    1/4 teaspoon nutmeg
    3/4 teaspoon mace
*1 1/2 cups raisins, finely
    chopped*
1 1/2 cups currants, plumped
    3/4 cup finely cut citron
    *3/4 cup candied orange and
    lemon peel, finely
    chopped*
    1/2 cup walnuts, chopped
1 1/2 cups soft bread crumbs
    *2 cups (1/2 pound) ground
    suet*
    1 cup brown sugar
    3 eggs, beaten
    6 Tablespoons currant jelly
    1/4 cup brandy or sherry

HARD SAUCE:

    1 cup butter, softened
    3 cups confectioners' sugar
    4 teaspoons vanilla
    1 egg, optional

"Served after a six-hour steam."

Sift dry ingredients, then mix in remaining ingredients. Pour into well-greased, 2-quart mold or two 1-quart molds. Steam 6 hours.

For sauce, mix all ingredients. Add 1 egg for fluffy hard sauce. Serve sauce with piping hot pudding.

Serves 16

Agnes Vastine
CHARLES CITY, IOWA

Mother's Date Pudding

4 eggs
2 cups sugar
2 cups dates, pitted and
    chopped
2 cups walnuts, chopped
1 Tablespoon flour
1 teaspoon baking powder

Beat eggs until light and lemon-colored. Add sugar and continue beating a few minutes. Stir in remaining ingredients. Grease and flour two 9-inch pie pans. Divide date mixture between pans and bake at 275 degrees about 40 minutes. Pudding will fall and be soft and chewy in the middle with a crunchy top. Serve with whipped cream or ice cream.

Serves 8
Easy

Dorothy H. Dines
DENVER, COLORADO

Mother's Carrot Pudding

PUDDING:

1/2 cup butter or margarine
1 1/4 cups sugar
2 eggs, separated
1 1/2 cups grated carrots
1 1/2 cups flour
1 teaspoon baking powder
1/2 teaspoon baking soda
1/2 teaspoon salt
1/4 cup milk
1 teaspoon lemon extract

GOLDEN PUDDING SAUCE:

4 Tablespoons flour
1 cup sugar
1/4 teaspoon salt
3 Tablespoons grated carrot
2 Tablespoons lemon juice
2 Tablespoons orange juice
4 Tablespoons butter
1 1/2 cups boiling water

Cream butter and sugar. Beat egg yolks into creamed mixture. Add grated carrots and sifted dry ingredients alternately with milk. Add lemon extract and fold in stiffly beaten egg whites. Place in well greased, 8-inch square pan. Bake at 350 degrees 55 minutes.

For sauce, mix flour and sugar. Add all ingredients but water and mix well. Add water and cook until thick and clear. Serve warm over pudding.

Serves 8–10
May do ahead

Celeste B. Shepard
CODY, WYOMING

Steamed Pear Pudding

1/2 cup shortening
1/2 cup sugar
1/2 cup honey
1/2 teaspoon vanilla
1/2 teaspoon lemon extract
2 eggs
1 3/4 cups flour, sifted before
    measuring
1 teaspoon baking powder
1 teaspoon salt
1/2 teaspoon nutmeg
1 teaspoon cinnamon
1/4 teaspoon ground cloves
2 cups fresh pears, peeled,
    cored and chopped
1 Tablespoon lemon juice
1 cup chopped nuts

Cream together shortening, sugar and honey. Add flavorings. Add eggs, 1 at a time, beating well after each addition. Sift flour with baking powder, salt and spices. Sprinkle pears with lemon juice. Add to creamed mixture alternately with dry ingredients. Add nuts. Pour into greased, 3-pound mold or two 1 1/2-pound molds. Cover tightly and steam 2–2 1/2 hours until done. Serve warm with spiced or plain hard sauce or whipped cream.

Serves 10–12

William E. Weiss
CODY, WYOMING

Lemon Mystery Pudding

1 cup sugar
1/4 cup flour
1/8 teaspoon salt
2 Tablespoons butter,
    melted
Juice from 2 lemons
Grated rind from
    1 lemon
3 eggs, separated
1 1/2 cups milk

Mix sugar, flour and salt. Stir in butter, lemon juice and rind, well-beaten egg yolks and milk. Beat until smooth. Fold in stiffly beaten egg whites. Turn mixture into 8 greased custard cups or greased 1 1/2-quart baking dish. Set in pan of hot water. Bake at 350 degrees 45 minutes.

Serves 8
Easy

Miriam Sample
BILLINGS, MONTANA

Marmalade Souffle

"This souffle does not flop and stays risen for ages."

3 heaping Tablespoons firm
   marmalade or jam
1 Tablespoon brandy
5 egg whites
   Pinch salt
1/2 cup sugar
1/2 cup slivered almonds,
   toasted

Stir marmalade and brandy until well mixed. Beat egg whites with salt until stiff and whisk in sugar. Fold marmalade mixture into whites. Pile mixture into buttered and sugared souffle dish. Sprinkle with almonds and bake at 400 degrees about 15 minutes or until top is brown. May serve with Grand Marnier Sauce (see index).

Serves 3–4

Mrs. Simon Hornby
LONDON, ENGLAND

Apricot or Prune Souffle

6 egg whites
1/4 cup sugar
1 cup pureed apricots or
   prunes (or dried apricots
   cooked with 1 cup sugar
   and pureed)
   Whipped cream
   Shaved almonds, toasted

Beat whites until stiff, gradually adding sugar. Fold in puree, stirring with large fork or flat wire whip. Butter and sprinkle with sugar a 2 1/2-quart double-boiler insert and turn in mixture. Butter the lid also. Cover and cook over gently boiling water 1 hour. Turn out on serving platter. Garnish with ring of whipped cream and shaved almonds or pass cream and coat souffle with almonds. Souffle can be kept waiting up to 40 minutes after cooking.

Serves 4–6
Easy

Miriam Sample
BILLINGS, MONTANA

Cold Lime Souffle with Berry Sauce

SOUFFLE:

1 envelope plain gelatin
1/4 cup cold water
6 eggs, separated
1 cup sugar
1 teaspoon grated lime rind
Juice of 2 medium limes
2–3 drops green food coloring
Pinch salt
1 cup heavy cream, whipped

BERRY SAUCE:

2 cups frozen raspberries or
strawberries, defrosted (or
3 cups fresh berries and
1/2 cup sugar)

"Attractive, light and refreshing."

Soak gelatin in water 5 minutes. Beat egg yolks with 1/2 cup sugar over boiling water until thickened. Add gelatin, rind, juice and food coloring and cook 5 minutes more, stirring constantly until thick and creamy. Cool thoroughly. Beat whites with salt until stiff and fold into gelatin mixture with second 1/2 cup of sugar. Fold in cream, pour into souffle dish and chill 4–5 hours or overnight.

For sauce, puree berries and strain. Serve cold. For fresh berries, puree with sugar. Serve souffle with sauce.

Serves 8–10
Must do ahead

Joan S. Richardson
LAKE FOREST, ILLINOIS

Peppermint Bavarian Cream

1 package unflavored gelatin
2 cups milk
1/2 teaspoon salt
1/4 pound red and white
peppermint candy,
crushed
1 cup heavy cream, whipped

Dissolve gelatin in 1/4 cup milk. Scald remaining milk in double-boiler insert with salt and candy, until candy melts. Remove from heat and stir in gelatin mixture. Cool. When partly thickened, fold in cream. Pour into chilled mold. Chill several hours or overnight.

Serves 4
Easy
Must do ahead

Katie Downes
ENGLEWOOD, NEW JERSEY

Guthrie Theatre Matinee Mousse

"This recipe takes just a few minutes to prepare, yet is very elegant."

6 ounces semi-sweet
  chocolate
2 eggs
2 Tablespoons strong hot
  coffee
1 Tablespoon Grand
  Marnier or rum
1/2 cup hot whole milk
1 cup heavy cream, slightly
  sweetened and whipped

Combine all but cream in blender and mix at high speed 2 minutes. Pour into small souffle dish or 4 to 6 mousse cups and chill until set. Garnish with whipped cream.

Serves 4
Easy
Must do ahead

Nancy How Girouard
GOLDEN VALLEY, MINNESOTA

Silver Lemon Mousse

CRUST:

2 cups fine graham
  cracker crumbs
2 Tablespoons melted
  butter
1 Tablespoon water

MOUSSE:

8 large eggs, separated
1/4 teaspoon salt
1 1/2 cups sugar
  Juice and grated rind of
  3 lemons
2 Tablespoons unflavored
  gelatin
1/3 cup cold water
1/2 cup boiling water
2 cups heavy cream,
  whipped
2 Tablespoons sugar

Mix crumbs with butter and water. Pat firmly into bottom and up sides of 10-inch spring form pan. Chill. Beat egg yolks with salt and 3/4 cup sugar until quite thick. Cook in double-boiler insert until thick, stirring well. Add lemon juice and cook 5 minutes longer. Soak gelatin in cold water 5 minutes. Add boiling water and stir until gelatin dissolves. Mix gelatin with yolk mixture. Remove from heat and cool unlit mixture starts to set. To speed cooling process, put insert in a pan of ice cubes and water, stirring often. Beat whites until frothy and add 3/4 cup sugar, 2 Tablespoons at a time. Continue beating until stiff peaks form. Set aside. With same beaters, beat yolk mixture 1 minute. Quickly fold egg whites, lemon rind and cooked mixture together and pour into prepared pan. Refrigerate. Before serving, whip cream with remaining sugar. Place pan right-side-up on serving plate and remove ring. Cover top and side with whipped cream.

Serves 16–20
Time-consuming
Must do ahead

Margot Belden Todd
CODY, WYOMING

Coffee Mousse

2 cups heavy cream
1/4 cup sugar
   4 egg whites, at room
     temperature
   2 Tablespoons instant coffee
   3 Tablespoons boiling water
   2 Tablespoons cold water
   1 envelope gelatin
     Grated sweet chocolate,
     optional

Whip cream until stiff, adding sugar gradually. Whip egg whites until stiff and fold into cream. Dissolve coffee in a small bowl with boiling water. Add cold water to gelatin, stir and quickly add to coffee. Stir until dissolved. Fold into cream mixture, 1 Tablespoon at a time. Pour into serving dish and refrigerate. Top with sweet chocolate.

Serves 6–8
Easy
Must do ahead

Mrs. C. H. Kibbee
SHERIDAN, WYOMING

Marron Mousse

1/4 cup water
2/3 cup sugar
   6 egg yolks
   1 cup marrons in syrup of
     vanilla, chopped
   1 teaspoon brandy
   2 cups heavy cream, whipped

Boil water and sugar together 5 minutes to make a syrup. Beat yolks and pour in syrup, beating constantly. Cook over hot water in double boiler until thick. Remove from water and beat until cool. Fold in marrons, brandy and cream and freeze. Serve frozen.

Serves 6
Easy
Must be frozen

Margo W. Stratfford
CODY, WYOMING

Arctic Mousse

1 1/4 cup graham cracker
    crumbs
1/4 cup sugar
1/3 cup margarine, melted
  1 (7-ounce) jar
    marshmallow cream
  2 (1-ounce) squares
    unsweetened chocolate,
    melted
  1 teaspoon vanilla
  2 Tablespoons milk
  1 cup heavy cream,
    whipped

Reserve a small portion of crumbs and combine remainder with sugar and margarine. Press onto bottom of 8-inch square pan. Mix next 3 ingredients. Gradually add milk, blending until smooth. Fold in cream. Pour over crust, sprinkle with reserved crumbs and freeze. Remove from freezer 10 minutes before serving.

Serves 6
Easy   *Anita Renee DiGiorgio*
Must be frozen   ELLICOTT CITY, MARYLAND

Corn Flake Ring

1/2 regular-sized box Corn
    Flakes (or 1/3 large box)
  1 cup pecans, chopped
  1 cup butter
  2 cups packed dark brown
    sugar
    Vanilla ice cream
    Butterscotch sauce,
    optional (see index)

Heavily butter ring mold. Place in freezer until very cold (may be done the night before). In a large mixing bowl, combine flakes and pecans. Bring butter and sugar to a slow boil over medium heat, pour mixture over flakes and pecans and mix together until flakes are evenly covered. Pack into mold. After 10 minutes, run a spatula around the edge, then invert mold on serving plate. Serve with vanilla ice cream and butterscotch sauce. Ring can be made in the morning. Refrigerate until right before serving.

Serves 8
Easy   *Mrs. Byron Ramsing*
May do ahead   CODY, WYOMING

Inez's Lemon Sherbet

"My grandmother's favorite summer dessert."

3/4 cup sugar
Dash salt
1 cup water
1/2 cup half and half
1/2 cup lemon juice
1/4 cup sugar
2 egg whites

Combine sugar, salt and water in saucepan. Cook over medium high heat 5 minutes. Cool. Add cream, then juice. Freeze firm in freezer tray. Break frozen mixture into chunks in chilled bowl. Beat with mixer until fluffy and smooth. Beat whites until very stiff, adding sugar. Fold into lemon mixture. Return to freezer tray and freeze firm.

Serves 6
Easy
Must be frozen

Betsy McGee
CODY, WYOMING

Strawberry Bombe

1 cup heavy cream
3/4 cup confectioners' sugar
1 cup strawberry pulp and juice, frozen or fresh
1 Tablespoon kirsch
1/2 cup shaved almonds, toasted
2 teaspoons vanilla
2 cups strawberry sherbet or ice

Whip cream, adding sugar last. Mix pulp, cream, kirsch, almonds and vanilla. Line a melon mold with strawberry sherbet, distributing evenly around sides and bottom. Fill cavity with strawberry mixture. Cover mold and freeze. Unmold just before serving and garnish with fresh whole strawberries.

Serves 10
Easy
Must be frozen

Margot Belden Todd
CODY, WYOMING

Selling Court's Strawberry Squares

"This was served by my friend at Selling Court, Faversham, England."

1 cup flour
1/4 cup brown sugar
3/4 cup chopped walnuts
1/2 cup butter, melted
2 egg whites
1 cup sugar
2 cups sliced fresh
   strawberries or 2 cups
   frozen berries, partially
   thawed and drained and
   sugar reduced to 2/3 cup
2 Tablespoons lemon juice
1 cup heavy cream, whipped
1/2 cup confectioners' sugar
1/2 teaspoon vanilla

Combine flour, brown sugar, nuts and butter. Spread evenly in 13 × 9 × 2-inch pan. Bake crumbs at 300 degrees about 20 minutes, stirring occasionally. Combine egg whites, sugar, berries and juice in large bowl. Beat 10 minutes. Whip cream with confectioners' sugar and vanilla until very stiff, then fold into berry mixture. Spoon over cooled crumbs. Freeze overnight and remove 5 minutes before serving.

Serves 12–20
Easy   *Katharine McMillan*
Must be frozen   INDIO, CALIFORNIA

Frozen Fruit Salad

2 cups sugar
1 cup water
2 (10-ounce) packages
   frozen strawberries,
   thawed, with juice
1 large can apricots,
   drained, cut up
1 large can crushed
   pineapple, with juice
4 bananas, cut up

Boil sugar and water to soft ball stage. Add syrup, while warm, to all fruit except bananas. Add bananas. Freeze.

Serves 12–15
Easy   *Nita Winterink*
Must do ahead   CHARLES CITY, IOWA

Enchanted Compote

COMPOTE:

2 cups raspberries
1/2 pound seedless grapes
9 peaches, peeled and thinly
 sliced
1/2 cup sugar

TOPPING:

1 cup heavy cream
1 Tablespoon sugar
2 Tablespoons maraschino
 liqueur
1 ounce unsweetened
 chocolate, grated

Sprinkle fruit with sugar. Place in layers in 10 × 6 1/2-inch baking dish. Chill at least 30 minutes.

Just before serving, whip cream with sugar and add liqueur. Spread over fruit and sprinkle chocolate on top. Place under broiler close to heat for 1 minute or until chocolate starts to melt.

Serves 6
Easy   *Mrs. Chauncey Keep Hutchins*
Must do ahead   LAKE FOREST, ILLINOIS

Brandied Fruits

1 (1-pound, 13-ounce) can
 Bartlett pear halves
1 (17-ounce) jar whole figs
1 (1-pound, 13-ounce) can
 sliced pineapple
1 (1-pound, 13-ounce) can
 cling peach halves
6 maraschino cherries
4 cups sugar
2 cups brandy
2 cinnamon sticks

"Makes a colorful gift in an old-fashioned glass canning jar."

Drain fruits and reserve syrups. Measure 6 cups combined syrups into saucepan. Add sugar, bring to a boil and cook 3 minutes. Cool. Add brandy and cinnamon. Pour over fruits in large glass or earthen jar. Cover and refrigerate at least 1 week. Fruit will keep several weeks. Serve with vanilla ice cream or whipped cream over fresh slices of angel food cake.

Yields 4 quarts
Easy   *Mildred Cowgill*
Must do ahead   CODY, WYOMING

Sugared Oranges with Grand Marnier

18 oranges
1/3 cup sugar, to taste
1 cup Grand Marnier

Carefully peel oranges, removing all white membrane. Cut horizontally into 3/8-inch slices. Layer in large, deep bowl, sprinkling each layer with a little sugar and some Grand Marnier. Pour remaining liqueur over top. Cover and refrigerate several hours.

Serves 12
Must do ahead

Miner's Delight Inn
ATLANTIC CITY, WYOMING

Mince Meat

2 pounds lean beef neck,
    chuck or stew meat or
    wild meat
1 cup meat juices
1/2 pound kidney suet,
    ground
1 pound currants
2 pounds raisins
4 pounds apples, chopped
1 1/2 pounds mixed candied
    fruit
2 pounds brown sugar
1 cup molasses
1 cup cherry or strawberry
    jam
2 teaspoons salt
1 teaspoon nutmeg
1 Tablespoon cinnamon
1 Tablespoon allspice
2 quarts sweet cider or
    fruit juice
    Rum or brandy, optional

Boil, cool and shred meat. Add remaining ingredients substituting brandy or rum for some of the cider, if desired, to improve flavor. Mix together and let stand about 1 week before making into pies. May be frozen immediately.

Yields 7 quarts
May be frozen
Must do ahead

Sandy Ellis
CODY, WYOMING

Refrigerator "Ready" Pie Crust

"Keeps in refrigerator, ready for use, for weeks."

1 pound lard, at room
  temperature
5 1/2–6 cups flour
1 teaspoon salt
Cold water

Cut lard into flour and salt until cornmeal consistency. Pack into coffee can, cover tightly and refrigerate until needed. Use 1 1/4 cups of mixture for a 1-crust pie, working in 1–2 Tablespoons water. For a double crust, use 2 1/4 cups mix and 2–3 Tablespoons water. Dough will be soft, short and easy to handle.

Yields 8 single crusts
Easy
May do ahead

Peg Frisby
CODY, WYOMING

Vinegar Pie Crust

"Keeps in refrigerator, ready for use, for weeks."

1 egg
1 Tablespoon vinegar
1 Tablespoon brown
  sugar
Water
2 1/2 cups flour
3/4 teaspoon salt
1/4 teaspoon baking
  powder
8 ounces lard

Break egg into a 1-cup measuring cup and beat with a fork. Add vinegar and brown sugar and blend well. Add water to make 1/2 cup liquid. Mix flour, salt and baking powder, then cut in lard until consistency of cornmeal. Add liquid mixture and blend quickly. Form into a ball, wrap in waxed paper and refrigerate 1 hour before rolling out into crusts.

Yields 4–5 crusts
Must do ahead

Carolyn Depue
WICKENBURG, ARIZONA

Paper Bag Apple Pie

FILLING:

6–8 apples, peeled and sliced
1/2 cup sugar
2 Tablespoons flour
1 teaspoon nutmeg
2 Tablespoons lemon juice
1 (9-inch) unbaked pie
crust

TOPPING:

1/2 cup sugar
1/2 cup flour
1/2 cup butter

Mix filling ingredients and mound into crust-lined pan. Combine topping ingredients until cornmeal consistency. Sprinkle over apples. Place in brown paper bag, folding over open edges and fastening with paper clips. Bake at 425 degrees 1 hour. Oven must be completely preheated to avoid burning the bag.

Serves 6–8
Easy   *Gina Guy*
May be frozen   PORTLAND, OREGON

Sour Cream Apple Pie

3 cups sliced raw apples
1 1/4 cups sugar (may be part
brown sugar)
1 cup sour cream
3 Tablespoons flour
1/8 teaspoon cinnamon,
optional
1/8 teaspoon salt
1 egg, beaten
1 unbaked (9-inch) deep-
dish or (10-inch) shallow
crust
1 cup brown sugar
4 Tablespoons margarine,
melted
1/2 cup flour
1/4 teaspoon cinnamon

Mix together first 7 ingredients and pour into crust. Bake at 350 degrees 30 minutes. Combine last 4 ingredients and sprinkle on top. Continue baking another 30 minutes or until topping is dark golden brown. Serve at room temperature.

Serves 6–8
Easy   *Mrs. Felix Bedlan*
                                   FAIRBURY, NEBRASKA

Cher-Apple Pie

2 recipes pie pastry,
  uncooked
4 cups sugar, to taste
4 Tablespoons flour
1 teaspoon cinnamon
4 cups fresh or frozen pie
  cherries
4 cups pared and sliced tart
  pie apples
4 Tablespoons butter
  Thin confectioners' sugar
  glaze, optional

Line a 9 × 13-inch pan with 1/2 pastry. Combine sugar, flour and cinnamon and add to fruits. Place in pan and dot with butter. Top with a whole crust or make a lattice crust. Bake at 400 degrees 20 minutes, then at 350 degrees 1 hour. Pie is attractive with glaze and excellent served with vanilla ice cream.

Serves 15
Easy
May be frozen

Marjorie Messenger
CODY, WYOMING

Marble-Top Chocolate Rum Pie

1/2 cup sugar
1 envelope unflavored
  gelatin
  Dash salt
1 cup milk
2 eggs, separated
6 ounces semi-sweet
  chocolate bits
1/4 cup light rum
1/4 cup sugar
1 cup heavy cream
1 teaspoon vanilla
1 (9-inch) baked pastry crust

In a saucepan, combine sugar, gelatin and salt. Stir in milk and beaten egg yolks. Cook and stir over low heat until slightly thick. Remove from heat and add chocolate bits, stirring until melted. Add rum and chill until partially set. Beat whites until soft peaks form. Gradually add sugar, beating until stiff peaks form. Fold into chocolate mixture. Whip cream with vanilla. Layer whipped cream and chocolate mixture in pastry shell, ending with whipped cream. Gently swirl top to marble. Chill until firm.

Serves 6–8
Easy
Must do ahead

Mrs. C.V. Whitney
SARATOGA SPRINGS, NEW YORK

Lemon Chess Pie

"A Southern dessert."

1/2 cup butter, softened
1 1/2 cups sugar
1 Tablespoon cornmeal
4 medium eggs
1/3 cup fresh lemon juice
Grated rind of 1 lemon
1 (9-inch) unbaked pie
crust

Thoroughly cream butter and sugar. Mix in cornmeal and add eggs, beating well after each addition. Add other ingredients and fill crust. Bake at 350 degrees 30–40 minutes until filling is set. Let stand 10 minutes before cutting.

Serves 6
Easy

Jane Dominick
CODY, WYOMING

Helen's Lemon Pie

FILLING:

1 cup plus 2 Tablespoons
sugar
7 1/2 Tablespoons cornstarch
1/4 teaspoon salt
1 7/8 cups water
3 egg yolks, slightly beaten
2 Tablespoons butter
2 teaspoons grated lemon
rind
1/3 cup plus 2 teaspoons
lemon juice

MERINGUE:

3 egg whites, at room
temperature
Pinch salt
1/2 teaspoon baking powder
1/2 cup superfine sugar
1/2 teaspoon vanilla
1 (9-inch) baked pie crust

Combine sugar, cornstarch and salt in double-boiler insert, then stir in water. Cook over boiling water until thickened, stirring constantly. Cover and cook 15 minutes more. Stir a little hot mixture into yolks. Return to insert and cook 2 minutes, stirring constantly. Add butter and cool. Add lemon rind and juice.

For meringue, beat whites until frothy and add salt and baking powder, beating until stiff but not dry. Add sugar gradually, sprinkling over the surface and beating thoroughly after each addition. Add vanilla. Fill crust with lemon mixture and cover with meringue, making sure meringue touches crust at all points. Make attractive swirls in meringue. Bake at 325 degrees about 20 minutes until light golden brown. Cool before serving.

Serves 6–8
Must do ahead

Helen Audier
CODY, WYOMING

Peanut Butter Pie

4 ounces cream cheese,
  softened
1 cup confectioners' sugar
1/2 cup peanut butter
1/2 cup milk
8 ounces non-dairy
  whipped topping
1 (9-inch) baked pie crust,
  plain or graham cracker
1/4 cup chopped peanuts

Slightly beat cream cheese, beat in sugar and peanut butter and slowly add milk. Carefully fold into whipped topping. Pour into crust, top with peanuts and freeze. Remove from freezer several minutes before serving and top with chocolate shavings.

Serves 8
Easy
Must be frozen

Dorothy Marchezak
EXPORT, PENNSYLVANIA

Pumpkin Pecan Mousse Pie

"A very special light dessert."

2 envelopes unflavored
  gelatin
1/3 cup cold water
1 (8-ounce) can pumpkin
2 teaspoons cinnamon
3 teaspoons pumpkin pie
  spice
1 cup sugar
4 eggs, separated
1/2 cup dark rum
1 cup confectioners' sugar
2 cups whipping cream
1 cup heavy cream
20–30 pecan halves
1 (10-inch) baked pie
  crust

In a double-boiler insert, soak gelatin in water 5–10 minutes. Beat pumpkin, spices and sugar until smooth. Heat gelatin over boiling water until melted. Beat egg yolks, add to gelatin mixture and stir. Cook until mixture begins to thicken and bubbles around edges slightly. Add rum, stir, remove from heat and let cool until consistency of unbeaten egg white. Stir occasionally. Beat whites until soft peaks form, then add 1/2 confectioners' sugar and beat until stiff peaks form. Fold gelatin mixture into pumpkin mixture until smooth. Gently fold whites into pumpkin mixture. Whip creams to soft peaks and add remaining confectioners' sugar, beating until stiff peaks form. Gently fold whipped cream into pumpkin mixture. Spoon into pie shell and swirl top into an attractive, peaked design. Top with pecan halves in a circular design, around the outside edge and in the middle. Chill 3–6 hours before serving. Pie may also be served as a frozen mousse. Let thaw 15–30 minutes after removing from freezer.

Serves 12–14
May be frozen
Must do ahead

James Herman
CODY, WYOMING

Blueberry Torte

CRUST:

1 cup flour
1/2 cup finely chopped walnuts
1/4 cup firmly packed brown
    sugar
1/2 cup butter

FILLING:

1 cup confectioners' sugar
1/2 cup butter, softened
1/4 teaspoon vanilla
2 eggs, separated
1 (8-ounce) can blueberry
    pie filling
1 cup heavy cream,
    sweetened and whipped

Combine flour, nuts and brown sugar. Cut in butter until mixture resembles coarse crumbs. Grease 7 1/2 × 12-inch baking dish and press mixture evenly over bottom. Bake at 400 degrees 15 minutes. Cool and chill.

For filling, cream together sugar, butter, vanilla and egg yolks, working until smooth. Beat egg whites until stiff but not dry and fold into yolk mixture. Spread evenly over crust, then spread pie filling evenly over top. Spread whipped cream for final layer. Chill.

Serves 8–10
Must do ahead

Darlene McCarty
CODY, WYOMING

Appeltaart

"This traditional pie is served in Holland with a cup of coffee topped with whipped cream."

CRUST:

1 1/4 cups flour
1/4 cup butter, softened
1/2 cup sugar
1 egg, beaten

FILLING:

6–8 apples, peeled, cored
and thinly sliced
1 teaspoon vanilla
1/2 cup sugar
1/2 teaspoon cinnamon
Juice of 1 lemon
1 cup raisins

TOPPING:

3/4 cup flour
1/2 cup sugar
1/4 cup butter

Mix together crust ingredients. Shape into ball and roll out to fit into greased, floured 10-inch spring form pan, lining sides.

Mix filling ingredients and spread in pan.

For topping, cut together ingredients to consistency of coarse crumbs. Place in a thick layer over apple mixture. Bake at 325 degrees 1 1/4 hours.

Serves 8–10
May be frozen

Carlou Stubbs
TUCSON, ARIZONA

Boysenberry Cobbler

1/4 cup shortening
1 cup sugar
1/8 teaspoon salt
2 teaspoons baking powder
1 cup flour
1 cup milk
1 (8-ounce) can
boysenberries with juice

Cream shortening with 1/2 sugar until fluffy. Add sifted dry ingredients alternately with milk. Beat until smooth. Pour into greased 8-inch pan or glass dish. Sprinkle berries on top. Pour juice over all and sprinkle with sugar. Bake at 375 degrees 45 minutes. Serve warm with cream, whipped cream or ice cream. May substitute purple plums for boysenberries.

Serves 4–6
Easy

Paddy Chase
CODY, WYOMING

Chocolate Roll

CAKE:

5 eggs, separated
1 cup sugar
1/4 cup flour
1/4 cup cocoa
1 teaspoon vanilla
1 cup whipping cream
1–2 Tablespoons sugar,
   to taste

CHOCOLATE SAUCE:

2 ounces unsweetened
   chocolate
2 Tablespoons butter
1 1/2 cups sugar
1/2 cup half and half

Grease a rimmed baking pan and line with greased waxed paper. Beat yolks with sugar 6 minutes or until light and fluffy. Mix flour and cocoa and add to yolks. Beat whites until stiff, adding vanilla last. Fold in whites. Spread evenly over prepared pan. Bake at 350 degrees 16–18 minutes. Cool 10 minutes, then turn out on waxed paper coated with confectioners' sugar. Remove waxed paper from cake and cover with damp cloth until thoroughly cooled. Whip cream, sweetened to taste, and spread over cake. Roll up like a jelly roll.

For sauce, melt chocolate and butter in double-boiler insert and add sugar and cream. Stir and cook about 10 minutes until well blended. Keep hot and serve over roll.

Serves 8–10
May be frozen

Elizabeth Frost
CODY, WYOMING

Pumpkin Roll

CAKE:

3 eggs, at room
   temperature
1 cup sugar
2/3 cup pumpkin pulp
1 teaspoon lemon juice
3/4 cup flour
2 teaspoons cinnamon
1 teaspoon ginger
1/2 teaspoon nutmeg
1/2 teaspoon salt
1 teaspoon baking powder

FILLING:

8 ounces cream cheese,
   softened
1/4 cup butter, softened
1 teaspoon vanilla
1 cup confectioners' sugar

Beat eggs 5 minutes, then beat in sugar. Stir in pumpkin and lemon juice. Sift dry ingredients and add to egg mixture. Grease and flour a jelly-roll pan (15 1/2 × 11 1/2 inches) and pour in batter evenly. Bake at 375 degrees 10–15 minutes. Turn out onto dish towel sprinkled with confectioners' sugar. Fold towel around cake and roll up. Refrigerate until cold.

For filling, cream all ingredients together. Unroll chilled cake and spread with filling using wet knife. Roll up, wrap in foil and freeze. Slice and serve while still frozen.

Serves 12
Must be frozen

Jean Hiatt
WHITTIER, CALIFORNIA

Nut Roll

"Sweet, like candy, but very light."

6 large eggs, separated
1/4 teaspoon salt
3/4 cup sugar
1 3/4 cups finely ground
 mixture of pecans,
 walnuts and peanuts
1 teaspoon baking powder
1/4 cup confectioners' sugar
2 cups heavy cream
2 Tablespoons sugar

Line a jelly-roll pan (15 1/2 × 10 1/2 inches) with waxed paper and grease the paper. Beat egg yolks with salt and sugar until thick and fluffy. Mix nuts and baking powder and fold into yolk mixture. Fold in stiffly beaten whites. Spread evenly in prepared pan. Bake at 375 degrees 15–20 minutes until golden brown and springy to touch. Remove from oven, cover with a cloth wrung out in cold water and refrigerate 1 hour. Loosen cake from pan, turn out on waxed paper dusted with confectioners' sugar and peel waxed paper off the top. Whip cream with sugar until very stiff and spread over nut cake. Roll up like a jelly roll, using waxed paper as a cover. Roll in damp cloth and refrigerate until serving.

Serves 10–12
Must do ahead

Margot Belden Todd
Cody, Wyoming

Almond Torte

"This recipe came with me from Germany where it has been in my family for generations."

CAKE:

3 Tablespoons bread
crumbs
12 eggs, separated, at room
temperature
1 Tablespoon rum,
optional
Grated rind and juice of
1 lemon
1 1/2 cups superfine sugar
2 cups ground almonds
1 Tablespoon flour

FILLING:

1/2 cup butter, softened
1/2 cup sugar
1 egg
4 ounces semi-sweet
chocolate, melted

TOPPING:

1 teaspoon instant coffee
2 cups heavy cream
2 Tablespoons sugar

DECORATION:

4 Tablespoons ground or
finely sliced almonds,
or half of each
Chocolate flakes

Grease a 10-inch springform pan and sprinkle with bread crumbs. Beat egg whites until very stiff. Mix yolks with rum, rind, juice and sugar, beating until foamy. Stir in almonds and flour until well blended, then fold in beaten whites and pour into prepared pan. Bake at 325 degrees 1 hour on middle oven rack. Cool cake on rack, remove ring and transfer to serving plate. Slice cake into 2 layers, using a thin piece of cardboard to lift off top half.

Beat filling ingredients to soft consistency, adding a little water if needed. Spread filling evenly over bottom and carefully replace top. This much may be done a day ahead and the cake refrigerated.

Make topping an hour or so before serving. Dissolve coffee in very little hot water, then cool. Start beating cream and gradually add coffee and sugar, beating until stiff. Cover top and sides of cake with topping. Decorate by sprinkling almonds and chocolate flakes on top and sides.

Serves 12
Must do ahead

Annaliese Oberreit
TETON VILLAGE, WYOMING

Applesauce Cake

1/2 cup butter or margarine,
    softened
1 cup sugar
1 egg, beaten
1 teaspoon cinnamon
1/4–1 teaspoon cloves, to taste
1 teaspoon nutmeg
1/2 teaspoon salt
1 teaspsoon baking soda
1 1/2 cups applesauce
1 cup each raisins and
    nuts, optional
2 cups flour

Cream butter and sugar. Add egg, spices and salt. Dissolve soda in a little warm water and beat into applesauce. Dredge raisins and nuts in flour. Combine and bake in tube pan at 350 degrees 45–60 minutes.

Serves 12
Easy
May be frozen

Mrs. Bart Rea
CASPER, WYOMING

Carrot Cake with Cream Cheese Icing

CAKE:

2 cups flour
2 teaspoons baking powder
1 1/2 teaspoons baking soda
1 1/2 teaspoons salt
2 teaspoons cinnamon
2 cups sugar
1 1/2 cups oil
4 eggs
2 cups grated carrots
1 (8 1/2-ounce) can
    crushed pineapple,
    drained
1 cup chopped nuts

Sift together first 5 ingredients. Combine sugar, oil and eggs and mix well with dry ingredients. Add carrots, pineapple and nuts. Bake in 9 × 13-inch pan or three 9-inch layer pans at 350 degrees 35–40 minutes. Cool. Zucchini may be substituted for carrots.

For icing, cream first 3 ingredients, then beat in sugar. Cake should be completely cool before icing.

Serves 12–15
Easy
May be frozen

Marilyn J. Miller
CODY, WYOMING

ICING:

1/2 cup butter, softened
8 ounces cream cheese
    softened
1 teaspoon vanilla
1 pound confectioners'
    sugar

Buffalo Bill and the Wild West Show cast members. *Courtesy of Buffalo Bill Historical Center, Cody, WY; P.6.550*

Hungarian Date Cake

1 teaspoon baking soda
1 cup chopped dates
1 1/4 cups boiling water
3/4 cup shortening
1 1/2 cups sugar
2 eggs
1 teaspoon vanilla
1 1/2 cups flour
1 teaspoon cinnamon
1/2 teaspoon salt
1/2 cup chopped pecans
6 ounces semi-sweet
  chocolate chips

Sprinkle soda over dates. Pour boiling water over dates and let stand for 5–10 minutes until plump. Cream shortening and 1 cup sugar. Add eggs and vanilla. Sift together flour, cinnamon and salt. Add date mixture to creamed mixture alternately with dry ingredients. Pour into greased 9 × 13-inch pan. Combine nuts, chips and remaining sugar for topping and sprinkle over batter. Bake at 350 degrees 25–30 minutes.

Serves 16

Mrs. C.V. Whitney
SARATOGA SPRINGS, NEW YORK

Huckleberry Walnut Cream Cake with Lemon Frosting

CAKE:

1 1/2 cups heavy cream
2 teaspoons vanilla
3 eggs
1 1/2 cups flour
1 1/2 cups sugar
2 teaspoons baking powder
1/4 teaspoon salt
1 cup finely chopped
  walnuts
1 cup huckleberries

FROSTING:

1 cup butter, softened
3 cups confectioners' sugar
2 Tablespoons lemon juice
1 teaspoon vanilla
4 egg yolks

Beat cream with vanilla until stiff. Beat eggs until thick and add to cream. Fold in sifted dry ingredients. Fold in nuts and berries. Pour into 2 greased, floured 8-inch or 9-inch cake pans. Bake at 350 degrees 30 minutes. Cool 10 minutes and remove from pans.

For frosting, beat first 4 ingredients together. Beat in yolks, 1 at a time. Refrigerate about 10 minutes until thickened. Frost thoroughly cooled cake and decorate with candied violets. Refrigerate.

Serves 12
Must do ahead

Beth E. Briggs
SHELBY, MONTANA

Lemon Delight Cake

CAKE:

1 package lemon cake
  mix
4 eggs
1 cup orange juice
1/2 cup oil
1 package instant lemon
  pudding

GLAZE:

1 small can frozen
  orange juice
  concentrate, thawed
2 cups confectioners'
  sugar

Blend cake ingredients, then beat at medium speed for 2 minutes. Spread batter in greased, floured 10-inch tube pan. Bake at 350 degrees 45 minutes. If serving without glaze, cool in pan about 15 minutes, then remove from pan.

For glaze, mix juice and sugar. Poke holes in cake with a toothpick. Pour glaze over hot cake and leave in pan until cake cools and glaze is absorbed. Cake should age several hours to a day before serving.

Serves 12–16
Must do ahead

Mrs. Atlee W. Davis
BARTOW, FLORIDA

Pineapple Cake

"Travels well without crumbling."

CAKE:

2 cups sugar
2 cups flour
2 teaspoons baking soda
1 cup chopped walnuts
1 (20-ounce) can
  crushed pineapple
  with syrup

Mix cake ingredients well. Pour into greased 9 × 13-inch pan. Bake at 350 degrees about 40 minutes. Cool in pan.

Combine frosting ingredients and beat until fluffy. Spread on cooled cake.

Serves 15
Easy
May be frozen

Pamela Stockton
CODY, WYOMING

FROSTING:

8 ounces cream cheese,
  softened
1 1/2–2 cups confectioners'
  sugar
1/4 cup butter, softened
1 teaspoon vanilla

Praline Pecan Cake New Orleans

CAKE:

1 package yellow (2-layer)
    cake mix
1 small package instant
    vanilla pudding and pie
    filling mix
4 large eggs, at room
    temperature
1/2 cup oil
1/4 cup liquid brown sugar
3/4 cup praline liqueur
1/2 cup bits of brickle
1/2 cup chopped pecans

GLAZE:

2 cups sifted confectioners'
    sugar
2 Tablespoons butter,
    softened
3–6 Tablespoons praline
    liqueur

Blend cake mix and pudding in large bowl. Add eggs, oil, brown sugar and liqueur. Beat at low speed until thoroughly mixed, then at medium speed 3–4 minutes. Stir in brickle and pecans. Pour into well greased, 10-inch tube or bundt pan and bake at 350 degrees 45–50 minutes until tester comes out clean.

Combine sugar and butter in small bowl and beat, adding liqueur gradually. Cool cake on rack 10 minutes, remove from pan, then pour glaze over cake and garnish with a few pecans and brickle bits.

Serves 10–12
Easy

Roberta Byrd
DALLAS, TEXAS

Sunshine Sponge Cake

"Light and tender as a fluffy cloud."

1 cup sifted cake flour
7 egg yolks
1 cup plus 3 Tablespoons
  sugar
2 Tablespoons water
1 1/2 Tablespoons lemon juice
1 1/2 teaspoons grated lemon
  rind
7 egg whites, at room
  temperature
1/4 teaspoon salt
1/2 teaspoon cream of tartar
1/2 teaspoon vanilla

Sift flour twice more. Beat egg yolks with 1/2 cup sugar and all the water, beating until very thick and creamy. Add lemon juice slowly, beating constantly. Mix in rind with a fork. Add flour, stirring until just blended. Beat whites with salt until foamy. Add cream of tartar and beat until stiff enough to hold peaks. Add remaining sugar, 2 Tablespoons at a time, beating at high speed until stiff peaks form and adding vanilla last. Fold yolk mixture into whites. Bake at 350 degrees 45–50 minutes in large, ungreased tube pan. Cool at least an hour before removing from pan.

Serves 10–12

Elizabeth Phelps Mills
EDGAR, MONTANA

Yule Cake

1/2 cup shelled Brazil nuts
1/2 cup walnut halves
1 (7 1/2-ounce) package
  pitted dates
1/2 cup red maraschino
  cherries, drained
1/2 cup green maraschino
  cherries, drained
3/4 cup flour
3/4 cup sugar
1/2 teaspoon salt
1/2 teaspoon baking powder
1 teaspoon vanilla
3 eggs, well beaten
Brandy

Line a glass loaf pan with waxed paper. Place nuts and fruits in a bowl. Mix dry ingredients and sift over fruit mixture. Stir. Add vanilla to eggs and combine with fruit mixture. There will be mostly fruit and nuts, not much batter. Spread in prepared pan. Bake at 275 degrees 1 1/2 hours. Cool and wrap in foil. Drizzle with 2 teaspoons brandy each day for 3 days. Keep tightly wrapped and refrigerated at least a week before serving.

Serves 12
Easy
Must do ahead

Marilyn Montville
CODY, WYOMING

Truffle Cake

"For chocoholics."

2/3 cup butter, salted or
    unsalted
  1 (12-ounce) bag chocolate
    chips
1 1/2 teaspoons flour
1 1/2 teaspoons sugar
  1/4 teaspoon salt
    4 eggs, separated

Melt butter and chips in double-boiler insert. Add flour, sugar and salt and stir thoroughly. Beat in egg yolks, 1 at a time. Beat whites until stiff, then fold into yolk mixture carefully. Pour into a deep, greased, floured, 8-inch cake or spring form pan. Bake at 325 degrees about 40 minutes until tester comes out clean. The cake will rise high and then shrink during cooling. Cool 15 minutes before cutting. May top with whipped cream.

Serves 8
Easy

Nancy Fees
CODY, WYOMING

Chocolate Cake with Fudge Frosting

CAKE:

2 1/2 cups flour
  2 teaspoons soda
1/2 teaspoon salt
  1 Tablespoon vinegar
  1 cup milk
  1 cup margarine, softened
  2 cups sugar
  2 eggs
1/2 cup cocoa
  1 cup hot water
  1 teaspoon vanilla

Sift together flour, soda and salt. Stir vinegar into milk and set aside. Cream margarine, adding sugar gradually. Add eggs and blend in cocoa. Add flour mixture alternately with milk and vinegar, mixing well. Add hot water and vanilla. Batter will be thin. Pour into greased, floured 9 × 13-inch pan or two 8-inch cake pans. Bake at 350 degrees 40–45 minutes.

For frosting, combine all but vanilla in saucepan and boil 2 minutes. Add vanilla and beat until thick enough to spread. When making a layer cake, whip 1 cup heavy cream with 2 Tablespoons sugar and spread between layers. Use frosting for top and sides.

FROSTING:

  1 ounce chocolate or
    2 Tablespoons cocoa
  1 cup sugar
1/3 cup milk
1/4 cup margarine
1/4 teaspoon salt
  1 teaspoon vanilla

Serves 10–14
May be frozen

Helen Helms
CODY, WYOMING

Chocolate Fudge-Sundae Cake

"This is a very rich cake with fudge sauce on the bottom."

CAKE:

1 cup all-purpose flour
2 teaspoons baking powder
1/2 teaspoon salt
2 Tablespoons cocoa
2/3 cup sugar
1/2 cup milk
2 Tablespoons butter,
    melted
1/2 cup chopped walnuts
1 teaspoon vanilla

TOPPING:

1 cup brown sugar
3 Tablespoons cocoa
1/4 teaspoon salt
1 1/4 cups boiling water
1 1/2 cups heavy cream,
    whipped

For cake, sift together dry ingredients. Add milk and butter and mix well. Add nuts and vanilla and mix again. Pour into greased 9-inch square pan and set aside.

For topping, mix sugar, cocoa and salt and sprinkle onto cake batter. Pour boiling water over the back of a spoon onto topping mixture, taking care not to disturb topping. Do not stir. Bake at 350 degrees 40–45 minutes. Serve warm or cold and topped with whipped cream.

Serves 12–16
Easy

James Herman
CODY, WYOMING

Chocolate-Zucchini Cake

2 eggs
1 3/4 cups sugar
1 cup buttermilk
1/2 cup oil
1 teaspoon vanilla
4 Tablespoons cocoa
1/2 teaspoon baking powder
1 teaspoon soda
1 teaspoon salt
2 1/2 cups flour
1 package instant vanilla
    pudding
2 cups finely grated
    zucchini
1 cup mini-chocolate chips
1/2–1 cup nuts, optional

Cream together first 5 ingredients. Sift together next 5 ingredients and add to creamed mixture. Add pudding and zucchini, mixing well. Pour into greased, floured 9 × 13-inch pan and sprinkle chips and nuts on top. Bake at 325 degrees 40–45 minutes until toothpick comes out clean.

Serves 14–16
Easy
May be frozen

L. Maxinne Hyatt
HYATTVILLE, WYOMING

Sour Cream Chocolate Cake

CAKE:

2 cups all-purpose flour
2 cups sugar
1 cup water
3/4 cup sour cream
1/4 cup butter, softened
1 1/4 teaspoons baking soda
1 teaspoon salt
1 teaspoon vanilla
1/2 teaspoon baking powder
2 eggs
4 ounces unsweetened
  baking chocolate,
  melted

In a large bowl, beat cake ingredients 30 seconds at low speed, scraping sides of the bowl constantly. Then beat 3 minutes at high speed. Pour into greased, floured cake pans, either three 8-inch or two 9-inch. Bake at 350 degrees 20–25 minutes, remove and cool on rack.

For frosting, melt butter and chocolate in double-boiler insert over barely simmering water. Remove from heat and cool. Add sugar, then blend in sour cream and vanilla, beating until smooth.

Serves 12
Easy

Kelly Howie
BIG HORN, WYOMING

FROSTING:

1/2 cup butter
4 ounces unsweetened
  baking chocolate
4 cups confectioners' sugar
1 cup sour cream
2 teaspoons vanilla

Sicilian Chocolate Cake

1/2 pound ricotta cheese
1 Tablespoon heavy cream
2 Tablespoons sugar
2 Tablespoons Triple Sec
1 ounce chocolate chipettes
1 frozen pound cake
1 package chocolate
  frosting mix

Beat ricotta, cream, sugar and liqueur until smooth. Add chipettes. Slice pound cake in 3 layers. Spread ricotta mixture on 2 layers and top with third layer. Spread chocolate frosting on top and sides. Refrigerate at least 6 hours before serving. Keeps well in refrigerator up to 4 days.

Serves 6–10
Easy
Must do ahead

Betsy McGee
CODY, WYOMING

Brown Sugar Pound Cake

"I hope you like the cake as much as I do."

CAKE:

1 cup butter, softened
1/2 cup vegetable shortening
5 eggs, at room
    temperature
1 pound plus 1 cup light
    brown sugar
3 1/2 cups flour
1/2 teaspoon baking powder
1 cup milk

Cream together butter and shortening. Add eggs, 1 at a time, creaming after each. Add sugar. Sift together flour and baking powder and add alternately with milk to sugar mixture. Bake at 325 degrees 1 1/4–1 1/2 hours in greased, floured tube pan.

For frosting, toast pecans in butter on thick broiler pan until brown. Let cool a little, then add sugar. Add enough milk to thin mixture to spreading consistency. Spread on top of cake. Some should drip down sides and center, but should not be spread anywhere except on top.

FROSTING:

1 cup chopped pecans
1/2 cup butter
1 pound confectioners'
    sugar
    Milk

Serves 12–15

Willard H. Scott, Jr.
NEW YORK, NEW YORK

Chocolate Pound Cake

"Easy to make and never fails to receive compliments."

3 1/3 cups flour, sifted
2 teaspoons instant coffee
1/2 cup cocoa
1/4 teaspoon salt
1/4 teaspoon baking powder
1 cup butter or margarine,
    softened
1/2 cup vegetable shortening
3 cups sugar
6 eggs
1 cup plus 2 Tablespoons
    milk
1 teaspoon vanilla

Combine flour, coffee, cocoa, salt and baking powder and set aside. Beat butter, shortening and sugar in large bowl until blended. Add eggs, 1 at a time, beating until fluffy. By hand, add dry ingredients alternately with milk and vanilla, beating after each addition until smooth. Pour into greased, floured 10-inch tube pan and bake in bottom third of oven at 325 degrees 1 hour and 20 minutes. Test for doneness. Cool on wire rack 10 minutes, remove from pan and let cool completely. Flavor improves if cake stands a day before serving.

Serves 18
Easy
Must do ahead

Carolyn Waller
CODY, WYOMING

Coconut Pound Cake

6 eggs, separated, at room
   temperature
1 cup shortening
1/2 cup margarine, softened
3 cups sugar
1/2 teaspoon almond extract
1/2 teaspoon coconut extract
3 cups sifted cake flour
1 cup milk
2 cups grated fresh
   coconut or canned
   flaked coconut

Beat egg yolks at high speed with shortening and margarine until well blended. Gradually add sugar, beating until light and fluffy. Add extracts and beat until blended. Add flour in thirds alternately with milk. Beat in coconut. Beat whites until stiff peaks form, fold into batter and pour into greased 10-inch tube pan. Bake at 300 degrees 2 hours until tester comes out clean. Cool on wire rack 15 minutes, remove from pan and cool. Wrap, refrigerate and serve next day. Make 12 cupcakes with remaining batter, baking at same temperature 45–60 minutes.

Serves 12–16
Must do ahead

Barbara M. Hassrick
WALPOLE, NEW HAMPSHIRE

Cream Cheese Pound Cake

1 1/2 cups butter, softened
3 cups sugar
8 ounces cream cheese,
   softened
6 eggs
3 cups flour
2 Tablespoons vanilla

Cream butter and sugar, then mix in cheese. Add eggs, 1 at a time, beating after each addition. Add flour and vanilla. Bake in greased, floured bundt or tube pan at 350 degrees about 1 hour and 15 minutes.

Serves 12
Easy

Linda T. Robinson
WEST YELLOWSTONE, MONTANA

Poppy Seed Pound Cake

1 cup butter, softened
2 3/4 cups sugar
6 eggs, separated
1/4 teaspoon baking soda
1/2 teaspoon salt
3 cups sifted flour
1 cup sour cream
2 Tablespoons poppy seeds
2 teaspoons vanilla
   Confectioners' sugar,
   optional

Cream butter and sugar. Add egg yolks, 1 at a time. Combine soda and salt with flour and sift twice more. Add flour mixture and sour cream alternately to butter and sugar mixture. Beat whites until stiff and fold into batter with poppy seeds and vanilla. Bake in greased, floured tube or bundt pan at 350 degrees 1 1/4–1 1/2 hours until tester comes out clean. Serve warm or, when cool, sprinkle with confectioners' sugar.

Serves 12–15
Easy

Ann Simpson
MCLEAN, VIRGINIA

Whipping Cream Pound Cake

3 cups sugar
1 cup butter, softened
6 eggs
1 teaspoon vanilla
3 cups sifted cake flour
1 cup heavy cream

Cream sugar and butter. Beat in eggs, 1 at a time. Add vanilla, then flour and cream alternately. Put into greased tube pan and place in cold oven. Turn oven to 325 degrees and bake 1 hour and 15 minutes.

Serves 10
Easy
May be frozen

Mrs. Atlee W. Davis
BARTOW, FLORIDA

Black Bottom Cupcakes

WHITE TOP:

8 ounces cream cheese,
  softened
1 egg
1/2 cup sugar
6 ounces chocolate chips

For top, combine first 3 ingredients and beat well. Stir in chips.

BLACK BOTTOM:

1 cup water
1/2 cup oil
1 Tablespoon vinegar
1 teaspoon vanilla
1 egg
1 1/2 cups flour
1 cup sugar
1 teaspoon baking soda
1/4 cup cocoa

For bottom, combine all ingredients and beat at least 2 minutes until cocoa is fully dissolved. To assemble cupcakes, measure 1 Tablespoon of black batter into paper-lined mini-muffin tins. Then top each with 1 teaspoon of white batter. Bake at 350 degrees 20 minutes.

Yields 48
Easy
May be frozen

Eloise L. Shaw
WORLAND, WYOMING

Fluffy White Frosting

1 2/3 cups sugar
1/2 cup water
1/3 teaspoon cream of tartar
1/2 cup egg whites at room
   temperature
1/2 teaspoon vanilla or
   almond extract

Combine sugar, water and cream of tartar in heavy saucepan and stir until smooth and sugar is dissolved. Cook 5–7 minutes over medium to high heat, without stirring, until syrup spins a fine thread from a metal spoon (240–270 degrees). Beat egg whites until very stiff, adding vanilla last. Beating at high speed, pour hot syrup into whites in a thin, continuous stream. Keep beating until mixture leaves a spoon almost clean and forms peaks. Note: for Creole Frosting, substitute 1 1/3 cups brown sugar for 1 2/3 cups white sugar.

**Yields enough for large tube
or 3-layer cake
Easy**

Margot Belden Todd
CODY, WYOMING

Minnehaha Frosting and Filling

"Wonderful with white cake."

1 1/2 cups sugar
1/2 teaspoon light corn syrup
2/3 cup boiling water
2 egg whites, stiffly beaten
1 teaspoon vanilla
6 figs, chopped
1/2 cup raisins, chopped
1/2 cup pecans or walnuts,
   chopped

Combine sugar, corn syrup and water. Bring quickly to a boil, stirring only until sugar is dissolved. Boil rapidly, without stirring, until a small amount of syrup forms a soft ball in cold water. Pour syrup in a fine stream over egg whites, beating constantly. Add vanilla and continue beating 10–15 minutes until frosting is cool and of spreading consistency. For filling, add enough frosting to fruit and nuts to make a filling that will spread easily. A little of the fruit and nuts may also be used with the frosting.

**Yields enough for
1 layer cake**

Mrs. Milward L. Simpson
CODY, WYOMING

Apple Brownies

1/2 cup butter, softened
1 cup sugar
1 egg, beaten
2 apples, peeled, cored and chopped
1/2 cup chopped pecans
1 cup flour
1/2 teaspoon soda
1/2 teaspoon baking powder
1/2 teaspoon cinnamon

Cream butter and sugar, beat in egg, then mix in apples and pecans. Sift dry ingredients and work into first mixture. Pour into buttered, 8 × 8-inch baking dish and bake at 350 degrees 40 minutes.

Yields 12–16

Mrs. Arnold H. Rohlfing
DARIEN, CONNECTICUT

My Mother's Brownies

BROWNIES:

1 cup butter or margarine, softened
2 cups sugar
1/2 teaspoon salt
4 eggs
4 ounces unsweetened chocolate
1 cup flour
1 cup chopped pecans or walnuts

ICING:

2 ounces unsweetened chocolate
1/2 cup firmly packed light brown sugar
1/4 cup water
1/4 teaspoon salt
2–3 Tablespoons butter or margarine
1 teaspoon vanilla
1 1/2–2 cups confectioners' sugar

Beat butter, sugar and salt together. Add eggs, 1 at a time, mixing well after each addition. Melt chocolate in double-boiler insert, add to butter mixture and blend well. Add flour and nuts. Pour into 2 greased, floured 8 × 8-inch baking pans and bake at 350 degrees 30–40 minutes. (They will appear undercooked, but harden as they cool.) Cool about 10 minutes, then loosen from sides of pans and turn onto waxed paper.

For icing, melt chocolate in double-boiler insert. Add sugar, water and salt. Slowly bring to a boil, boil 1 minute and remove from heat. Add butter, vanilla and confectioners' sugar until icing is of spreading consistency. If too stiff, add a few drops of hot water. Spread icing over brownies.

Yields 24

Jane Dominick
CODY, WYOMING

Cowboy Bars

2 cups brown sugar
3 cups flour
1/2 teaspoon salt
1 teaspoon soda dissolved
  in 1 cup hot water
1 teaspoon cinnamon
1 teaspoon baking powder
2 eggs, beaten
1 cup oil
1 cup raisins
1/2 cup chopped walnuts,
  optional
1 cup confectioners' sugar

Without stirring, put all ingredients but last 2 in a bowl. Mix lightly and spread in greased, floured 17 × 11-inch pan. Bake at 350–375 degrees 15–20 minutes. Glaze with thin layer of confectioners' sugar that has been thinned with enough water to spreading consistency. Cut in squares.

Yields 36–48
Easy   *Mrs. Leo N. Chase*
May be frozen   Jackson, Wyoming

Oatmeal Bars

BARS:

1 cup quick oats
1 1/2 cups boiling water
1/2 cup margarine
1 cup brown sugar
1 cup sugar
2 eggs
1 1/2 cups flour
1 teaspoon soda
1/2 teaspoon salt

Mix oats, water and margarine and let stand 20 minutes. Cream together sugars and eggs and add to oat mixture. Stir in flour, soda and salt, then spread in greased jelly-roll pan and bake at 350 degrees 25 minutes.

For topping, boil sugar, cream and margarine 1 1/2 minutes, stir in nuts and coconut and spread on bars.

Yields 49   *Mrs. Spike Van Cleve*
Easy   Big Timber, Montana

TOPPING:

1 cup brown sugar
4 Tablespoons cream
6 Tablespoons margarine
1/2 cup chopped nuts
1/2 cup shredded coconut

7-Sin Bars

1/2 cup butter
1 teaspoon vanilla
1 cup graham cracker
  crumbs
1 cup shredded coconut
1 (6-ounce) package
  semi-sweet chocolate
  chips
1 (6-ounce) package
  butterscotch chips
1 can sweetened condensed
  milk
1 cup chopped pecans

Melt butter in 9 × 12-inch baking pan. Stir in vanilla. Sprinkle crumbs into pan, then sprinkle in coconut and both kinds of chips. Pour milk over all and top with pecans. Bake at 350 degrees 25 minutes. Turn oven off and leave another 5 minutes. Cool, then refrigerate several hours before cutting in squares.

Yields 24
Easy
Must do ahead

Clair Lindgren Buchanan
BOULDER, COLORADO

Twice-Baked Pecan Squares

"As yummy as pecan pie."

1/2 cup butter or margarine,
  softened
1/2 cup firmly packed dark
  brown sugar
1 cup flour
2 eggs
1 cup firmly packed light
  brown sugar
1 cup coarsely chopped
  pecans
1/2 cup flaked coconut
2 Tablespoons flour
1 teaspoon vanilla
Pinch salt
Confectioners' sugar

Cream butter and dark brown sugar until light and fluffy. Add flour and mix well. Press mixture evenly into greased, 13 × 9 × 2-inch baking pan and bake at 350 degrees 20 minutes. Beat eggs until frothy, then gradually add light brown sugar, beating until smooth and thick. Combine pecans, coconut and flour and stir well. Combine egg mixture, nut mixture, vanilla and salt, mix well and spread over crust. Bake at 350 degrees 20 minutes until golden brown. Cool, then sprinkle with confectioners' sugar.

Yields 36–48
Easy
May be frozen

Marilyn Fisher
EL DORADO, ARKANSAS

Polka Daters

"Chocolaty and chewy."

1 1/4 cups (8-ounce package)
    chopped dates
1 cup hot water
1 cup margarine, softened
1 1/4 cups sugar
2 eggs
1 3/4 cups flour
1 1/2 teaspoons baking soda
1 teaspoon vanilla
6 ounces chocolate chips
1/2 cup chopped pecans

Mix dates and water. Set aside to cool. Beat margarine, sugar and eggs until creamy. Gradually stir in flour and baking soda. Stir in date mixture. Add vanilla and half the chips. Spread in greased 15 × 10 × 1-inch pan. Top with remaining chips and pecans. Bake at 350 degrees 30 minutes. Cool and cut into bars.

Yields 30
Easy

Mrs. John F. Giles, III
DALLAS, TEXAS

Apricot-Coconut Balls

"Distinctive flavors and textures."

1 1/2 cups dried apricots,
    ground
2 2/3 cups flaked coconut
3/4 cup sweetened
    condensed milk
Confectioners' sugar

Combine apricots and coconut, add milk and blend well, using hands. Shape into small balls and roll in sugar. Let stand about 2 hours until firm before serving. Balls may be stored at room temperature 3–4 days.

Yields 5 dozen
Easy
Must do ahead

Nancy L. Allen
WHEATLAND, WYOMING

Brown Lace Cookies

1/2 cup butter, softened
2 cups firmly packed
  brown sugar
2 eggs, beaten
1 teaspoon vanilla
1/2 cup flour
1 teaspoon baking powder
2 cups pecans, chopped

Cream butter and sugar. Add eggs and vanilla, beating well. Sift flour and baking powder together and add to creamed mixture with nuts. Chill 1 hour. Place sheet of foil on baking sheet. Drop by half teaspoonfuls 3 inches apart. (They will spread while baking.) Bake at 400 degrees 6 minutes. Cool before removing from foil.

Yields 6–7 dozen
Easy
Must do ahead

Mrs. C.V. Whitney
SARATOGA SPRINGS, NEW YORK

"Forgotten" Cookies

2 egg whites
1/2 teaspoon cream of tartar
1/8 teaspoon mint flavoring
1/8 teaspoon red or green
  food coloring
3/4 cup sugar
1 1/2 ounces chocolate chips
1/2 cup chopped nuts

Beat whites with cream of tartar, mint flavoring and food coloring until frothy. Slowly add sugar, 1 Tablespoon at a time, and beat until stiff. Fold in chips and nuts. Drop on baking sheets lined with foil and then waxed paper. Place cookies in 375-degree oven, turn off heat and leave overnight. This may be done early in the morning and removed in the evening.

Yields 30
Easy
Must do ahead

Mrs. Gerald G. Sabine
SAN LEANDRO, CALIFORNIA

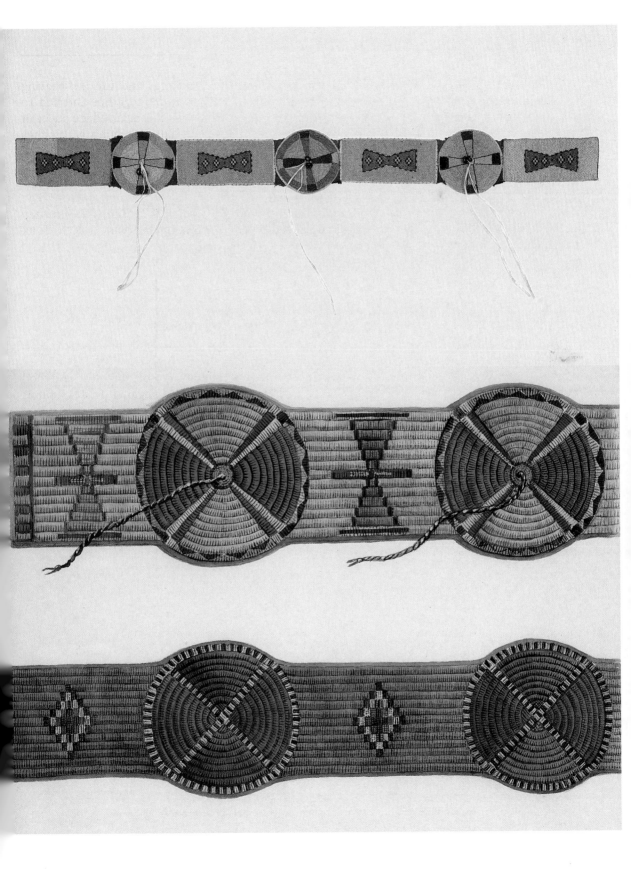

Top: Blanket strip, ca. 1910, Cree/Northern Plains. Courtesy of *Buffalo Bill Historical Center, Cody, WY; Gift of Mr. and Mrs. William Henry Harrison; NA.203.178.* Middle and Bottom: Two sections of Crow beaded blanket strip ca. 1924–1926. *Courtesy of Buffalo Bill Historical Center, Cody, WY; 9.66.30*

Old Fashioned Ginger Cookies

1 1/2 cups sugar
1 cup lard
1 teaspoon salt
2 eggs, slightly beaten
1 teaspoon baking soda
1/4 cup hot water
1/2 cup molasses
1 Tablespoon ginger
1 Tablespoon cinnamon
4 cups flour
Raisins, plumped in warm water for a few minutes

Cream sugar, lard and salt. Add eggs and mix well. Dissolve soda in water and add. Stir in molasses. Add ginger and cinnamon with first 2 cups of flour and mix well. Stir in remaining flour. Refrigerate. Cut into gingerbread men or circles. Decorate with raisins. Bake at 350 degrees 5–8 minutes. If cookies become hard, soften by storing with apple slices.

Yields 30
Must do ahead

Mrs. Don Kurtz
CODY, WYOMING

Honey Whole Wheat Chip Chews

"A great snack any time."

1 cup butter, softened
1/2 cup honey
1 cup sugar
2 eggs
1 teaspoon vanilla
1 3/4 cups whole wheat flour
1 cup white flour
1 teaspoon salt
1/2 teaspoon baking soda
2 teaspoons cinnamon
2 cups instant oatmeal
1 cup chopped walnuts
1 cup chocolate chips

Cream butter, honey and sugar until light. Beat in eggs and vanilla. Add flours, soda, salt, cinnamon and oatmeal and mix well. Blend in nuts and chips. Using a 1/3-cup measure, drop on greased baking sheet. Flatten with a fork until cookie is about 4 inches in diameter. Bake at 375 degrees 10–12 minutes. Cool 3–5 minutes before removing from sheets. Cool on paper towel on a flat surface.

Yields 24–30 large cookies
Easy
May be frozen

Ray Jarrett
BILLINGS, MONTANA

"Mother, I Forgot" Cookies

"For those no-time-to-bake emergencies."

3 cups quick rolled oats
1 cup chocolate chips
1/4 cup coconut
1/4 cup chopped nuts
2 cups sugar
3/4 cup margarine or butter
1/2 cup evaporated milk

Mix first 4 ingredients in large bowl. Bring remaining ingredients to a rapid boil and boil 1 1/2 minutes. Pour hot mixture over mixture in bowl and stir until chocolate melts. Drop by teaspoonfuls on waxed paper.

Yields 24
Easy

Mrs. Arne G. Sandberg
CODY, WYOMING

Mrs. Zisman's Whipcrackers

"Hide these from your roommate."

4 cups flour
1 teaspoon salt
1 cup butter or margarine
1 envelope quick dry yeast
1/4 cup lukewarm water
1 egg
2 egg yolks
1 cup sour cream
1 teaspoon vanilla
1 cup sugar
1/4 teaspoon cinnamon

Sift flour and salt into large bowl and cut in butter. In a separate bowl, soak yeast in water according to directions. Beat eggs together and combine with yeast, sour cream and vanilla. Mix thoroughly into flour mixture. Cover and let rise in refrigerator 2 hours. Place dough on lightly sugared bread board. Sprinkle sugar lightly over dough and roll out to a 10 × 12-inch rectangle. Fold dough to center from each side. Roll out and fold again, using a little more sugar. Fold a total of 4 times, sprinkling sugar on dough and board each time and using about 3/4 cup of sugar in all. Cut in 3/4 × 4-inch strips. Add cinnamon to remaining sugar and sprinkle over strips. Give each strip a hard twist to resemble a hairpin. Bake at 375 degrees 20 minutes on ungreased baking sheets until light brown.

Yields 36
Time-consuming
Must do ahead

Nancy Fees
CODY, WYOMING

Pecan Puffs

"Rich and devastating."

1/2 cup butter, softened
2 Tablespoons sugar
1 teaspoon vanilla
1 cup sifted flour
1 cup ground pecan meats
Confectioners' sugar

Beat butter until soft and blend in sugar until creamy. Add vanilla and flour and stir in pecans. Roll into small balls, place on greased baking sheet and bake at 300 degrees 45 minutes. Remove and roll in confectioners' sugar, then roll again after cooling.

Yields 20
Easy

Frannie Robinson
ROSWELL, GEORGIA

Pecan Sugar Cookies

2 cups sifted flour
1 teaspoon salt
1/2 teaspoon soda
1 cup vegetable shortening
or butter, softened
1/2 cup sugar
1/2 cup brown sugar
1 egg, beaten slightly
1 teaspoon vanilla
1/2 cup chopped pecans
1/2 cup pecan halves

Sift together flour, salt and soda. Cream shortening and sugars until very smooth. Beat in egg, add sifted flour mixture and mix well. Add vanilla and chopped nuts. For small cookies, form 1/2 teaspoon of dough into a small ball. Arrange 12 balls on ungreased baking sheet. Press each ball flat with bottom of a small glass dipped in sugar. Top each cookie with a pecan half. Bake at 350 degrees 15 minutes until golden.

Yields 6–8 dozen
Easy

Marjorie Messenger
CODY, WYOMING

Blueberry Sauce

"Terrific served with ice cream after a heavy meal."

1 1/2 cups fresh or frozen
    blueberries
1/4 cup sugar
3/4 teaspoon cinnamon
1/4 teaspoon nutmeg

Mix all ingredients together in saucepan. Cook over low heat about 10 minutes, stirring frequently. Serve hot or cold.

Serves 4–6
Easy
May do ahead

William E. Weiss
CODY, WYOMING

Chocolate Sauce

"Wonderful for ice cream sundaes."

6 ounces chocolate chips
1 cup miniature
    marshmallows
1 small can evaporated
    milk

Put all ingredients in glass jar. Cover jar with lid and place in pan of very hot water. Stir frequently until chips dissolve. Cool and refrigerate or serve hot.

Serves 8
Easy

Anita Renee DiGiorgio
ELLICOTT CITY, MARYLAND

Creme Fraiche

8 ounces heavy cream
3 Tablespoons yogurt
2 teaspoons buttermilk

Mix ingredients thoroughly with wire whisk and bake at 100 degrees 8 hours or overnight. Chill.

Serves 6
Easy
Must do ahead

Nan Thorne Fogle
BOULDER, COLORADO

Grand Marnier Sauce

"An elegant touch for any fresh fruit."

5 egg yolks
1/2 cup sugar
1/4 cup Grand Marnier
1 cup heavy cream, whipped
   with 2 Tablespoons sugar

Mix yolks and sugar in double-boiler insert over gently boiling water. Whisk until pale yellow and remove from heat. Add half the liqueur and cool. Fold cream into egg mixture and add remaining liqueur. Let stand 3 hours before serving or refrigerate for later use.

Serves 10–12
Easy
Must do ahead

Temptations
CODY, WYOMING

Rum Butter Sauce

1 cup sugar
2 Tablespoons cornstarch
1 cup boiling water
1/2 cup lemon juice
   Grated rind of 1 lemon
1/2 cup butter
2 Tablespoons brandy
1/4 teaspoon nutmeg
1/2 cup light rum
2 Tablespoons dark rum

Blend sugar and cornstarch in boiling water. Cook, stirring constantly, over medium heat until mixture begins to thicken. Add remaining ingredients and cook 2 minutes, stirring constantly. Serve hot over mince pie, pound cake or puddings.

Yields 3 cups
Easy

Mrs. B. J. Fullmer
BROOKFIELD, VERMONT

Index